❑ Contents ■

"Tell Me a Riddle"

Women Writers
Texts and Contexts

SERIES EDITORS

SERIES BOARD

THOMAS L. ERSKINE
Salisbury State University

MARTHA BANTA
University of California at Los Angeles

CONNIE L. RICHARDS
Salisbury State University

BARBARA T. CHRISTIAN
University of California at Berkeley

PAUL LAUTER
Trinity College

VOLUMES IN THE SERIES

"Tell Me a Riddle"

☐ TILLIE OLSEN ■

Edited and with an introduction by
DEBORAH SILVERTON ROSENFELT

R
Rutgers University Press
New Brunswick, New Jersey

Library of Congress Cataloging-in-Publication Data

Olsen, Tillie.
    Tell me a riddle / Tillie, Olsen ; edited and with an introduction by
Deborah Silverton Rosenfelt.
        p.   cm. — (Women writers : texts and contexts)
    Includes bibliographical references.
    ISBN 0-8135-2136-X (cloth) — ISBN 0-8135-2137-8 (pbk.)
    1. Cancer—Patients—United States—Fiction.   2. Married people—
United States—Fiction.   3. Working class—United States—Fiction.
4. Aged women—United States—Fiction.   5. Olsen, Tillie. Tell me a riddle.
I. Rosenfelt, Deborah Silverton.   II. Title.   III. Series: Women writers
(New Brunswick, N.J.)
PS3565.L82T45   1995
813'.54—dc20   94-29813
                                                                        CIP

British Cataloging-in-Publication information available

For Miranda

☐ Introduction

Introduction

> How much it takes to become a writer. Bent . . . ,
> circumstances, time, development of craft—but beyond
> that: how much conviction as to the importance of what
> one has to say, one's right to say it. And the will,
> the measureless store of belief in oneself to be able to
> come to, cleave to, find the form for one's own life
> comprehensions. Difficult for any male not born into a
> class that breeds such confidence.
> Almost impossible for a girl, a woman.
> TILLIE OLSEN,
> *Silences*

Tillie Olsen's life spans more than eighty years of this century.
Born in Nebraska in 1912 or 1913, she lives today, as she has
for many years, in a third-floor walk-up apartment in cooperative housing in San Francisco, still the modestly priced multicultural community envisioned by its longshoremen's union
founders. Writer, scholar, teacher, activist, mother, she has
touched the lives of others through her presence as well as
through her prose. Her legacy of published work is not large:
in the thirties, two poems, two essays, a story; in the forties,
columns for the *People's World*, a leftist newspaper; subsequently, the work she is known for today—*Tell Me a Riddle*
(1962), a volume of short fiction; *Yonnondio*, a novel written in the thirties but not published until 1974; "Requa I"
(1970), a short story, intended as the first section of a longer
work; *Silences* (1978), a collection of critical essays as intricately webbed as a poem. A poem and a short story written
when Olsen was in her teens were published for the first time
in 1993. She also edited a "daybook and reader," *Mother to
Daughter, Daughter to Mother* (1984), a gathering of words
from 120 writers—mothers and daughters, including herself

3

and her daughter Julie Olsen Edwards—and wrote or co-wrote several short essays and prefaces. Though Olsen has written less than her readers might wish, her fiction is highly regarded for its transformative vision and consummate craft. As Robert Coles observed in a review of *Tell Me a Riddle,* "Everything she has written has become almost immediately a classic."[1]

Olsen: Her Life and Her Work

Tillie Olsen's parents, Samuel Lerner and Ida Beber Lerner, were born and raised in Russia.[2] Like many other young people of their time, they saw in socialism the promise of a world free from religious superstition and from the divisiveness of narrow ethnic identities, as well as from the political oppressions of the tsarist regime. As Jews, they were close to the Bund, a Jewish socialist organization with a humanist and internationalist perspective; this radical humanism informs the grandmother's passionate rejection of traditional Jewish religious practice in "Tell Me a Riddle": "Tell them to write: Race, human; Religion, none."[3] They participated in the 1905 Revolution, a mass uprising protesting the tyranny of the tsarist regime in Russia and calling for democratizing measures. When the revolution failed and Samuel faced imprisonment and exile in Siberia, he fled to this country, where he and Ida were married. Samuel Lerner eventually became the secretary of the Nebraska Socialist Party, and the six Lerner children grew up in a home where the struggles for survival of their working-class immigrant family were understood in the context of global human struggles for survival and dignity. As Elaine Orr writes, the young Tillie Lerner

> came to know the United States both as a place of promise and as a country economically, socially, racially, and sexually divided. Around her she saw farmers suffering from a depressed agricultural industry and miners and packinghouse workers (among them her father) who were beginning to organize against management. Thus her first memories were colored by labor struggles, the realities of the workplace, the desire of laborers for a job and dignity, and a growing Ameri-

> can socialism. . . . Woven into Olsen's young consciousness
> . . . was . . . her parents' immigrant identity, the Yiddish ideal
> of enlightenment they embodied, and a spirit of hope, for free-
> dom and justice that had imbued their lives in Russia. (23)

The second of six children, Tillie Lerner left high
school after the eleventh grade to earn a living. She took
a series of jobs—tie presser, mother's helper, hack writer,
model, ice-cream packer, book clerk, waitress, punch-press
operator. Today, she points out to those who speak of her as
a high school dropout that she received more education than
most of the women of this era. In *Silences,* she notes that
"two-thirds of the illiterate in the world today are women," and
asks: "How many of us who are writers have mothers, grandmothers, of limited education; awkward, not at home, with the
written word, however eloquent they may be with the spoken
one? Born a generation or two before, we might have been
they."[4] Olsen's love of learning began early and persisted; she
read voraciously in Omaha's Carnegie Library, especially fiction, and like other working-class readers, she found a world
of literature and social thought in the Little Blue Books, inex-
pensive miniature editions of authors ranging from Plato to
Marx, their contents shaped by the socialist background of
Kansas publisher Emanuel Haldeman-Julius. Harriet Monroe
had begun publishing *Poetry* in 1912, and Olsen was introduced in its pages to the work of midwesterners and modern-
ists like Sandburg, Stevens, Eliot, Yeats, Joyce, and Lowell.
Both her formal schooling and her informal learning—not
just her reading, but her attendance at local events like visits
from poet Carl Sandburg or Eugene Debs, the eloquent leader
of the Socialist Party; her absorption of the discussions about
politics and history in her home, her attentiveness to the
nuances of voice and experience in the world about her—
informed her use of language and shaped her consciousness.
    It was a surprisingly diverse world—native-born and
newly immigrant midwestern workers, visiting socialist activists and intellectuals, black families in the Lerner's integrated
neighborhood. The young Tillie Lerner seems to have been,
very early, "one on whom nothing is lost," a favorite phrase of
hers from Henry James (*Silences* 62, 147); her ability to recall

and inscribe the rhythms of language—the cadences of Black sermons, the multiethnic exchanges of factory workers, the inflections of Yiddish-influenced English—make her prose a particularly rich evocation of multicultural America. Olsen's democratic use of language, as Constance Coiner argues in her essay in this casebook, expresses an inclusive social vision that insists on dignity and equality for all human life. Olsen sees her work as part of a "larger tradition of social concern," which included for her as a young reader writers ranging from Tolstoy, Chekhov, and Victor Hugo to Rebecca Harding Davis, Elizabeth Madox Roberts, and Walt Whitman. In the Notes for her essay on Harding Davis's *Life in the Iron Mills* (1861, reprinted by The Feminist Press in 1972), Olsen tells how at fifteen, her encounter with the story, published anonymously in *The Atlantic Monthly,* reminded her, "'Literature can be made out of the lives of despised people,'" and "You, too, must write.'"[5]

Olsen's commitment to writing and her social engagement unfolded simultaneously. Responding to the struggles for survival of those around her, and influenced by the socialist ideals of her parents, Olsen became a political activist in her teens. She joined the Young People's Socialist League and in 1931 the Young Communist League. In the 1930s, when America was in the midst of a devastating depression, communism seemed to many to offer a more humane, and more socially successful, vision than the laissez-faire capitalism of the pre–New Deal United States. Her work took her to Kansas City, where she was jailed for helping to organize a strike in a packing house. She contracted pleurisy while working in a tie factory; in jail, she developed incipient tuberculosis, and she went for a period of recovery to Faribault, Minnesota. There, she became pregnant and began work on the novel that would become *Yonnondio.* As Pearlman and Werlock put it, "When Olsen left Minnesota for California in the spring of 1933 . . . she took with her the commitments of a political activist, a writer, and a mother" (18–19).

In California, Olsen remained politically engaged throughout most of the thirties. She also met and eventually married Jack Olsen, himself a YCL activist. Both participated in the great union-building efforts of those years, and in 1934,

6

they were arrested for taking part in the San Francisco maritime strike, one of the most important strikes of American labor history. In the same year, Olsen had published "The Iron Throat," part of the opening chapter of *Yonnondio*, in *The Partisan Review*; its power won her immediate recognition, and she responded to the encouragement of Lincoln Steffens by producing accounts of the strike ("The Strike") and of her arrest ("Thousand Dollar Vagrant"). Also in 1934, she published two poems, "I Want You Women up North to Know" and "There Is a Lesson," the first protesting the exploitation of women workers in the sweatshops of the southwestern garment industry; the second castigating fascist massacres in Austria and prophesying revolution.

In her thirties writing, Olsen voices the angers and longings, the hopes and capacities of working people—men, women, and children. The perspectives and experiences of women are particularly significant in her work: in *Yonnondio*, as I maintain in my essay here, she brings to the masculinist world of the left proletarian novel an account of familial life only rarely articulated in the genre. *Yonnondio* tells the story of a working-class midwestern family, the Holbrooks, who struggle to survive by moving from a mining town in Wyoming, to a farm in South Dakota, and finally to the slaughterhouses of a city much like Omaha, Nebraska. The novel creates in Mazie Holbrook, the young daughter, and in her mother Anna a figure who reappears throughout Olsen's work, both fiction and criticism: a woman potentially an artist/activist, silenced by poverty, by the willingly assumed burdens of caring for others, and by the expectations associated with her gender.

As the decade wore on, and Olsen bore her second daughter, she became increasingly absorbed in the balancing act of mothering her family and working for pay, though she did not relinquish her activist commitments. She left off work on *Yonnondio*, putting aside the completed chapters, not rediscovering them and preparing them for publication until the 1970s. In the forties, she bore two more daughters. Her experiences as a mother have made her one of motherhood's most powerful and influential chroniclers; few other writers have rendered so fully the profound contradictions of maternality:

its calling forth of all one's love, patience, humor, and sometimes, when the resources for furthering growth are nonexistent, despair; its absorption of one's attention, time, thought; its transformation of one's creative capacities from the boldly visionary to the carefully nurturant. This theme resonates in *Yonnondio* and is central to the stories of *Tell Me a Riddle*. It receives its most devastating articulation in *Silences:* "And indeed, in our century as in the last, until very recently almost all distinguished achievement has come from childless women" (31). Yet motherhood also deepened Olsen's passion for a society that would nurture rather than inhibit human growth.

It was not until the 1950s that Olsen began to write fiction again. The 1950s were a time of relative material prosperity for many, but it was also an era haunted by the memory of the terrible holocausts of World War II and by the pervasive threat of nuclear annihilation. The Cold War against the Soviet Union provided the context in which the anti-Communist inquisitions of Senator Joseph McCarthy and his ilk could flourish. Congress, the courts, businesses, most labor unions, the entertainment industry, the academic world—all collaborated in the vigorous repression of the left activist politics and culture of the previous decades. Jack Olsen was called to testify before the House Un-American Activities Committee, where he asserted his intention to "resist with all of my power efforts of this committee to curtail our freedoms."[6] He was blacklisted from his work in the Warehousemen's Union, and began all over again as a printer's apprentice. The FBI followed Tillie Olsen from job to job; she was fired after each of their appearances.

Ironically, this was also a time of passage from Olsen's busiest mother-work-activist years, when "the simplest circumstances for creation did not exist," to the moment when, her youngest child in school, she was able to snatch the necessary moments to write. In 1954 she enrolled in a writing class at San Francisco State University, almost finishing one story, "I Stand Here Ironing," and completing the first draft of a second, "Hey Sailor, What Ship?" On the basis of this work, she received a Stegner Fellowship in creative writing to Stanford, and there, "as the exiled homesick come home," she

found "the comradeship of books and writing human beings."[7] In her eight months of "freed time" at Stanford, she
completed "Hey Sailor, What Ship?", wrote "O Yes," and finished the first third of "Tell Me a Riddle." She describes this
period in both personal and social terms in the passage from
First Drafts, Last Drafts and the excerpt from *Silences,* both
included here.

Olsen continued to struggle with the circumstances
imposing silence in her own writing life: the need to work
for pay; the interruptions occasioned by family life; the loss
of the habit of writing, of the feeling of being "peopled" by
her characters. She seems to have suffered, too, from what
she calls in *Silences,* quoting Louise Bogan, "The knife of
the perfectionist attitude in art and life"; "woman, economic,
perfectionist causes—all inextricably intertwined," she writes
(9). "Requa I," published in 1970, was her first story in almost
ten years, and its linguistic density suggests something of the
perfectionist labor that created it. A stylistically complex work
set in the depression era, "Requa" narrates a thirteen-year-old
boy's slow recovery from the devastating loss of his mother.
Though "Requa" is literally the American-Indian place-name
of the North Pacific town where the boy, Stevie, comes to live
with his clumsily nurturant uncle, a worker in a junkyard,
the word also connotes a requiem, a commemoration of the
dispossessed and forgotten. Written, as Blanche Gelfant puts
it, "after long silence," "Requa" implies, in its simultaneous
difficulty and beauty of form, an order won from disorder.
Its final coherence, wrought from a chaos of fragments, blank
spaces, catalogues of junkyard sounds and implements, ultimately draws a parallel, as Gelfant suggests, between "a
child's renewed will to live" and "an artist's recovered power
to write."[8]

Silence, or rather, the reclamation of lives and words
from silence, from silencing, becomes Olsen's greatest theme,
enacted in the rhythms of her life, documented in her essays
on the lives, work, and words of others. *Yonnondio: From the
Thirties* was reclaimed from silence, pieced together in 1972–
73 from manuscripts written in the thirties, by the older
writer, "in arduous partnership" with "that long ago young
writer."[9] The novel—actually the opening section of what

had been a more ambitious project—takes its name from a poem by Walt Whitman that Olsen draws on for the novel's epigraph:

> *Lament for the aborigines . . .*
> A song, a poem of itself—*the word itself a dirge . . .*
> (Race of the woods, the landscapes free and the falls!
> No picture, poem, statement, passing them to the future:)
> Yonnondio! Yonnondio!—unlimn'd they disappear;
> To-day gives place, and fades—the cities, farms, and
>   factories fade;
> A muffled sonorous sound, a wailing word is borne through
>   the air for a moment,
> Then blank and gone and still, and utterly lost.

Yonnondio's title and epigraph, invoking a vanished American Indian culture, link it not only to "Requa I" but to the essays Olsen was also writing in the sixties and seventies, essays that simultaneously theorized the effects of silencings in writers' lives and that pay a special respect to writers who have rescued the otherwise invisible and silent lives of others from oblivion. As Olsen says toward the conclusion of *Silences*, it was "an attempt, as later were 'One Out of Twelve,' 'Rebecca Harding Davis,' and now the rest of this book, to expand the too sparse evidence on the relationship between circumstances and creation." (262). For Olsen, creativity is a human gift accorded to most of us; the "circumstances" of gender, of race, and of class—"the great unexamined" (*Silences* 264)—are what deform and impede its expression.

At the end of the 1971 talk for the Modern Language Association that became the second chapter of *Silences*, Olsen called on those present to join her in the task of reclamation; her emphasis on women as writers, as readers, as teachers marks her deepening response to and her growing importance for the feminist criticism and culture taking shape during the seventies:

> You who teach, read writers who are women. There is a whole literature to be re-estimated, revalued. . . .

Read, listen to, living women writers; our new as well as
our established, often neglected ones. Not to have audience is
a kind of death.

Read the compass of women writers in our infinite variety. Not only those who tell us of ourselves as "the other half,"
but also those who write of the other human dimensions,
realms.

Teach women's lives through the lives of the women who
wrote the books, as well as through the books themselves. . . .

Help create writers, perhaps among them yourselves.

(44–45)

Olsen's work as a scholar and teacher during this time
exemplifies her commitment to her own mandates. She com-
piled influential reading lists of neglected writings for the
Radical Teacher and the *Women's Studies Newsletter,* and she
helped identify "lost" texts for reprinting by The Feminist
Press, the first of many small presses devoted to the writings
of women. One of these was the story that had been so important to her as a young girl—Rebecca Harding Davis's *Life in
the Iron Mills*. Olsen's "Biographical Interpretation" of Harding Davis's life and work richly recreates the world in which
her predecessor lived and wrote, arguing that Davis's literary
gifts diminished as she assumed the prescribed, and desired,
roles of wife and mother as well as the burden of writing for
money. In commenting on Rebecca Harding Davis's last years,
Olsen hypothesizes a secret life reminiscent not only of the
grandmother's in "Tell Me a Riddle" but also of her own sense
of life buried within her during her non-writing years: "Probably to the end of her days, a creature unknown to those
around her lived on in Rebecca, a secret creature still hungry
to know; living . . . ecstatically in nature. . . ; 'with her own
people, elsewhere' in the . . . red-brick house" (151).

In 1978, Olsen published *Silences,* an innovative collection that includes her previous essays, an extended gloss
on them, and excerpts from the work of other writers, culled
from her "jottings"—hundreds, maybe thousands of note-
cards and scraps on which over the years she recorded passages to remember. *Silences* catalogues all the various forms

of silencing that befall writers—especially, though not exclusively, women; especially, though not exclusively, those who must struggle for sheer survival.

Tillie Olsen's life and work form a bridge between the activism and culture of the "red decade" of the thirties and the movements of the sixties and seventies, especially the women's movement, which provided an eager audience for her work. An important influence on the feminist writers, critics, and students of the seventies and eighties, Olsen has also contributed to "the larger tradition of social concern" both as a writer of fiction and a scholar and teacher whose efforts have been crucial to the democratization of the American literary canon.

Tell Me a Riddle *and "Tell Me a Riddle"*

"Tell Me a Riddle" is the title story of Olsen's only collection, published in 1962. The other stories are "I Stand Here Ironing," "Hey Sailor, What Ship?" and "O Yes," all written in the 1950s. Originally conceived as sections of a novel, the stories portray the lives of members of an extended family over three generations. David and Eva of "Tell Me a Riddle" are the first generation; their children—Clara, Vivi, Hannah, Sammy, Helen, and Davy, killed in World War II—the second generation; and Jeannie and Carol, Helen and Lennie's children, representative of the third. All the stories explore the interrelatedness of the "private sphere" and the "public"; set within the home, constructed from the rhythms and language of daily familial life, they constantly expand their scope to illustrate the location of the family within a larger set of social relations. In "I Stand Here Ironing" a mother broods in a sustained monologue on the ways in which growing up in anxious poverty has affected, perhaps limited, her daughter's capacities; at the conclusion her fierce prayer is that her child's will to live is strong enough to transcend the hard soil of her youth: "Only help her to know—help make it so there is cause for her to know—that she is more than this dress on the ironing board, helpless before the iron."[10] In the elegaic "Hey Sailor, What Ship?" an old sailor friend of Lennie's and Helen's comes to shore on leave and collapses of alcoholism and illness in their home before disappearing once again; the very intrusiveness of his visit measures the degree of loss the story records, the loss of an earlier time when men and women—including Lennie and Whitey, the sailor—united to struggle as progressive union activists for better working conditions and for a better world. In "O Yes" Helen sadly watches her daughter grow increasingly estranged from her closest friend, who is Black, as the formal and informal tracking system of the American public school system intrudes on the less racially differentiated world of early childhood.

The most sustained and complex of the pieces in the *Riddle* volume, "Tell Me a Riddle" addresses some of the deepest concerns of western culture: the nature of human bonding; the quest for, in Olsen's words, "coherence, transport, meaning"; the aspiration toward justice; the confrontation with death. The ethical and spiritual dimensions of these themes cannot be severed from the social and historical. Like Olsen's other work, the novella celebrates the endurance of human love and of the passion for justice, in spite of the pain inflicted and the capacities wasted by poverty, racism, and a patriarchal social order, and in spite of the horrors of the Holocaust and the war and the new possibilities for nuclear destruction. Its power derives from a distillation of such themes in evocative and precise language that makes poetic and performative use of the specific rhythms and idioms of Yiddish-born English, and from a structure that only gradually reveals the relevance to the lives of one poor aging immigrant Jewish couple of a past embracing the great struggles and great horrors of modern history. In its slow unfolding of that past and in its final revelation of Eva's passionate idealism, the novella invites its readers to recognize how deeply they are embedded in the processes of history, to meditate on the "circumstances" of class, race, and gender as the soil which nurtures or impedes human achievement; and to acknowledge, as David does, the discrepancy between what is—including perhaps their own complicity with injustice—and what should be.

"Tell Me a Riddle" begins with an argument between an old man and woman, married forty-seven years, a deadly battle of wills over whether or not to sell their home and move to a cooperative run by his lodge. The conflict is shaped by the different ways poverty has affected the man and the woman. David longs to be free from responsibility and fretting about money, so that he can use "the vitality still in him"; Eva, remembering the desperation and humiliation of years of making do with remade clothes and begged meat bones, vows to "let him wrack his head for how they would live," for she "would not exchange her solitude for anything." "Never again to be forced to move to the rhythms of others" is a refrain echoing through the text. David longs to be surrounded by friends; Eva longs only to be left alone. The years of struggle to keep her family fed and clothed have transformed her capacity for engagement in the lives of others into its obverse: the terrible need for solitude, for "reconciled peace."

When Eva falls ill, and the illness turns out to be terminal cancer, David finds himself compelled to become a caretaker himself. Concealing the seriousness of Eva's condition from her, but fearing to stay home alone with her in her dying, he takes her on a pilgrimage, first to visit a daughter and her family in Ohio, and then to Venice, California, which in those years was home to a community of older, working-class Jews. As her condition deteriorates, Eva becomes delirious, pouring out fragments of poetry and song from her youth. Tended in her illness not only by David but by her granddaughter, Jeannie, a nurse, Eva passes on to Jeannie the legacy of her earlier years. It is crucial to the way "Riddle" works as art that Olsen reveals the dimensions of that legacy only gradually; only gradually do we realize that this grouchy, sick grandmother, this silent bitter woman who wants only solitude, was once an orator in the 1905 revolution, that she and her husband met in the prison camps of Siberia, that she had once publicly articulated a passionate vision of human possibility and human liberty. Through this narrative strategy, Olsen suggests the tragic dimensions of social silencings: those imposed upon working class people by physical and intellectual deprivation, isolation, and routinized work; and those imposed upon women by role-related demands and patriarchal ideologies antagonistic to the act of creative articulation. Read this way, Eva's final utterances in "Tell Me a Riddle," her coming to speech again at last, become an act of resistance and creation, both cathartic and political.

Eva's deathbed oration forces David—and the reader—to acknowledge not only what has been lost and destroyed in her, but what has been lost and destroyed in the complacent yet troubled American society of the 1950s, with its grasping for material well-being, its atomic nightmares, its repression of the radical culture of the past. The narrative form of "Riddle" itself is secretive, riddling; unfolding in the present, the narrative is continuously disrupted by intimations of the past, a past only divulged in brief revelations and fragments of conversation and memory, as though it is too complex, too different, for the present to contain, but too important to utterly repress. As the past becomes ever more intrusive, embracing revolutionary vision and experience and the "monstrous shapes" of history that intervened between the thirties and the fifties—the holocaust, the war, the atomic bombing of Hiroshima and Nagasaki—this narrative counterpoint reveals that Eva's withdrawal, though grounded in her personal circumstances, has deeper causes still: a terrible anguish over the course of modern history, and an overpowering sense of the disparity between the revolutionary idealism that inspired her youthful activism and the complacency of contemporary life. One of the resonant words of "Riddle" is "betrayal," and David's changed consciousness at the novella's conclusion must encompass "the bereavement and betrayal he had sheltered—compounded through the years—hidden even from himself." His final reconciliation with his dying wife must take place within a historical context that she has forced him to acknowledge, to remember. In dying, Eva awakens David (and the community of readers who share his acceptance of things as they are) from a numb accommodation into potential opposition. Her rage at contemporary waste and injustice exemplified by the pollution of Los Angeles and the confinement of her friend Mrs. Mays to a single, inadequate room emerges finally not as odd but as appropriate, as necessary.

"Riddle" addresses profound issues of consciousness, asking how the passionately humanistic vision of a progressive moment in history can survive and be transmitted to a new generation in a different historical moment. While the motif of illness is grounded in the literal and autobiographical—Olsen had watched her own mother die a similar death—it also functions as an emblem of this radical humanist's profound alienation from the post-war order. Richard Ohmann argues that a certain "structure of feeling" characterized American fiction from the end of World War II through the mid-seventies, inscribed in narrative patterns in which "social contradictions were easily displaced into images of personal illness" (390). He notes a pattern in which illness becomes an alternative to an acceptance of distorted social relations—male supremacy, class domination, competitiveness, individualism. For Ohmann, the basic story on which fiction of the era plays variations is "the movement into illness and toward recovery."[11] Eva's cancer, the source of her physical disintegration and the sign of her refusal to accept fifties America, links her to other postwar heroes whose illness is a response to an apparently untransformable social order; but for her, there is no personal recovery, no accommodation. Like Whitey, the sailor in "Hey Sailor, What Ship?" whose alcoholism dooms him as surely as Eva's cancer dooms her, Eva is tragically anachronistic as the repository of revolutionary consciousness, an actor in a textual order structured by the plot of her expulsion from that order. Yet the narrative that leads to her death is produced by the same narrative act that redeems her life from the silence to which fifties culture had consigned the radical past.[12]

Critical Responses and Casebook Materials

The best commentator on Olsen's fiction is Olsen herself; passages from *Silences* provide both a context for the writing of the fiction and a more direct articulation of many of its themes. In the first chapter of *Silences*, "Silences in Literature" (originally published in *Harper's Magazine* in 1965 and included here) Olsen explores the "unnatural silences" that impede human creativity and testifies to the silencings in her own life. Readers may perhaps recognize Eva in its evocation of those among the silenced "whose waking hours are all struggle for existence; the barely educated; the illiterate; women." Also included is Olsen's statement from *First Drafts, Last Drafts: Forty Years of the Creative Writing Program at Stanford*, a compressed discussion of her time at Stanford and of the era and events that underlie the writing of "Tell Me a Riddle."

For a work of such complexity and power, "Tell Me a Riddle" has generated surprisingly little sustained criticism. The *Tell Me a Riddle* volume received excellent reviews, including one by Dorothy Parker in *Esquire*[13] and one in the *New York Times Book Review*.[14] "Tell Me a Riddle" received the O. Henry Award for the Best American Short Story of 1961; reprinted in numerous anthologies and translated into many languages, its status as one of the great American short stories of our time remains secure. Yet Robert Coles, another admirer of the *Riddle* stories, is also correct in noting that Olsen has been "spared celebrity."[15] As Mickey Pearlman and Abby H. P. Werlock point out in their book-length study of Olsen,

> She is often not a reference point in discussions of American writers of either gender. It is unusual, to say the least, that a writer so admired by a large number of other writers and general readers is missing so completely from scholarly studies by Americans. (xii)

Serious and sustained critical treatment of Olsen has come largely from feminist critics and writers, for whom her work resonates with particular poignancy: she anticipated and indeed helped formulate some of the crucial issues of contemporary feminism, especially the tensions between motherhood and other forms of productive activity. The critical reactions to Olsen's work have been chronicled in Kay Hoyle Nelson's helpful introduction to *The Critical Response to Tillie Olsen*. Nelson suggests that "over the decades the critical response . . . has moved from descriptive to celebratory to analytical."[16] The trajectory of Olsen criticism may not be quite so clear as Nelson implies. The celebratory began in the thirties, as she herself demonstrates, when Robert Cantwell praised the young Tillie Lerner's first published section of *Yonnondio* as "a work of early genius," with "metaphors startling in their brilliance,"[17] and recent work, including theoretically sophisticated analysis, can still be celebratory of Olsen's achievement, as is Constance Coiner's essay in this volume. It is true, though, that sustained work on Olsen began in the late seventies with essentially descriptive overviews, and has led to more complex "rereadings" in the late eighties and early nineties, including Pearlman and Werlock's 1991 volume in the Twayne series, which offers respectful critiques of Olsen's major writings while problematizing the "fragmented quality of her sparse output" (ix). In the interim, critics have explored various specific dimensions of her work—the contextual, the spiritual, the esthetic—and have elucidated particular themes, narrative patterns, and clusters of imagery.

Two important early overviews of Olsen, Ellen Cronan Rose's "Limning: Or Why Tillie Writes"[18] and Catherine R. Stimpson's "Tillie Olsen: Witness as Servant,"[19] both written in the mid-seventies, explore the relationship of Olsen's work to feminist consciousness. Rose cautions against reading the fiction as a feminist statement and finds a disparity between the emphasis on the struggles of women in Olsen's talks and what Rose perceives as a broader vision in her fiction that bestows esthetic form on the otherwise inchoate struggles for meaning common to all human life. Rose seems to have felt the need to rescue Olsen from too exclusive an embrace by the community of feminist readers and writers who claimed her as a source of inspiration in the early seventies. Stimpson finds Olsen working toward a synthesis of literature, feminism, and other forms of radical analysis; she also assumes the pervasiveness of a deeply political passion in Olsen, a grief and rage over "the loss of talent, love, promise, energy, adventurousness, power, and creativity" and a commitment to bear witness to those losses in a way that will alter the circumstances of future generations. This tension between an emphasis on Olsen's humanism and universality on the one hand and the specificity of her circumstances as a working-class woman with political commitments on the other reappears frequently in Olsen criticism; yet it seems necessary only because American literary criticism has so often claimed the incompatibility of art and politics, of an encompassing imaginative vision and a specific cultural location.

A number of critics have examined the social and autobiographical contexts—the soil, in Olsen's words—in which her work took root. The stories of *Tell Me a Riddle* use Olsen's life experience, as Linda Pratt demonstrates in her essay here. Pratt shows how the structure of Olsen's family coincides with the structure of the family in the *Riddle* stories, noting the resemblance to Olsen's mother, and to her death from cancer, in Eva and her fate. The pioneering essay in this regard was Selma Burkom and Margaret Williams's "De-Riddling Tillie Olsen's Writings," which offered an overview located in the autobiographical circumstances of her life. Reprinting for the first time two of her poems from the thirties, Burkom and Williams discuss in some detail Olsen's roots in the American left. As with Rose, their concern is to demonstrate how Olsen manages to transcend the political and the propagandistic to render "the complexity of reality" through a realism "not narrowly 'social' but broadly humanistic" (79). My own essay, "From the Thirties," included here, is indebted to Burkom and Williams's research; however, in locating Olsen as a working-class woman coming to voice within a tradition of American socialism and Marxism, I tried to explore and reclaim the dimensions of that legacy that have nurtured cultural expression, as well as to investigate the contradictions facing women writing within the left. In attending to the historical and class contexts and ideological conflicts that shaped Olsen's work, I offer a reading I later designated as "materialist feminist."[20] Constance Coiner addresses some of the same issues in her writings on Olsen and Meridel Le Sueur and develops them further in her forthcoming book for Oxford University Press.[21]

Another dimension of Olsen's life that has received critical attention is her Jewish background and its relation to her fiction. Jacqueline Mintz and Rose Kamel place Olsen in a tradition of Jewish American women writers, examining the influence of the eastern European Jewish heritage on Olsen's representation of women and family life.[22] Elenore Lester, writing in the Jewish journal *Midstream*, rebukes Olsen for repressing the issue of ethnic identity in *Yonnondio,* but John Clayton and Bonnie Lyons argue for the importance of radical Jewish humanism to her vision, a vision that embodies, in Lyons's words, "both the messianic hope and universal world-view of a particular kind of secular Jew."[23] Linda Pratt offers a more sophisticated version of Lester's critique in the essay included here. She researches the specificity of Olsen's heritage as a secular and socialist jew in the Midwest, at a moment when anti-Semitism would have reminded her of her marginality in a predominantly Christian world and when the upwardly mobile religious Jewish community would have had little use for the secular, indeed, proudly atheist traditions of leftist Yiddishkeit. Pratt wonders, provocatively, if this dual marginalization might help account for the assimilated quality of the Holbrooks in *Yonnondio,* while in "Tell Me a Riddle," written years later in a different era, Olsen can at last pay tribute to and draw on the language and experiences of the revolutionary Jewish midwesterners of her parents' generation. Olsen herself resists this interpretation; she feels that the universalizing of the Holbrooks owes more to the internationalism of the left than to internal conflicts over her Jewish identity—an identity unimportant in her secular family of origin.

A number of critics have responded to "Tell Me a Riddle" as a work of spiritual significance. In the first important book-length study of Olsen, *Tillie Olsen and a Feminist Spiritual Vision,* Elaine Orr offers a reading that emphasizes the transformative and visionary dimensions of her work. Orr argues that Olsen's writings invite religious comprehension because they celebrate the "miracle and sanctity of each human life" and affirm a hoped-for world in which renewal and rebirth arise from brokenness and discontinuity (xvi–xvii). For Orr, Olsen's work is in effect an inspirational text, calling forth a response best described in terms of the insights of feminist theologians like Nelle Morton and Rosemary Ruether. Such feminist thinkers find transformative possibilities in the dailiness of human life, in attentiveness to women's personal experience, and in the acts of human nurturance often but not inevitably associated with maternality. In the chapter from Orr's book included here, she explores a trinity of images associated in Olsen with the reconstruction of individual identity in relation to human community: journeying, blossoming, and piecing. Naomi Jacobs makes a similar argument, but identifies a different cluster of imagery based on "the four prescientific elements: earth, air, fire, water."[24]

Joanne Trautmann Banks's essay comparing "Tell Me a Riddle" with Tolstoy's "The Death of Ivan Illich" explores how each text inscribes the processes and meanings of dying. Banks, who writes for *Literature and Medicine* as a professor of literature in a medical school, told Olsen in a letter how hundreds of her students have read the story "as they seek to understand terminal illness in an intelligent, humane context . . . they've become better doctors because of it."[25] Her essay, included here, contrasts the stylistic modes of the two texts while suggesting the evolution in each of a language appropriate to each character's spiritual labor in dying.

Olsen's explorations of the hidden experience of maternality in all its power and ambivalence have been noted by a number of critics. One of the few to bring a psychoanalytic feminist perspective to bear on "Tell Me a Riddle," Judith Kegan Gardiner argues that the novella is akin to other contemporary women's fictions of the maternal deathbed in its representation of an embittered maternal figure dying of a "disease of nurturance gone sour, digestive cancer," but different in its vision of potential healing between generations of women. Jeanne's acceptance of her grandmother, Gardiner argues, "breaches the alienation shown in . . . other fictions"; the novella "cuts the noose of the mother knot by weaving a more complex and lovely tie between the generations."[26] The chapter on "Motherhood as Source and Silencer of Creativity" from Mara Faulkner's book included here uses concepts of multiple vision and "organic feminist criticism"; Faulkner deliberately places herself in opposition to postmodernist silencings of contextual concerns, conjoining an interest in contexts with a concern for literary style. Like Orr, she locates three constellations of images in "Tell Me a Riddle"—here, hunger, stone, and flood—seeing them as elaborating a pattern of blight-fruit possibility that pervades Olsen's work as a whole.

For Rachel Blau DuPlessis, the mother-daughter dyad in "Tell Me a Riddle" links it with other texts by contemporary women writers that feature a daughter artist and a mother whose creative capacities are blocked or frustrated. One of the pioneering critical studies of contemporary fiction by women, DuPlessis's *Writing beyond the Ending: Narrative Strategies of Twentieth-Century Women Writers* (1985) brings a materialist feminist analysis to the study of narrative. DuPlessis argues that modern women writers have developed narrative strategies that escape the limits of their nineteenth-century predecessors' narratives: their bifurcation into either romance plots or plots of bildung (development) and quest, and their resolutions either in a heroine's marriage or in her death. The chapter included here examines the figure of the female artist as reconstructed in contemporary women's fictions, inviting us to view Eva as a silenced artist whose last work is the "cantata" she composes in dying. In this reading the granddaughter's practice of her art, similar in its ethical motivation to Eva's, will realize the creative potential left unfulfilled in the grandmother's life.

Constance Coiner's essay applies the poetics of Mikhail Bakhtin to *Tell Me a Riddle,* drawing also on feminist versions of reader-response theory. She demonstrates how Olsen's commitments to social change are elaborated in her linguistic strategies: a democratization of style that, as in Eva's dying "cantata," draws on many voices simultaneously, rather than privileging a univocal narrator; and an open-endedness that invites readers into the text as participants and actors in the making of meaning and the remaking of culture. My essay, "Rereading Tillie Olsen in an Age of Deconstruction," not included here, is in dialogue with Coiner's, as well as with my own earlier work on Olsen. Rereading Olsen at the close of the Reagan–Bush years, an era comparable in many ways to the 1950s when the *Riddle* stories were written, I found in them a sense of loss and alienation that no doubt reflected my own malaise. Reading them through lenses ground in part by the deconstructions of post-modernism—that is, the emphasis on texts as linguistic structures participating in the dominant discourses of an era and inscribing dualistically some of its ideologies—I argued that Olsen's stories both oppose the oppressions and repressions of their era and unwillingly accede in their narrative structure to some of the era's constructions of gender and race. For example, though Jeanne is enriched by and becomes the bearer of her grandmother's legacy, I sensed in her portrayal a diminution, even a domestication, of Eva's revolutionary rage. Yet the stories exist for us primarily as affirmations, the narrative act that created them defying the forces of silence.

It is certain that readers and critics will continue to find much to debate, much to enlighten, and much to inspire in Tillie Olsen's work. To paraphrase her injunction to readers at the outset of her edition of *Life in the Iron Mills:* You are about to give the life of your reading to an American classic. . . . Remember, as you begin to read: these lives, brought here for the first time into literature, unknown, invisible.

☐ *Notes* ∎

1. Robert Coles, "Reconsideration," *New Republic* (December 6, 1975): 30.

2. My discussion of Olsen's life draws on the following sources: personal interviews with Tillie Olsen conducted in 1980 and in 1992 and a lengthy phone conversation in 1994; transcripts of interviews with Olsen conducted in 1986 and graciously supplied by Constance Coiner; Selma Burkom and Margaret Williams, "De-Riddling Tillie Olsen's Writing," *San Jose Studies* 2 (February 1976): 64–83; Elaine Neil Orr, *Tillie Olsen and a Feminist Spiritual Vision* (Jackson: University Press of Mississippi, 1987); and Mickey Pearlman and Abby H. P. Werlock, *Tillie Olsen* (Boston: G. K. Hall, 1991). Subsequent references to these sources typically appear in the text.

3. I use italics for the volume of stories, *Tell Me a Riddle* (Philadelphia: Lippincott, 1961; New York: Dell, Delta, 1989), and quotation marks for the novella, "Tell Me a Riddle." References to the other *Riddle* stories in the text refer to the 1989 edition.

4. Tillie Olsen, *Silences* (New York: Delacorte Press/Seymour Lawrence, 1978), 184. Subsequent references appear in the text.

5. "A Biographical Interpretation," in Rebecca Harding Davis, *Life in the Iron Mills and Other Stories* (Old Westbury, N.Y.: The Feminist Press, 1972, 1985), 157–158. Subsequent references appear in the text.

6. Quoted in Pearlman and Werlock, *Tillie Olsen,* 26.

7. Personal Statement in *First Drafts, Last Drafts: Forty Years of the Creative Writing Program at Stanford University,* prepared by William McPheron with the assistance of Amor Towles (Stanford: Stanford University Libraries, 1989). Included in this volume.

8. Blanche H. Gelfant, "After Long Silence: Tillie Olsen's

'Requa,'" *Women Writing in America: Voices in Collage* (Hanover, N.H.: University Press of New England, 1984), 70.

9. *Yonnondio: From the Thirties* (New York: Delacorte Press/Seymour Lawrence, 1974), viii. Subsequent references appear in the text.

10. "I Stand Here Ironing," in *Tell Me a Riddle* (New York: Dell Delta, 1989), 12.

11. "The Shaping of a Canon: U.S. Fiction 1960–1975," in Robert van Hallberg, ed. *Canons* (Chicago: University of Chicago Press, 1983), passim.; quotations 390, 395–396.

12. Parts of this analysis appear in somewhat different form in my essay, "Rereading *Tell Me a Riddle* in the Age of Deconstruction," in Shelley Fisher Fishkin and Elaine Hedges, eds., *Listening to 'Silences': New Essays in Feminist Criticism* (New York: Oxford University Press, 1994).

13. Dorothy Parker, "Book Reviews," review of *Tell Me a Riddle, Esquire* (June 1962): 64.

14. William H. Peden, "Dilemmas of Day-to-Day Living," review of *Tell Me a Riddle, New York Times Book Review* (November 12, 1961): 54.

15. Coles, 30.

16. "Introduction," Kay Hoyle Nelson and Nancy Huse, eds., *The Critical Response to Tillie Olsen* (New York: Greenwood Press, forthcoming), 16.

17. Cited in Nelson, *The Critical Response*, 5.

18. Ellen Cronan Rose, "Limning: Or Why Tillie Writes," *Hollins Critic* 13.2 (April 1976): 1–13.

19. Catherine R. Stimpson, "Tillie Olsen: Witness as Servant." *Polit: A Journal for Literature and Politics* 1.2 (Fall 1977): 1–12.

20. Judith Newton and Deborah Rosenfelt, "Introduction: Toward a Materialist-Feminist Criticism," *Feminist Criticism and Social Change: Sex, Class, and Race in Literature and Culture* (New York: Methuen, 1985).

21. "Literature of Resistance: The Intersection of Feminism and the Communist Left in Meridel Le Sueur and Tillie Olsen," in Lennard J. Davis and M. Bella Mirabella, eds., *Left Politics and the Literary Profession* (New York: Columbia University Press, 1990); Constance Coiner, *Better Red: The Writing and Resistance of Tillie*

Olsen and Meridel Le Sueur (New York: Oxford University Press, 1995).

22. Jacqueline A. Mintz, "The Myth of the Jewish Mother in Three Jewish, American, Female Writers," *Centennial Review* 22 (1978): 346–55; Rose Yalow Kamel, "Riddles and Silences: Tillie Olsen's Autobiographical Fiction," in *Aggravating the Conscience: Jewish-American Literary Mothers in the Promised Land* (New York: Peter Lang Publishing, 1988), 81–114.

23. Elenore Lester, "The Riddle of Tillie Olsen," *Midstream* (January 1975): 75–79; John Clayton, "Grace Paley and Tillie Olsen: Radical Jewish Humanists," *Response: A Contemporary Jewish Review* 46 (1984): 37–52; Bonnie Lyons, "Tillie Olsen: The Writer as Jewish Woman," *Studies in American Jewish Literature* 5 (1986): 89–102; quotation 93.

24. Naomi M. Jacobs, "Earth, Air, Fire and Water in 'Tell Me a Riddle'," *Studies in Short Fiction* 23 (Fall 1986): 401.

25. Joanne Trautmann Banks, Letter to Tillie Olsen, May 10, 1990.

26. Judith Kegan Gardiner, "A Wake for Mother: The Maternal Deathbed in Women's Fiction," *Feminist Studies* 4 (June 1978): 146–65; quotation page 163.

1912 or 1913	Tillie Lerner is born in Wahoo, Omaha, or Mead, Nebraska, the second of six children.
1929–1930	Leaves high school after eleventh grade; seeks work in Stockton, California.
1931	Relocates to Midwest; joins Young Communist League; organizes workers in Kansas City, Kansas; contracts incipient tuberculosis.
1932	Moves to Faribault, Minnesota; begins *Yonnondio;* gives birth to daughter, Karla.
1933	Moves back to California; settles permanently in San Francisco.
1934	Arrested for participating in San Francisco Maritime Strike; publishes "The Iron Throat," "The Strike," "Thousand Dollar Vagrant," "There Is a Lesson," and "I Want You Women Up North to Know."
1935	Attends American Writers Congress in New York.
1936	Begins relationship with Jack Olsen.
1938	Daughter Julie born.
1943	Daughter Katherine Jo born. Marries Jack Olsen.
1948	Daughter Laurie born.
1953–1954	Writes "I Stand Here Ironing"; begins "Hey Sailor, What Ship?" Enrolls in creative writing course at San Francisco State University.
1955–1956	Attends Stanford University on Stegner fellowship in creative writing; completes "Hey

Adapted from *Tillie Olsen* by Mickey Pearlman and Abby H. P. Werlock (Boston: G. K. Hall, 1991).

	Sailor, What Ship?" and "O Yes"; works on "Tell Me a Riddle."
1956	Publishes "Help Her to Believe" ("I Stand Here Ironing").
1957	Publishes "Hey Sailor, What Ship?" and "Baptism" ("O Yes").
1959	Receives Ford Foundation grant in literature.
1960	Publishes "Tell Me a Riddle."
1961	"Tell Me a Riddle" receives O. Henry first prize for best American short story. *Tell Me a Riddle* (the book) published.
1962–1964	Receives fellowship from Radcliffe Institute for Independent Study.
1969–1970	Visiting Professor and Writer in Residence, Amherst College.
1970	"Requa I" published; reprinted in *Best American Short Stories of 1971*, dedicated to Olsen.
1971	Teaches first "women in literature" class and creative writing seminar at Stanford University.
1972	At MacDowell Writers' Colony in New Hampshire, working on recovered manuscript of *Yonnondio* and on biographical interpretation, "Rebecca Harding Davis, Her Life and Times," published in *Life in the Iron Mills*.
1973–1974	Writer in residence, Massachusetts Institute of Technology.
1974	Publishes *Yonnondio*. Distinguished visiting professor, University of Massachusetts, Boston.
1975–1976	American Academy and National Institute of Arts and Letters award for distinguished contribution to American letters; Guggenheim Fellowship.
1978	Publishes *Silences*.

28

1979	Awarded honorary Litt. D. by University of Nebraska (first of six honorary degrees).
1980	International visiting scholar, Norway; Radcliffe centennial visitor and lecturer. Film version of *Tell Me a Riddle,* directed by Lee Grant.
1981	May 18 proclaimed Tillie Olsen Day in San Francisco.
1983	Tillie Olsen week; symposium, 5 Quad Cities Colleges, Iowa and Illinois.
1983–1984	Awarded Senior Fellowship, National Endowment for the Humanities.
1984	Publishes *Mother to Daughter, Daughter to Mother.*
1985–1986	Bunting Fellow, Radcliffe College
1986	Hill Visiting Professor, University of Minnesota.
1987	Gund Professor, Kenyon College, Gambier, Ohio. Regents lecturer, University of California at Los Angeles.
1989	Jack Olsen dies.
1991	Receives Mari Sandoz Award, Nebraska Library Association.
1994	Receives Rea Award for the Short Story ($25,000 to writers contributing significantly to the short story as an art form).

Tell Me a Riddle

The edition of "Tell Me a Riddle" included here is the 1989 Delta reprint, the most recent version of the text. Olsen has gradually revised "Tell Me a Riddle" since its first publication in 1961, most notably to eliminate language like "man" and "mankind," substituting the more generic and inclusive "human" and "humankind." In the first edition, Eva's quotation from the old socialist hymn, "These Things Shall Be," included the line "all that may plant man's lordship firm"; this line was omitted in subsequent versions. These revisions suggest the influence of feminist critiques of sexist language; they support Olsen's inclusive and democratic vision.

The first edition lacked the hopeful and prophetic subtitle, "These Things Shall Be," included in all subsequent versions. Another interesting change is the alteration of Eva's wish to "journey to her self" to a longing instead to "journey on." The motive behind this change may be guessed by noting another emendation to the same passage when Olsen excerpts it for *Mother to Daughter, Daughter to Mother.* In all editions of the full text, Eva searches for "coherence, transport, meaning." In the daybook, she seeks "coherence, transport, community" (198). Olsen's revisions move the text away from a privileging of the isolated self and develop further the implicit longing for a community and a commitment larger than self or biological family.

❑ Tell Me a Riddle

"These Things Shall Be"*
(1956–1960)

I

For forty-seven years they had been married.
How deep back the stubborn, gnarled roots of the quarrel reached, no one could say—but only now, when
tending to the needs of others no longer shackled them
together, the roots swelled up visible, split the earth between them, and the tearing shook even to the children, long since grown.

Why now, why now? wailed Hannah.

As if when we grew up weren't enough, said
Paul.

Poor Ma. Poor Dad. It hurts so for both of them,
said Vivi. They never had very much; at least in old age
they should be happy.

Knock their heads together, insisted Sammy; tell
'em: you're too old for this kind of thing; no reason not
to get along now.

From *Tell Me a Riddle* (New York: Delta, 1989).

*Poem by John Addington Symonds, sung in the British labor and socialist
movements, and in progressive social and religious movements in the United
States.

Lennie wrote to Clara: They've lived over so much together; what could possibly tear them apart?

Something tangible enough.

Arthritic hands, and such work as he got, occasional. Poverty all his life, and there was little breath left for running. He could not, could not turn away from this desire: to have the troubling of responsibility, the fretting with money, over and done with; to be free, to be *care*free where success was not measured by accumulation, and there was use for the vitality still in him. There was a way. They could sell the house, and with the money join his lodge's Haven, cooperative for the aged. Happy communal life, and was he not already an official; had he not helped organize it, raise funds, served as a trustee?

But she—would not consider it.

"What do we need all this for?" he would ask loudly, for her hearing aid was turned down and the vacuum was shrilling. "Five rooms" (pushing the sofa so she could get into the corner) "furniture" (smoothing down the rug) "floors and surfaces to make work. Tell me, why do we need it?" And he was glad he could ask in a scream.

"Because I'm use't."

"Because you're use't. This is a reason, Mrs. Word Miser? Used to can get unused!"

"Enough unused I have to get used to already. . . . Not enough words?" turning off the vacuum a moment to hear herself answer. "Because soon enough we'll need only a little closet, no windows, no furniture, nothing to make work, but for worms. Because now I want room. . . . Screech and blow like you're doing, you'll need that closet even sooner. . . . Ha, again!"

for the vacuum bag wailed, puffed half up, hung stubbornly limp. "This time fix it so it stays; quick before the phone rings and you get too important-busy."

But while he struggled with the motor, it seethed in him. Why fix it? Why have to bother? And if it can't be fixed, have to wring the mind with how to pay the repair? At the Haven they come in with their own machines to clean your room or your cottage; you fish, or play cards, or make jokes in the sun, not with knotty fingers fight to mend vacuums.

Over the dishes, coaxingly: "For once in your life, to be free, to have everything done for you, like a queen."

"I never liked queens."

"No dishes, no garbage, no towel to sop, no worry what to buy, what to eat."

"And what else would I do with my empty hands? Better to eat at my own table when I want, and to cook and eat how I want."

"In the cottages they buy what you ask, and cook it how you like. *You* are the one who always used to say: better mankind born without mouths and stomachs than always to worry for money to buy, to shop, to fix, to cook, to wash, to clean."

"How cleverly you hid that you heard. I said it then because eighteen hours a day I ran. And you never scraped a carrot or knew a dish towel sops. Now— for you and me—who cares? A herring out of a jar is enough. But when *I* want, and nobody to bother." And she turned off her ear button, so she would not have to hear.

But as *he* had no peace, juggling and rejuggling the money to figure: how will I pay for this now?; prying out the storm windows (there they take care of this); jolting in the streetcar on errands (there I would not have to ride to take care of this or that); fending the patronizing relatives just back from Florida (at the Haven it matters what one is, not what one can afford), he gave *her* no peace.

"Look! In their bulletin. A reading circle. Twice a week it meets."

"Haumm," her answer of not listening.

"A reading circle, Chekhov they read that you like, and Peretz.* Cultured people at the Haven that you would enjoy."

"Enjoy!" She tasted the word. "Now, when it pleases you, you find a reading circle for me. And forty years ago when the children were morsels and there was a Circle, did you stay home with them once so I could go? Even once? You trained me well. I do not need others to enjoy. Others!" Her voice trembled. "Because *you* want to be there with others. Already it makes me sick to think of you always around others. Clown, grimacer, floormat, yesman, entertainer, whatever they want of you."

And now it was he who turned the television loud so he need not hear.

Old scar tissue ruptured and the wounds festered anew. Chekhov indeed. She thought without softness of that young wife, who in the deep night hours while she nursed the current baby, and perhaps held another in her lap, would try to stay awake for the only time there was to read. She would feel again the weather of the outside on his cheek when, coming late from a meet-

---

*Isaac Loeb Peretz, turn-of-the-century Russian writer of fiction in Yiddish.

ing, he would find her so, and stimulated and ardent, sniffing her skin, coax: "I'll put the baby to bed, and you—put the book away, don't read, don't read."

That had been the most beguiling of all the "don't read, put your book away" her life had been. Chekhov indeed!

"Money?" She shrugged him off. "Could we get poorer than once we were? And in America, who starves?"

But as still he pressed:

"Let me alone about money. Was there ever enough? Seven little ones—for every penny I had to ask—and sometimes, remember, there was nothing. But always *I* had to manage. Now *you* manage. Rub your nose in it good."

But from those years she had had to manage, old humiliations and terrors rose up, lived again, and forced her to relive them. The children's needings; that grocer's face or this merchant's wife she had had to beg credit from when credit was a disgrace; the scenery of the long blocks walked around when she could not pay; school coming, and the desperate going over the old to see what could yet be remade; the soups of meat bones begged "for-the-dog" one winter. . . .

Enough. Now they had no children. Let *him* wrack his head for how they would live. She would not exchange her solitude for anything. *Never again to be forced to move to the rhythms of others.*

For in this solitude she had won to a reconciled peace.

Tranquillity from having the empty house no longer an enemy, for it stayed clean—not as in the days when it was her family, the life in it, that had seemed the enemy: tracking, smudging, littering, dirtying, engaging her in endless defeating battle—and on whom her endless defeat had been spewed.

The few old books, memorized from rereading; the pictures to ponder (the magnifying glass superimposed on her heavy eyeglasses). Or if she wishes, when he is gone, the phonograph, that if she turns up very loud and strains, she can hear: the ordered sounds and the struggling.

Out in the garden, growing things to nurture. Birds to be kept out of the pear tree, and when the pears are heavy and ripe, the old fury of work, for all must be canned, nothing wasted.

And her once social duty (for she will not go to luncheons or meetings) the boxes of old clothes left with her, as with a life-practised eye for finding what is still wearable within the worn (again the magnifying glass superimposed on the heavy glasses) she scans and sorts—this for rag or rummage, that for mending and cleaning, and this for sending away.

Being able at last to live within, and not move to the rhythms of others, as life had forced her to: denying; removing; isolating; taking the children one by one; then deafening, half-blinding—and at last, presenting her solitude.

And in it she had won to a reconciled peace.

Now he was violating it with his constant campaigning: *Sell the house and move to the Haven.* (You sit, you sit—there too you could sit like a stone.) He was making of her a battleground where old grievances tore. (Turn on your ear button—I am talking.) And stubbornly she resisted—so that from wheedling, reasoning, manipulation, it was bitterness he now started with.

38

And it came to where every happening lashed up a quarrel.

"I will sell the house anyway," he flung at her one night. "I am putting it up for sale. There will be a way to make you sign."

The television blared, as always it did on the evenings he stayed home, and as always it reached her only as noise. She did not know if the tumult was in her or outside. Snap! she turned the sound off. "Shadows," she whispered to him, pointing to the screen, "look, it is only shadows." And in a scream: "Did you say that you will sell the house? Look at me, not at that. I am no shadow. You cannot sell without me."

"Leave on the television. I am watching."

"Like Paulie, like Jenny, a four-year-old. Staring at shadows. *You cannot sell the house.*"

"I will. We are going to the Haven. There you would not hear the television when you do not want it. I could sit in the social room and watch. You could lock yourself up to smell your unpleasantness in a room by yourself—for who would want to come near you?"

"No, no selling." A whisper now.

"The television is shadows. Mrs. Enlightened! Mrs. Cultured! A world comes into your house—and it is shadows. People you would never meet in a thousand lifetimes. Wonders. When you were four years old, yes, like Paulie, like Jenny, did you know of Indian dances, alligators, how they use bamboo in Malaya? No, you scratched in your dirt with the chickens and thought Olshana* was the world. Yes, Mrs. Unpleasant, I will

---

* Olsen's invented name for a typical village of tsarist Russia.

sell the house, for there better can we be rid of each other than here."

She did not know if the tumult was outside, or in her. Always a ravening inside, a pull to the bed, to lie down, to succumb.

"Have you thought maybe Ma should let a doctor have a look at her?" asked their son Paul after Sunday dinner, regarding his mother crumpled on the couch, instead of, as was her custom, busying herself in Nancy's kitchen.

"Why not the President too?"

"Seriously, Dad. This is the third Sunday she's lain down like that after dinner. Is she that way at home?"

"A regular love affair with the bed. Every time I start to talk to her."

Good protective reaction, observed Nancy to herself. The workings of hos-til-ity.

"Nancy could take her. I just don't like how she looks. Let's have Nancy arrange an appointment."

"You think she'll go?" regarding his wife gloomily. "All right, we have to have doctor bills, we have to have doctor bills." Loudly: "Something hurts you?"

She startled, looked to his lips. He repeated: "Mrs. Take It Easy, something hurts?"

"Nothing. . . . Only you."

"A woman of honey. That's why you're lying down?"

"Soon I'll get up to do the dishes, Nancy."

"Leave them, Mother, I like it better this way."

"Mrs. Take It Easy, Paul says you should start ballet. You should go to see a doctor and ask: how soon can you start ballet?"

"A doctor?" she begged. "Ballet?"

"We were talking, Ma," explained Paul, "you don't seem any too well. It would be a good idea for you to see a doctor for a checkup."

"I get up now to do the kitchen. Doctors are bills and foolishness, my son. I need no doctors."

"At the Haven," he could not resist pointing out, "a doctor is *not* bills. He lives beside you. You start to sneeze, he is there before you open up a Kleenex. You can be sick there for free, all you want."

"Diarrhea of the mouth, is there a doctor to make you dumb?"

"Ma. Promise me you'll go. Nancy will arrange it."

"It's all of a piece when you think of it," said Nancy, "the way she attacks my kitchen, scrubbing under every cup hook, doing the inside of the oven so I can't enjoy Sunday dinner, knowing that half-blind or not, she's going to find every speck of dirt. . . ."

"Don't, Nancy, I've told you—it's the only way she knows to be useful. What did the *doctor* say?"

"A real fatherly lecture. Sixty-nine is young these days. Go out, enjoy life, find interests. Get a new hearing aid, this one is antiquated. Old age is sickness only if one makes it so. Geriatrics, Inc."

"So there was nothing physical."

"Of course there was. How can you live to yourself like she does without there being? Evidence of a kidney disorder, and her blood count is low. He gave her a diet, and she's to come back for follow-up and lab work. . . . But he was clear enough: Number One prescription—start living like a human being. . . . When I think of your dad, who could really play the invalid with

41

that arthritis of his, as active as a teenager, and twice as much fun. . . ."

"You didn't tell me the doctor says your sickness is in you, how you live." He pushed his advantage. "Life and enjoyments you need better than medicine. And this diet, how can you keep it? To weigh each morsel and scrape away each bit of fat, to make this soup, that pudding. There, at the Haven, they have a dietician, they would do it for you."

She is silent.

"You would feel better there, I know it," he says gently. "There there is life and enjoyments all around."

"What is the matter, Mr. Importantbusy, you have no card game or meeting you can go to?"—turning her face to the pillow.

For a while he cut his meetings and going out, fussed over her diet, tried to wheedle her into leaving the house, brought in visitors:

"I should come to a fashion tea. I should sit and look at pretty babies in clothes I cannot buy. This is pleasure?"

"Always you are better than everyone else. The doctor said you should go out. Mrs. Brem comes to you with goodness and you turn her away."

"Because *you* asked her to, she asked me."

"They won't come back. People you need, the doctor said. Your own cousins I asked; they were willing to come and make peace as if nothing had happened. . . ."

"No more crushers of people, pushers, hypocrites,

42

around me. No more in *my* house. You go to
them if you like."

"Kind he is to visit. And you, like ice."

"A babbler. All my life around babblers. Enough!"

"She's even worse, Dad? Then let her stew a while,"
advised Nancy. "You can't let it destroy you; it's a psychological thing, maybe too far gone for any of us to help."

So he let her stew. More and more she lay silent
in bed, and sometimes did not even get up to make the
meals. No longer was the tongue-lashing inevitable if
he left the coffee cup where it did not belong, or forgot
to take out the garbage or mislaid the broom. The birds
grew bold that summer and for once pocked the pears,
undisturbed.

A bellyful of bitterness and every day the same
quarrel in a new way and a different old grievance the
quarrel forced her to enter and relive. And the new torment: I am not really sick, the doctor said it, then why
do I feel so sick?

One night she asked him: "You have a meeting
tonight? Do not go. Stay . . . with me."

He had planned to watch "This Is Your Life," but
half sick himself from the heavy heat, and sickening
therefore the more after the brooks and woods of the
Haven, with satisfaction he grated:

"Hah, Mrs. Live Alone And Like It wants company all of a sudden. It doesn't seem so good the time of
solitary when she was a girl exile in Siberia. 'Do not go.
Stay with me.' A new song for Mrs. Free As A Bird. Yes,
I am going out, and while I am gone chew this alone-
ness good, and think how you keep us both from where
if you want people, you do not need to be alone."

"Go, go. All your life you have gone without me."

After him she sobbed curses he had not heard in years, old-country curses from their childhood: Grow, oh shall you grow like an onion, with your head in the ground. Like the hide of a drum shall you be, beaten in life, beaten in death. Oh shall you be like a chandelier, to hang, and to burn. . . .

She was not in their bed when he came back. She lay on the cot on the sun porch. All week she did not speak or come near him; nor did he try to make peace or care for her.

He slept badly, so used to her next to him. After all the years, old harmonies and dependencies deep in their bodies; she curled to him, or he coiled to her, each warmed, warming, turning as the other turned, the nights a long embrace.

It was not the empty bed or the storm that woke him, but a faint singing. *She* was singing. Shaking off the drops of rain, the lightning riving her lifted face, he saw her so; the cot covers on the floor.

"This is a private concert?" he asked. "Come in, you are wet."

"I can breathe now," she answered; "my lungs are rich." Though indeed the sound was hardly a breath.

"Come in, come in." Loosing the bamboo shades. "Look how wet you are." Half helping, half carrying her, still faint-breathing her song.

A Russian love song of fifty years ago.

He had found a buyer, but before he told her, he called together those children who were close enough to come. Paul, of course, Sammy from New Jersey, Hannah from Connecticut, Vivi from Ohio.

With a kindling of energy for her beloved visitors,

she arrayed the house, cooked and baked. She was not prepared for the solemn after-dinner conclave, they too probing in and tearing. Her frightened eyes watched from mouth to mouth as each spoke.

His stories were eloquent and funny of her refusal to go back to the doctor; of the scorned invitations; of her stubborn silence or the bile "like a Niagara"; of her contrariness: "If I clean it's no good how I cleaned; if I don't clean, I'm still a master who thinks he has a slave."

(Vinegar he poured on me all his life; I am well marinated; how can I be honey now?)

Deftly he marched in the rightness for moving to the Haven; their money from social security free for visiting the children, not sucked into daily needs and into the house; the activities in the Haven for him; but mostly the Haven for *her:* her health, her need of care, distraction, amusement, friends who shared her interests.

"This does offer an outlet for Dad," said Paul; "he's always been an active person. And economic peace of mind isn't to be sneezed at, either. I could use a little of that myself."

But when they asked: "And you, Ma, how do you feel about it?" could only whisper:

"For him it is good. It is not for me. I can no longer live between people."

"You lived all your life *for* people," Vivi cried.

"Not with." Suffering doubly for the unhappiness on her children's faces.

"You have to find some compromise," Sammy insisted. "Maybe sell the house and buy a trailer. After forty-seven years there's surely some way you can find to live in peace."

"There is no help, my children. Different things we need."

"Then live alone!" He could control himself no longer. "I have a buyer for the house. Half the money for you, half for me. Either alone or with me to the Haven. You think I can live any longer as we are doing now?"

"Ma doesn't have to make a decision this minute, however you feel, Dad," Paul said quickly, "and you wouldn't want her to. Let's let it lay a few months, and then talk some more."

"I think I can work it out to take Mother home with me for a while," Hannah said. "You both look terrible, but especially you, Mother. I'm going to ask Phil to have a look at you."

"Sure," cracked Sammy. "What's the use of a doctor husband if you can't get free service out of him once in a while for the family? And absence might make the heart . . . you know."

"There was something after all," Paul told Nancy in a colorless voice. "That was Hannah's Phil calling. Her gall bladder. . . . Surgery."

"Her *gall* bladder. If that isn't classic. 'Bitter as gall'—talk of psychosom——"

He stepped closer, put his hand over her mouth, and said in the same colorless, plodding voice. "We have to get Dad. They operated at once. The cancer was everywhere, surrounding the liver, everywhere. They did what they could . . . at best she has a year. Dad . . . we have to tell him."

II

Honest in his weakness when they told him, and that she was not to know. "I'm not an actor. She'll know right away by how I am. Oh that poor woman. I am old too, it will break me into pieces. Oh that poor woman. She will spit on me; 'So my sickness was how I live.' Oh Paulie, how she will be, that poor woman. Only she should not suffer. . . . I can't stand sickness, Paulie, I can't go with you."

But went. And play-acted.

"A grand opening and you did not even wait for me. . . . A good thing Hannah took you with her."

"Fashion teas I needed. They cut out what tore in me; just in my throat something hurts yet. . . . Look! so many flowers, like a funeral. Vivi called, did Hannah tell you? And Lennie from San Francisco, and Clara; and Sammy is coming." Her gnome's face pressed happily into the flowers.

It is impossible to predict in these cases, but once over the immediate effects of the operation, she should have several months of comparative well-being.

The money, where will come the money?

Travel with her, Dad. Don't take her home to the old associations. The other children will want to see her.

The money, where will I wring the money?

Whatever happens, she is not to know. No, you can't ask her to sign papers to sell the house; nothing to upset her. Borrow instead, then after. . . .

I had wanted to leave you each a few dollars to make life easier, as other fathers do. There will be nothing left now. (Failure! you and your "business is exploitation." Why didn't you make it when it could be made?—Is that what you're thinking of me, Sammy?)

47

Sure she's unreasonable, Dad—but you have to stay with her; if there's to be any happiness in what's left of her life, it depends on you.

Prop me up, children, think of me, too. Shuffled, chained with her, bitter woman. No Haven, and the little money going. . . . How happy she looks, poor creature.

The look of excitement. The straining to hear everything (the new hearing aid turned full). Why are you so happy, dying woman?

How the petals are, fold on fold, and the gladioli color. The autumn air.

Stranger grandsons, tall above the little gnome grandmother, the little spry grandfather. Paul in a frenzy of picture-taking before going.

She, wandering the great house. Feeling the books; laughing at the maple shoemaker's bench of a hundred years ago used as a table. The ear turned to music.

"Let us go home. See how good I walk now." "One step from the hospital," he answers, "and she wants to fly. Wait till Doctor Phil says."

"Look—the birds too are flying home. Very good Phil is and will not show it, but he is sick of sickness by the time he comes home."

"Mrs. Telepathy, to read minds," he answers; "read mine what it says: when the trunks of medicines become a suitcase, then we will go."

The grandboys, they do not know what to say to us. . . . Hannah, she runs around here, there, when is there time for herself?

Let us go home. Let us go home.

Musing; gentleness—*but for the incidents of the rabbi in the hospital, and of the candles of benediction.*

Of the rabbi in the hospital:

Now tell me what happened, Mother.

From the sleep I awoke, Hannah's Phil, and he stands there like a devil in a dream and calls me by name. I cannot hear. I think he prays. Go away, please, I tell him, I am not a believer. Still he stands, while my heart knocks with fright.

You scared *him,* Mother. He thought you were delirious.

Who sent him? Why did he come to *me?*

It is a custom. The men of God come to visit those of their religion they might help. The hospital makes up the list for them—race, religion—and you are on the Jewish list.

Not for rabbis. At once go and make them change. Tell them to write: Race, human; Religion, none.

And of the candles of benediction:

Look how you have upset yourself, Mrs. Excited Over Nothing. Pleasant memories you should leave.

Go in, go back to Hannah and the lights. Two weeks I saw candles and said nothing. But she asked me.

So what was so terrible? She forgets you never did, she asks you to light the Friday candles and say the benediction like Phil's mother when she visits. If the candles give her pleasure, why shouldn't she have the pleasure?

Not for pleasure she does it. For emptiness. Because his family does. Because all around her do.

That is not a good reason too? But you did not
hear her. For heritage, she told you. For the boys,
from the past they should have tradition.

Superstition! From our ancestors, savages, afraid
of the dark, of themselves: mumbo words and magic
lights to scare away ghosts.

She told you: how it started does not take away
the goodness. For centuries, peace in the house it
means.

Swindler! does she look back on the dark centuries? Candles bought instead of bread and stuck into
a potato for a candlestick? Religion that stifled and
said: in Paradise, woman, you will be the footstool
of your husband, and in life—poor chosen Jew—
ground under, despised, trembling in cellars. And
cremated. And cremated.*

This is religion's fault? You think you are still an
orator of the 1905 revolution?** Where are the pills
for quieting? Which are they?

Heritage. How have we come from our savage
past, how no longer to be savages—this to teach. To
look back and learn what humanizes—this to teach.
To smash all ghettos that divide us—not to go back,
not to go back—this to teach. Learned books in the
house, will humankind live or die, and she gives to
her boys—superstition.

Hannah that is so good to you. Take your pill,
Mrs. Excited For Nothing, swallow.

---

* Alludes to Yiddish folk saying, the basis of Peretz's story, "A Good Marriage,"
and to the cremations in Nazi concentration camps.
** Broad uprising against the regime of Tsar Nicholas II that temporarily ini-
tiated a series of democratizing concessions.

Heritage! But when did I have time to teach? Of
Hannah I asked only hands to help.
Swallow.
Otherwise—musing; gentleness.

Not to travel. To go home.
The children want to see you. We have to show
them you are as thorny a flower as ever.
Not to travel.
Vivi wants you should see her new baby. She sent
the tickets—airplane tickets—a Mrs. Roosevelt she
wants to make of you. To Vivi's we have to go.

A new baby. How many warm, seductive babies. She
holds him stiffly, *away* from her, so that he wails. And a
long shudder begins, and the sweat beads on her
forehead.
"Hush, shush," croons the grandfather, lifting
him back. "You should forgive your grandmamma, little
prince, she has never held a baby before, only seen
them in glass cases. Hush, shush."
"You're tired, Ma," says Vivi. "The travel and the
noisy dinner. I'll take you to lie down."
(*A long travel from, to, what the feel of a baby
evokes.*)

In the airplane, cunningly designed to encase from motion (no wind, no feel of flight), she had sat severely
and still, her face turned to the sky through which they
cleaved and left no scar.
So this was how it looked, the determining, the
crucial sky, and this was how man moved through it,
remote above the dwindled earth, the concealed human
life. Vulnerable life, that could scar.

There was a steerage ship of memory that shook across a great, circular sea; clustered, ill human beings; and through the thick-stained air, tiny fretting waters in a window round like the airplane's—sun round, moon round. (The round thatched roofs of Olshana.) Eye round—like the smaller window that framed distance the solitary year of exile when only her eyes could travel, and no voice spoke. And the polar winds hurled themselves across snows trackless and endless and white—like the clouds which had closed together below and hidden the earth.

Now they put a baby in her lap. Do not ask me, she would have liked to beg. Enough the worn face of Vivi, the remembered grandchildren. I cannot, cannot. . . .

Cannot what? Unnatural grandmother, not able to make herself embrace a baby.

She lay there in the bed of the two little girls, her new hearing aid turned full, listening to the sound of the children going to sleep, the baby's fretful crying and hushing, the clatter of dishes being washed and put away. They thought she slept. Still she rode on.

It was not that she had not loved her babies, her children. The love—the passion of tending—had risen with the need like a torrent; and like a torrent drowned and immolated all else. But when the need was done— oh the power that was lost in the painful damming back and drying up of what still surged, but had nowhere to go. Only the thin pulsing left that could not quiet, suffering over lives one felt, but could no longer hold nor help.

On that torrent she had borne them to their own lives, and the riverbed was desert long years now. Not there would she dwell, a memoried wraith. Surely that was not all, surely there was more. Still the springs, the springs were in her seeking. Somewhere an older power that beat for life. Somewhere coherence, transport, meaning. If they would but leave her in the air now stilled of clamor, in the reconciled solitude, to journey on.

And they put a baby in her lap. Immediacy to embrace, and the breath of *that* past: warm flesh like this that had claims and nuzzled away all else and with lovely mouths devoured; hot-living like an animal— intensely and now; the turning maze; the long drunkenness; the drowning into needing and being needed. Severely she looked back—and the shudder seized her again, and the sweat. Not that way. Not there, not now could she, not yet. . . .

And all that visit, she could not touch the baby.

"Daddy, is it the . . . sickness she's like that?" asked Vivi. "I was so glad to be having the baby—for her. I told Tim, it'll give her more happiness than anything, being around a baby again. And she hasn't played with him once."

He was not listening, "Aahh little seed of life, little charmer," he crooned, "Hollywood should see you. A heart of ice you would melt. Kick, kick. The future you'll have for a ball. In 2050 still kick. Kick for your grandaddy then."

Attentive with the older children; sat through their performances (command performance; we command you to be the audience); helped Ann sort autumn leaves to find the best for a school program; listened gravely to Richard tell about his rock collection, while her lips mutely formed the words to remember: *igneous, sedi-*

mentary, metamorphic; looked for missing socks, books, and bus tickets; watched the children whoop after their grandfather who knew how to tickle, chuck, lift, toss, do tricks, tell secrets, make jokes, match riddle for riddle. (Tell me a riddle, Grammy. I know no riddles, child.) Scrubbed sills and woodwork and furniture in every room; folded the laundry; straightened drawers; emptied the heaped baskets waiting for ironing (while he or Vivi or Tim nagged: You're supposed to rest here, you've been sick) but to none tended or gave food—and could not touch the baby.

After a week she said: "Let us go home. Today call about the tickets."

"You have important business, Mrs. Inahurry? The President waits to consult with you?" He shouted, for the fear of the future raced in him. "The clothes are still warm from the suitcase, your children cannot show enough how glad they are to see you, and you want home. There is plenty of time for home. We cannot be with the children at home."

"Blind to around you as always: the little ones sleep four in a room because we take their bed. We are two more people in a house with a new baby, and no help."

"Vivi is happy so. The children should have their grandparents a while, she told to me. I should have my mommy and daddy. . . ."

"Babbler and blind. Do you look at her so tired? How she starts to talk and she cries? I am not strong enough yet to help. Let us go home."

(To reconciled solitude.)

For it seemed to her the crowded noisy house was listening to her, listening for her. She could feel it like a

*great ear pressed under her heart. And everything
knocked: quick constant raps: let me in, let me in.*

*How was it that soft reaching tendrils also be-
came blows that knocked?*

C'mon, Grandma, I want to show you. . . .

Tell me a riddle, Grandma. (*I know no riddles.*)

Look, Grammy, he's so dumb he can't even find
his hands. (Dody and the baby on a blanket over
the fermenting autumn mould.)

I made them—for you. (Ann) (Flat paper dolls
with aprons that lifted on scalloped skirts that
lifted on flowered pants; hair of yarn and great
ringed questioning eyes.)

Watch me, Grandma. (Richard snaking up the
tree, hanging exultant, free, with one hand at
the top. Below Dody hunching over in pretend-
cooking.) (*Climb too, Dody, climb and look.*)

Be my nap bed, Grammy. (The "No!" too late.)
Morty's abandoned heaviness, while his fingers
ladder up and down her hearing-aid cord to his
drowsy chant: eentsiebeentsiespider. (*Children
trust.*)

It's to start off your own rock collection, Grandma. That's a trilobite fossil, 200 million years old
(millions of years on a boy's mouth) and that
one's obsidian, black glass.

Knocked and knocked.

Mother, I *told* you the teacher said we had to
bring it back all filled out this morning. Didn't you
even ask Daddy? Then tell *me* which plan and I'll
check it: evacuate or stay in the city or wait for
you to come and take me away. (Seeing the look of

straining to hear.) It's for Disaster, Grandma. (*Children trust.*)

Vivi in the maze of the long, the lovely drunkenness. The old old noises: baby sounds; screaming of a mother flayed to exasperation; children quarreling; children playing; singing; laughter.

And Vivi's tears and memories, spilling so fast, half the words not understood.

She had started remembering out loud deliberately, so her mother would know the past was cherished, still lived in her.

Nursing the baby: My friends marvel, and I tell them, oh it's easy to be such a cow. I remember how beautiful my mother seemed nursing my brother, and the milk just flows. . . . Was that Davy? It must have been Davy. . . .

Lowering a hem: How did you ever . . . when I think how you made everything we wore . . . Tim, just think, seven kids and Mommy sewed everything . . . do I remember you sang while you sewed? That white dress with the red apples on the skirt you fixed over for me, was it Hannah's or Clara's before it was mine?

Washing sweaters: Ma, I'll never forget, one of those days so nice you washed clothes outside; one of the first spring days it must have been. The bubbles just danced while you scrubbed, and we chased after, and you stopped to show us how to blow our own bubbles with green onion stalks . . . you always. . . .

"Strong onion, to still make you cry after so many years," her father said, to turn the tears into laughter.

While Richard bent over his homework: Where is it now, do we still have it, the Book of the Martyrs? It always seemed so, well—exalted, when you'd put it on

56

the round table and we'd all look at it together; there was even a halo from the lamp. The lamp with the beaded fringe you could move up and down; they're in style again, pulley lamps like that, but without the fringe. You know the book I'm talking about, Daddy, the Book of Martyrs, the first picture was a bust of Spartacus . . . Socrates? I wish there was something like that for the children, Mommy, to give them what you. . . . (And the tears splashed again.)

(What I intended and did not? Stop it, daughter, stop it, leave that time. And he, the hypocrite, sitting there with tears in his eyes—it was nothing to you then, nothing.)

. . . The time you came to school and I almost died of shame because of your accent and because I knew you knew I was ashamed; how could I? . . . Sammy's harmonica and you danced to it once, yes you did, you and Davy squealing in your arms. . . . That time you bundled us up and walked us down to the railway station to stay the night 'cause it was heated and we didn't have any coal, that winter of the strike, you didn't think I remembered that, did you, Mommy? . . . How you'd call us out to see the sunsets. . . .

Day after day, the spilling memories. Worse now, questions, too. Even the grandchildren: Grandma, in the olden days, when you were little. . . .

It was the afternoons that saved.

While they thought she napped, she would leave the mosaic on the wall (of children's drawings, maps, calendars, pictures, Ann's cardboard dolls with their great ringed questioning eyes) and hunch in the girls' closet on the low shelf where the shoes stood, and the girls' dresses covered.

For that while she would painfully sheathe against the listening house, the tendrils and noises that knocked, and Vivi's spilling memories. Sometimes it helped to braid and unbraid the sashes that dangled, or to trace the pattern on the hoop slips.

Today she had jacks and children under jet trails to forget. Last night, Ann and Dody silhouetted in the window against a sunset of flaming man-made clouds of jet trail, their jacks ball accenting the peaceful noise of dinner being made. Had she told them, yes she had told them of how they played jacks in her village though there was no ball, no jacks. Six stones, round and flat, toss them out, the seventh on the back of the hand, toss, catch and swoop up as many as possible, toss again. . . .

Of stones (repeating Richard) there are three kinds: earth's fire jetting; rock of layered centuries; crucibled new out of the old (*igneous, sedimentary, metamorphic*). But there was that other—frozen to black glass, never to transform or hold the fossil memory . . . (let not my seed fall on stone). There was an ancient man who fought to heights a great rock that crashed back down eternally*—eternal labor, freedom, labor . . . (stone will perish, but the word remain). And you, David, who with a stone slew, screaming: Lord, take my heart of stone and give me flesh.**

---

* Alludes to the myth of Sisyphus, who was punished eternally in Tartarus for reporting the whereabouts of Zeus, king of the gods, to the father of the maiden Zeus had seized.

** Alludes to the biblical story of David's triumph over the giant Philistine, Goliath; Samuel I : 17. The quotation, which Olsen heard in a black church, paraphrases Ezekiel 11 : 19: "I shall remove the heart of stone from their bodies and give them a heart of flesh."

Who was screaming? Why was she back in the
common room of the prison, the sun motes dancing in
the shafts of light, and the informer being brought in, a
prisoner now, like themselves. And Lisa leaping, yes,
Lisa, the gentle and tender, biting at the betrayer's
jugular. Screaming and screaming.

No, it is the children screaming. Another of Paul
and Sammy's terrible fights?

In Vivi's house. Severely: you are in Vivi's house.

Blows, screams, a call: "Grandma!" For her? Oh
please not for her. Hide, hunch behind the dresses
deeper. But a trembling little body hurls itself beside
her—surprised, smothered laughter, arms surround
her neck, tears rub dry on her cheek, and words too soft
to understand whisper into her ear (Is this where you
hide too, Grammy? It's my secret place, we have a secret now).

And the sweat beads, and the long shudder
seizes.

It seemed the great ear pressed inside now, and the
knocking. "We have to go home," she told him, "I grow
ill here."

"It's your own fault, Mrs. Bodybusy, you do not
rest, you do too much." He raged, but the fear was in
his eyes. "It was a serious operation, they told you to
take care. . . . All right, we will go to where you can
rest."

But where? Not home to death, not yet. He had
thought to Lennie's, to Clara's; beautiful visits with
each of the children. She would have to rest first, be
stronger. If they could but go to Florida—it glittered before him, the never-realized promise of Florida. Califor-

nia: of course. (The money, the money, dwindling!) Los
Angeles first for sun and rest, then to Lennie's in San
Francisco.

He told her the next day. "You saw what Nancy
wrote: snow and wind back home, a terrible winter.
And look at you—all bones and a swollen belly. I called
Phil: he said: 'A prescription, Los Angeles sun and
rest.'"

She watched the words on his lips. "You have
sold the house," she cried, "that is why we do not go
home. That is why you talk no more of the Haven, why
there is money for travel. After the children you will
drag me to the Haven."

"The Haven! Who thinks of the Haven any more?
Tell her, Vivi, tell Mrs. Suspicious: a prescription, sun
and rest, to make you healthy. . . . And how could I sell
the house without *you?*"

At the place of farewells and greetings, of winds of coming and winds of going, they say their good-byes.

They look back at her with the eyes of others before them: Richard with her own blue blaze; Ann with
the nordic eyes of Tim; Morty's dreaming brown of a
great-grandmother he will never know; Dody with the
laughing eyes of him who had been her springtide love
(who stands beside her now); Vivi's, all tears.

The baby's eyes are closed in sleep.
Good-bye, my children.

III

It is to the back of the great city he brought her, to the
dwelling places of the cast-off old. Bounded by two lines

of amusement piers to the north and to the south, and between a long straight paving rimmed with black benches facing the sand—sands so wide the ocean is only a far fluting.

In the brief vacation season, some of the boarded stores fronting the sands open, and families, young people and children, may be seen. A little tasselled tram shuttles between the piers, and the lights of roller coasters prink and tweak over those who come to have sensation made in them.

The rest of the year it is abandoned to the old, all else boarded up and still; seemingly empty, except the occasional days and hours when the sun, like a tide, sucks them out of the low rooming houses, casts them onto the benches and sandy rim of the walk—and sweeps them into decaying enclosures once again.

A few newer apartments glint among the low bleached squares. It is in one of these Lennie's Jeannie has arranged their rooms. "Only a few miles north and south people pay hundreds of dollars a month for just this gorgeous air, Grandaddy, just this ocean closeness."

She had been ill on the plane, lay ill for days in the unfamiliar room. Several times the doctor came by—left medicine she would not take. Several times Jeannie drove in the twenty miles from work, still in her Visiting Nurse uniform, the lightness and brightness of her like a healing.

"Who can believe it is winter?" he asked one morning. "Beautiful it is outside like an ad. Come, Mrs. Invalid, come to taste it. You are well enough to sit in here, you are well enough to sit outside. The doctor said it too."

But the benches were encrusted with people, and the sands at the sidewalk's edge. Besides, she had seen the far ruffle of the sea: "there take me," and though she leaned against him, it was she who led.

Plodding and plodding, sitting often to rest, he grumbling. Patting the sand so warm. Once she scooped up a handful, cradling it close to her better eye; peered, and flung it back. And as they came almost to the brink and she could see the glistening wet, she sat down, pulled off her shoes and stockings, left him and began to run. "You'll catch cold," he screamed, but the sand in his shoes weighed him down—he who had always been the agile one—and already the white spray creamed her feet.

He pulled her back, took a handkerchief to wipe off the wet and the sand. "Oh no," she said, "the sun will dry," seized the square and smoothed it flat, dropped on it a mound of sand, knotted the kerchief corners and tied it to a bag—"to look at with the strong glass" (for the first time in years explaining an action of hers)—and lay down with the little bag against her cheek, looking toward the shore that nurtured life as it first crawled toward consciousness the millions of years ago.

He took her one Sunday in the evil-smelling bus, past flat miles of blister houses, to the home of relatives. Oh what is this? she cried as the light began to smoke and the houses to dim and recede. Smog, he said, everyone knows but you. . . . Outside he kept his arms about her, but she walked with hands pushing the heavy air as if to open it, whispered: who has done this? sat down suddenly to vomit at the curb and for a long while refused to rise.

One's age as seen on the altered face of those known in youth. Is this they he has come to visit? This Max and Rose, smooth and pleasant, introducing them to polite children, disinterested grandchildren, "the whole family, once a month on Sundays. And why not? We have the room, the help, the food."

Talk of cars, of houses, of success: this son that, that daughter this. And *your* children? Hastily skimped over, the intermarriages, the obscure work—"my doctor son-in-law, Phil"—all he has to offer. She silent in a corner. (Car-sick like a baby, he explains.) Years since he has taken her to visit anyone but the children, and old apprehensions prickle: "no incidents," he silently begs, "no incidents." He itched to tell them. "A very sick woman," significantly, indicating her with his eyes, "a very sick woman." Their restricted faces did not react. "Have you thought maybe she'd do better at Palm Springs?" Rose asked. "Or at least a nicer section of the beach, nicer people, a pool." Not to have to say "money" he said instead: "would she have sand to look at through a magnifying glass?" and went on, detail after detail, the old habit betraying of parading the queerness of her for laughter.

After dinner—the others into the living room in men- or women-clusters, or into the den to watch TV— the four of them alone. She sat close to him, and did not speak. Jokes, stories, people they had known, beginning of reminiscence, Russia fifty-sixty years ago. Strange words across the Duncan Phyfe table: *hunger; secret meetings; human rights; spies; betrayals; prison; escape*—interrupted by one of the grandchildren: "Commercial's on; any Coke left? Gee, you're missing a real hair-raiser." And then a granddaughter (Max proudly: "look at her, an American queen") drove them home on

her way back to U.C.L.A. No incident—except that
there had been no incidents.

The first few mornings she had taken with her the
magnifying glass, but he would sit only on the benches,
so she rested at the foot, where slatted bench shadows
fell, and unless she turned her hearing aid down, other
voices invaded.

Now on the days when the sun shone and she
felt well enough, he took her on the tram to where
the benches ranged in oblongs, some with tables for
checkers or cards. Again the blanket on the sand in the
striped shadows, but she no longer brought the magnifying glass. He played cards, and she lay in the sun and
looked towards the waters; or they walked—two blocks
down to the scaling hotel, two blocks back—past chili-
hamburger stands, open-doored bars, Next-to-New and
perpetual rummage sale stores.

Once, out of the aimless walkers, slow and shuf-
fling like themselves, someone ran unevenly towards
them, embraced, kissed, wept: "dear friends, old friends."
A friend of *hers,* not his: Mrs. Mays who had lived next
door to them in Denver when the children were small.

Thirty years are compressed into a dozen sentences; and the present, not even in three. All is told:
the children scattered; the husband dead; she lives in a
room two blocks up from the sing hall—and points to
the domed auditorium jutting before the pier. The leg?
phlebitis; the heavy breathing? that, one does not ask.
She, too, comes to the benches each day to sit. And tomorrow, tomorrow, are they going to the community
sing? Of course he would have heard of it, everybody
goes—the big doings they wait for all week. They have

never been? She will come to them for dinner tomorrow and they will all go together.

So it is that she sits in the wind of the singing, among the thousand various faces of age.

    She had turned off her hearing aid at once they came into the auditorium—as she would have wished to turn off sight.

    One by one they streamed by and imprinted on her—and though the savage zest of their singing came voicelessly soft and distant, the faces still roared—the faces densened the air—chorded into

children-chants, mother-croons, singing of the chained love serenades, Beethoven storms, mad Lucia's scream drunken joy-songs, keens for the dead, work-singing

> *while from floor to balcony to dome a bare-footed sore-covered little girl threaded the sound-thronged tumult, danced her ecstasy of grimace to flutes that scratched at a cross-roads village wedding*

Yes, faces became sound, and the sound became faces; and faces and sound became weight—pushed, pressed

"Air"—her hands claw his.

    "Whenever I enjoy myself. . . ." Then he saw the gray sweat on her face. "Here. Up. Help me, Mrs. Mays," and they support her out to where she can gulp the air in sob after sob.

    "A doctor, we should get for her a doctor."

    "Tch, it's nothing," says Ellen Mays, "I get it all the time. You've missed the tram; come to my place. Fix your hearing aid, honey . . . close . . . tea. My view.

See, she *wants* to come. Steady now, that's how." Adding mysteriously: "Remember your advice, easy to keep your head above water, empty things float. Float."

The singing a fading march for them, tall woman with a swollen leg, weaving little man, and the swollen thinness they help between.

The stench in the hall: mildew? decay? "We sit and rest then climb. My gorgeous view. We help each other and here we are."

The stench along into the slab of room. A washstand for a sink, a box with oilcloth tacked around for a cupboard, a three-burner gas plate. Artificial flowers, colorless with dust. Everywhere pictures foaming: wedding, baby, party, vacation, graduation, family pictures. From the narrow couch under a slit of window, sure enough the view: lurching rooftops and a scallop of ocean heaving, preening, twitching under the moon.

"While the water heats. Excuse me . . . down the hall." Ellen Mays has gone.

"You'll live?" he asks mechanically, sat down to feel his fright; tried to pull her alongside.

She pushed him away. "For air," she said; stood clinging to the dresser. Then, in a terrible voice:

After a lifetime of room. Of many rooms.

Shhh.

You remember how she lived. Eight children. And now one room   like a coffin.

She pays rent!

Shrinking the life of her   into one room   like a coffin   Rooms and rooms like this   I lie on the quilt and hear them talk

Please, Mrs. Orator-without-Breath.

Once you went for coffee   I walked   I saw   A

Balzac   a Chekhov to write it   Rummage   Alone   On
scraps
     Better old here than in the old country!
     On scraps   Yet they sang like   like   Wondrous!
Humankind   one has to believe   So strong   for what?
To rot   not grow?
     Your poor lungs beg you. They sob between each
word.
     Singing.   Unused   the life in them. She   in this
poor room   with her   pictures   Max   You   The
children   Everywhere unused the life   And who
has meaning?   Century after century   still all in
us   not   to grow?
     Coffins, rummage, plants: sick woman. Oh lay
down. We will get for you the doctor.
     "And when will it end. Oh, *the end.*" *That* night-
mare thought, and this time she writhed, crumpled
against him, seized his hand (for a moment again the
weight the soft distant roaring of humanity) and on the
strangled-for breath, begged: "Man . . . we'll destroy
ourselves?"
     And looking for answer—in the helpless pity and
fear for her (for *her*) that distorted his face—she understood the last months, and knew that she was dying.

     IV

"Let us go home," she said after several days.
     "You are in training for a cross-country run? That
is why you do not even walk across the room? Here, like
a prescription Phil said, till you are stronger from the
operation. You want to break doctor's orders?"
     She saw the fiction was necessary to him, was

silent; then: "At home I will get better. If the doctor here says?"

"And winter? And the visits to Lennie and to Clara? All right," for he saw the tears in her eyes, "I will write Phil, and talk to the doctor."

Days passed. He reported nothing. Jeannie came and took her out for air, past the boarded concessions, the hooded and tented amusement rides, to the end of the pier. They watched the spent waves feeding the new, the gulls in the clouded sky; even up where they sat, the wind-blown sand stung.

She did not ask to go down the crooked steps to the sea.

Back in her bed, while he was gone to the store, she said: "Jeannie, this doctor, he is not one I can ask questions. Ask him for me, can I go home?"

Jeannie looked at her, said quickly: "Of course, poor Granny. You want your own things around you, don't you? I'll call him tonight. . . . Look, I've something to show you," and from her purse unwrapped a large cookie, intricately shaped like a little girl. "Look at the curls—can you hear me well, Granny?—and the darling eyelashes. I just came from a house where they were baking them."

"The dimples, there in the knees," she marveled, holding it to the better light, turning, studying, "like art. Each singly they cut, or a mold?"

"Singly," said Jeannie, "and if it is a child only the mother can make them. Oh Granny, it's the likeness of a real little girl who died yesterday—Rosita. She was three years old. *Pan del Muerto,* the Bread of the Dead. It was the custom in the part of Mexico they came from."

Still she turned and inspected. "Look, the hollow

in the throat, the little cross necklace. . . . I think for
the mother it is a good thing to be busy with such
bread. You know the family?"

Jeannie nodded. "On my rounds. I nursed . . . Oh
Granny, it is like a party; they play songs she liked to
dance to. The coffin is lined with pink velvet and she
wears a white dress. There are candles. . . ."

"In the house?" Surprised, "They keep her in the
house?"

"Yes, said Jeannie, "and it *is* against the health
law. The father said it will be sad to bury her in this
country; in Oaxaca they have a feast night with candles
each year; everyone picnics on the graves of those they
loved until dawn."

"Yes, Jeannie, the living must comfort themselves." And closed her eyes.

"You want to sleep, Granny?"

"Yes, tired from the pleasure of you. I may keep
the Rosita? There stand it, on the dresser, where I can
see; something of my own around me."

In the kitchenette, helping her grandfather unpack the
groceries, Jeannie said in her light voice:

"I'm resigning my job, Grandaddy."

"Ah, the lucky young man. Which one is he?"

"Too late. You're spoken for." She made a pyra-
mid of cans, unstacked, and built again.

"Something is wrong with the job?"

"With me. I can't be"—she searched for the
word—"What they call professional enough. I let myself feel things. And tomorrow I have to report a
family. . . ." The cans clicked again. "It's not that, either. I just don't know what I want to do, maybe go
back to school, maybe go to art school. I thought if you

went to San Francisco I'd come along and talk it over with Momma and Daddy. But I don't see how you can go. She wants to go home. She asked me to ask the doctor."

The doctor told her himself. "Next week you may travel, when you are a little stronger." But next week there was the fever of an infection, and by the time that was over, she could not leave the bed—a rented hospital bed that stood beside the double bed he slept in alone now.

Outwardly the days repeated themselves. Every other afternoon and evening he went out to his new-found cronies, to talk and play cards. Twice a week, Mrs. Mays came. And the rest of the time, Jeannie was there.

By the sickbed stood Jeannie's FM radio. Often into the room the shapes of music came. She would lie curled on her side, her knees drawn up, intense in listening (Jeannie sketched her so, coiled, convoluted like an ear), then thresh her hand out and abruptly snap the radio mute—still to lie in her attitude of listening, concealing tears.

Once Jeannie brought in a young Marine to visit, a friend from high-school days she had found wandering near the empty pier. Because Jeannie asked him to, gravely, without self-consciousness, he sat himself crosslegged on the floor and performed for them a dance of his native Samoa.

Long after they left, a tiny thrumming sound could be heard where, in her bed, she strove to repeat the beckon, flight, surrender of his hands, the fluttering footbeats, and his low plaintive calls.

Hannah and Phil sent flowers. To deepen her

pleasure, he placed one in her hair. "Like a girl," he said, and brought the hand mirror so she could see. She looked at the pulsing red flower, the yellow skull face; a desolate, excited laugh shuddered from her, and she pushed the mirror away—but let the flower burn.

The week Lennie and Helen came, the fever returned. With it the excited laugh, and incessant words. She, who in her life had spoken but seldom and then only when necessary (never having learned the easy, social uses of words), now in dying, spoke incessantly.

In a half-whisper: "Like Lisa she is, your Jeannie. Have I told you of Lisa who taught me to read? Of the highborn she was, but noble in herself. I was sixteen; they beat me; my father beat me so I would not go to her. It was forbidden, she was a Tolstoyan.* At night, past dogs that howled, terrible dogs, my son, in the snows of winter to the road, I to ride in her carriage like a lady, to books. To her, life was holy, knowledge was holy, and she taught me to read. They hung her. Everything that happens one must try to understand why. She killed one who betrayed many. Because of betrayal, betrayed all she lived and believed. In one minute she killed, before my eyes (there is so much blood in a human being, my son), in prison with me. All that happens, one must try to understand.

"The name?" Her lips would work. "The name that was their pole star; the doors of the death houses fixed to open on it; I read of it my year of penal servitude. Thuban!" very excited, "Thuban, in ancient

---

*Follower of the novelist Tolstoy, who opposed the private ownership of property and supported the dignity of peasant life.

Egypt the pole star. Can you see, look out to see it,
Jeannie, if it swings around *our* pole star that seems to
us not to move.

"Yes, Jeannie, at your age my mother and grandmother had already buried children . . . yes, Jeannie, it
is more than oceans between Olshana and you . . . yes,
Jeannie, they danced, and for all the bodies they had they
might as well be chickens, and indeed, they scratched
and flapped their arms and hopped.

"And Andrei Yefimitch, who for twenty years had
never known of it and never wanted to know, said as if
he wanted to cry: but why my dear friend this malicious laughter?" Telling to herself half-memorized
phrases from her few books. "Pain I answer with tears
and cries, baseness with indignation, meanness with
repulsion . . . for life may be hated or wearied of, but
never despised."*

Delirious: "Tell me, my neighbor, Mrs. Mays,
the pictures never lived, but what of the flowers? Tell
them who ask: no rabbis, no ministers, no priests, no
speeches, no ceremonies: ah, false—let the living comfort themselves. Tell Sammy's boy, he who flies, tell
him to go to Stuttgart and see where Davy has no
grave. And what? . . . And what? where millions have
no graves—save air."

In delirium or not, wanting the radio on; not
seeming to listen, the words still jetting, wanting the
music on. Once, silencing it abruptly as of old, she began to cry, unconcealed tears this time. "You have pain,
Granny?" Jeannie asked.

---

*Both passages come from Chekhov, "Ward No. 6."

"The music," she said, "still it is there and we do not hear; knocks, and our poor human ears too weak. What else, what else we do not hear?"

Once she knocked his hand aside as he gave her a pill, swept the bottles from her bedside table: "no pills, let me feel what I feel," and laughed as on his hands and knees he groped to pick them up.

Nighttimes her hand reached across the bed to hold his.

A constant retching began. Her breath was too faint for sustained speech now, but still the lips moved:

> *When no longer necessary   to injure others* *
> *Pick   pick pick   Blind chicken*
> *As a human being   responsibility* **

"David!" imperious, "Basin!" and she would vomit, rinse her mouth, the wasted throat working to swallow, and begin the chant again.

She will be better off in the hospital now, the doctor said.

He sent the telegrams to the children, was packing her suitcase, when her hoarse voice startled. She had roused, was pulling herself to sitting.

"Where now?" she asked. "Where now do you drag me?"

---

* From Chekhov's "Rothschild's Fiddle."

** From letter by Ida Lerner, Olsen's mother: "As a human being who carries responsibility for action, I think as a duty to the community we must try to understand each other."

"You do not even have to have a baby to go this time," he soothed, looking for the brush to pack. "Remember, after Davy you told me—worthy to have a baby for the pleasure of the ten-day rest in the hospital?"

"Where now? Not home yet?" Her voice mourned. "Where *is* my home?"

He rose to ease her back. "The doctor, the hospital," he started to explain, but deftly, like a snake, she had slithered out of bed and stood swaying, propped behind the night table.

"Coward," she hissed, "runner."

"You stand," he said senselessly.

"To take me there and run. Afraid of a little vomit."

He reached her as she fell. She struggled against him, half slipped from his arms, pulled herself up again.

"Weakling," she taunted, "to leave me there and run. Betrayer. All your life you have run."

He sobbed, telling Jeannie. "A Marilyn Monroe to run for her virtue. Fifty-nine pounds she weighs, the doctor said, and she beats at me like a Dempsey. Betrayer, she cries, and I running like a dog when she calls; day and night, running to her, her vomit, the bed-pan. . . ."

"She needs you, Grandaddy," said Jeannie. "Isn't that what they call love? I'll see if she sleeps, and if she does, poor worn-out darling, we'll have a party, you and I: I brought us rum babas."

They did not move her. By her bed now stood the tall hooked pillar that held the solutions—blood and dex-

74

trose—to feed her veins. Jeannie moved down the hall
to take over the sickroom, her face so radiant, her grandfather asked her once: "you are in love?" (Shameful the
joy, the pure overwhelming joy from being with her
grandmother; the peace, the serenity that breathed.)
"My darling escape," she answered incoherently, "my
darling Granny"—as if that explained.

Now one by one the children came, those that were
able. Hannah, Paul, Sammy. Too late to ask: and what
did you learn with your living, Mother, and what do we
need to know?

Clara, the eldest, clenched:

*Pay me back, Mother, pay me back for all you
took from me. Those others you crowded into your
heart. The hands I needed to be for you, the heaviness, the responsibility.*

*Is this she? Noises the dying make, the crablike
hands crawling over the covers. The ethereal
singing.*

*She hears that music, that singing from child-
hood; forgotten sound—not heard since, since. . . .
And the hardness breaks like a cry: Where did we
lose each other, first mother, singing mother?*

*Annulled: the quarrels, the gibing, the harshness
between; the fall into silence and the withdrawal.*

*I do not know you, Mother. Mother, I never
knew you.*

Lennie, suffering not alone for her who was dying, but for that in her which never lived (for that
which in him might never come to live). From him too,

unspoken words: *good-bye Mother who taught me to mother myself.*

Not Vivi, who must stay with her children; not Davy, but he is already here, having to die again with *her* this time, for the living take their dead with them when they die.

Light she grew, like a bird, and, like a bird, sound bubbled in her throat while the body fluttered in agony. Night and day, asleep or awake (though indeed there was no difference now) the songs and the phrases leaping.

And he, who had once dreaded a long dying (from fear of himself, from horror of the dwindling money) now desired her quick death profoundly, for *her* sake. He no longer went out, except when Jeannie forced him; no longer laughed, except when, in the bright kitchenette, Jeannie coaxed his laughter (and she, who seemed to hear nothing else, would laugh too, conspiratorial wisps of laughter).

Light, like a bird, the fluttering body, the little claw hands, the beaked shadow on her face; and the throat, bubbling, straining.

He tried not to listen, as he tried not to look on the face in which only the forehead remained familiar, but trapped with her the long nights in that little room, the sounds worked themselves into his consciousness, with their punctuation of death swallows, whimpers, gurglings.

> *Even in reality* (swallow) *life's lack of it*
> *Slaveships   deathtrains   clubs   eeenough*
> *The bell   summon what enables*

78,000 in one minute (whisper of a scream)
78,000 human beings   we'll destroy ourselves? *

"Aah, Mrs. Miserable," he said, as if she could hear, "all your life working, and now in bed you lie, servants to tend, you do not even need to call to be tended, and still you work. Such hard work it is to die? Such hard work?"

The body threshed, her hand clung in his. A melody, ghost-thin, hovered on her lips, and like a guilty ghost, the vision of her bent in listening to it, silencing the record instantly he was near. Now, heedless of his presence, she floated the melody on and on.

"Hid it from me," he complained, "how many times you listened to remember it so?" And tried to think when she had first played it, or first begun to silence her few records when he came near—but could reconstruct nothing. There was only this room with its tall hooked pillar and its swarm of sounds.

No man one   except through others
Strong   with the not yet   in the now
Dogma dead   war dead   one country

"It helps, Mrs. Philosopher, words from books? It helps?" And it seemed to him that for seventy years she had hidden a tape recorder, infinitely microscopic, within her, that it had coiled infinite mile on mile, trapping every song, every melody, every word read, heard,

---

* The italicized passage contains references to the ships that transported slaves from Africa to America, to the trains that took millions of Jews and other Nazi victims to the concentration camps, and to the dropping of the atomic bomb on Hiroshima.

and spoken—and that maliciously she was playing back only what said nothing of him, of the children, or their intimate life together.

"Left us indeed, Mrs. Babbler," he reproached, "you who called others babbler and cunningly saved your words. A lifetime you tended and loved, and now not a word of us, for us. Left us indeed? Left me."

And he took out his solitaire deck, shuffled the cards loudly, slapped them down.

> *Lift high   banner of reason* (tatter of an orator's voice)
>   *justice   freedom   light*
> *Humankind   life worthy   capacities*
> *Seeks* (blur of shudder) *belong   human being*

"Words, words," he accused, "and what human beings did *you* seek around you, Mrs. Live Alone, and what humankind think worthy?"

Though even as he spoke, he remembered she had not always been isolated, had not always wanted to be alone (as he knew there had been a voice before this gossamer one; before the hoarse voice that broke from silence to lash, make incidents, shame him—a girl's voice of eloquence that spoke their holiest dreams). But again he could reconstruct, image, nothing of what had been before, or when, or how, it had changed.

Ace, queen, jack. The pillar shadow fell, so, in two tracks; in the mirror depths glistened a moonlike blob, the empty solution bottle. And it worked in him: *of reason and justice and freedom . . . Dogma dead:* he remembered the full quotation, laughed bitterly. "Hah, good you do not know what you say; good Victor Hugo died and did not see it, his twentieth century."

Deuce, ten, five. Dauntlessly she began a song of their youth of belief:

These things shall be, a loftier race
than e'er the world hath known shall rise
with flame of freedom in their souls
and light of knowledge in their eyes

King, four, jack "In the twentieth century, hah!"

They shall be gentle, brave and strong
to spill no drop of blood, but dare
all . . .
on earth and fire and sea and air

"To spill no drop of blood, hah! So, cadaver, and you too, cadaver Hugo, 'in the twentieth century ignorance will be dead, dogma will be dead, war will be dead, and for all mankind one country—of fulfilment?' Hah!"

And every life (long strangling cough) *shall be a song* *

The cards fell from his fingers. Without warning, the bereavement and betrayal he had sheltered—compounded through the years—hidden even from himself—revealed itself,
> uncoiled,
> released,
> *sprung*

---

* The italicized passages are all fragments from Hugo's "These Things Shall Be." The last verse is: "New arts shall bloom of loftier mould,/ And mightier music thrill the skies,/ And every life shall be a song/ When all the earth is paradise."

and with it the monstrous shapes of what had actually happened in the century.

A ravening hunger or thirst seized him. He groped into the kitchenette, switched on all three lights, piled a tray—"you have finished your night snack, Mrs. Cadaver, now I will have mine." And he was shocked at the tears that splashed on the tray.

"Salt tears. For free. I forgot to shake on salt?"

Whispered: "Lost, how much I lost."

Escaped to the grandchildren whose childhoods were childish, who had never hungered, who lived un-ravaged by disease in warm houses of many rooms, had all the school for which they cared, could walk on any street, stood a head taller than their grandparents, tow-ered above—beautiful skins, straight backs, clear straightforward eyes. "Yes, you in Olshana," he said to the town of sixty years ago, "they would seem nobility to you."

And was this not the dream then, come true in ways undreamed? he asked.

And are there no other children in the world? he answered, as if in her harsh voice.

And the flame of freedom, the light of knowledge?

And the drop, to spill no drop of blood?

And he thought that at six Jeannie would get up and it would be his turn to go to her room and sleep, that he could press the buzzer and she would come now; that in the afternoon Ellen Mays was coming, and this time they would play cards and he could marvel at how rouge can stand half an inch on the cheek; that in the evening the doctor would come, and he could beg him to be merciful, to stop the feeding solutions, to let her die.

To let her die, and with her their youth of belief
out of which her bright, betrayed words foamed;
stained words, that on her working lips came stainless.

Hours yet before Jeannie's turn. He could press
the buzzer and wake her to come now; he could take a
pill, and with it sleep; he could pour more brandy into
his milk glass, though what he had poured was not yet
touched.

Instead he went back, checked her pulse, gently
tended with his knotty fingers as Jeannie had taught.

She was whimpering; her hand crawled across
the covers for his. Compassionately he enfolded it, and
with his free hand gathered up the cards again. Still
was there thirst or hunger ravening in him.

That world of their youth—dark, ignorant, terrible with hate and disease—how was it that living in it,
in the midst of corruption, filth, treachery, degradation,
they had not mistrusted man nor themselves; had believed so beautifully, so . . . falsely?

"Aaah, children," he said out loud, "how we believed, how we belonged." And he yearned to package
for each of the children, the grandchildren, for everyone,
that joyous certainty, that sense of mattering, of mov-
ing and being moved, of being one and indivisible with
the great of the past, with all that freed, ennobled. Package it, stand on corners, in front of stadiums and on
crowded beaches, knock on doors, give it as a fabled gift.

"And why not in cereal boxes, in soap packages?"
he mocked himself. "Aah. You have taken my senses,
cadaver."

Words foamed, died unsounded. Her body
writhed; she made kissing motions with her mouth.
(Her lips moving as she read, pouring over the Book

of Martyrs, the magnifying glass superimposed over
the heavy eyeglasses.) *Still she believed*? "Eva!" he
whispered. "Still you believed? You lived by it? These
Things Shall Be?"

"One pound soup meat," she answered distinctly,
"one soup bone."

"My ears heard you. Ellen Mays was witness:
'Humankind . . . one has to believe.'" Imploringly:
"Eva!"

"Bread, day-old." She was mumbling. "Please, in
a wooden box . . . for kindling. The thread, hah, the
thread breaks. Cheap thread"—and a gurgling, enormously loud, began in her throat.

"I ask for stone; she gives me bread—day-old."
He pulled his hand away, shouted: "Who wanted questions? Everything you have to wake?" Then dully, "Ah,
let me help you turn, poor creature."

Words jumbled, cleared. In a voice of crowded
terror:

"Paul, Sammy, don't fight.

"Hannah, have I ten hands?

"How can I give it, Clara, how can I give it if I
don't have?"

"You lie," he said sturdily, "there was joy too."
Bitterly: "Ah how cheap you speak of us at the last."

As if to rebuke him, as if her voice had no relationship with her flaring body, she sang clearly, beautifully, a school song the children had taught her when
they were little; begged:

"Not look   my hair   where they cut. . . ."

(The crown of braids shorn.)* And instantly he

---

*Reference to the Orthodox Jewish custom of cutting off the bride's hair and
replacing it with a wig, and to the cutting off of prisoners' hair in Siberia.

left the mute old woman poring over the Book of the
Martyrs; went past the mother treading at the sewing
machine, singing with the children; past the girl in her
wrinkled prison dress, hiding her hair with scarred
hands, lifting to him her awkward, shamed, imploring
eyes of love; and took her in his arms, dear, personal,
fleshed, in all the heavy passion he had loved to rouse
from her.

"Eva!"

Her little claw hand beat the covers. How much,
how much can a man stand? He took up the cards, put
them down, circled the beds, walked to the dresser,
opened, shut drawers, brushed his hair, moved his hand
bit by bit over the mirror to see what of the reflection he
could blot out with each move, and felt that at any moment he would die of what was unendurable. Went to
press the buzzer to wake Jeannie, looked down, saw
on Jeannie's sketch pad the hospital bed, with *her;* the
double bed alongside, with him; the tall pillar feeding
into her veins, and their hands, his and hers, clasped,
feeding each other. And as if he had been instructed he
went to his bed, lay down, holding the sketch (as if it
could shield against the monstrous shapes of loss, of betrayal, of death) and with his free hand took hers back
into his.

So Jeannie found them in the morning.

That last day the agony was perpetual. Time after time
it lifted her almost off the bed, so they had to fight to
hold her down. He could not endure and left the room;
wept as if there never would be tears enough.

Jeannie came to comfort him. In her light voice
she said: Grandaddy, Grandaddy don't cry. She is not
there, she promised me. On the last day, she said she

would go back to when she first heard music, a little girl on the road of the village where she was born. She promised me. It is a wedding and they dance, while the flutes so joyous and vibrant tremble in the air. Leave her there, Grandaddy, it is all right. She promised me. Come back, come back and help her poor body to die.

For my mother, my father,
and
Two of that generation
Seevya and Genya*
Infinite, dauntless, incorruptible

Death deepens the wonder

---

* Seevya Dinkin and Genya Gorelick, two activist immigrant women of Olsen's parents' generation. Genya Gorelick *was* an orator in the 1905 Revolution.

◻ Background
to the Story

Silences in Literature

Originally an unwritten talk, spoken from notes at the Radcliffe Institute in 1962 as part of a weekly colloquium of members. Edited from the taped transcription, it appears here as published in *Harper's Magazine,* October 1965.
    (Several omitted lines have been restored; an occasional name or phrase and a few footnotes have been added.)

Silences

Literary history and the present are dark with silences: some the silences for years by our acknowledged great; some silences hidden; some the ceasing to publish after one work appears; some the never coming to book form at all.

What is it that happens with the creator, to the creative process, in that time? What *are* creation's needs for full functioning? Without intention of or pretension to literary scholarship, I have had special need to learn all I could of this over the years, myself so nearly remaining mute and having to let writing die over and over again in me.

These are not *natural* silences—what Keats called *agonie ennuyeuse* (the tedious agony)—that necessary time for renewal, lying fallow, gestation, in the natural cycle of creation. The silences I speak of here are unnatural: the unnatural thwarting of what struggles to come into being, but cannot. In the old, the obvious parallels: when the seed strikes stone; the soil will not sustain; the spring is false; the time is drought or blight or infestation; the frost comes premature.

The great in achievement have known such silences— Thomas Hardy, Melville, Rimbaud, Gerard Manley Hopkins. They tell us little as to why or how the creative working atrophied and died in them—if ever it did.

From *Silences* (New York: Delacorte Press/Seymour Lawrence, 1978), 5–21. Introductory note and all footnotes are Olsen's.

"Less and less shrink the visions then vast in me," writes Thomas Hardy in his thirty-year ceasing from novels after the Victorian vileness to his *Jude the Obscure*. ("So ended his prose contributions to literature, his experiences having killed all his interest in this form"—the official explanation.) But the great poetry he wrote to the end of his life was not sufficient to hold, to develop the vast visions which for twenty-five years had had expression in novel after novel. People, situations, interrelationships, landscape—they cry for this larger life in poem after poem.

It was not visions shrinking with Hopkins, but a different torment. For seven years he kept his religious vow to refrain from writing poetry, but the poet's eye he could not shut, nor win "elected silence to beat upon [his] whorled ear." "I had long had haunting my ear the echo of a poem which now I realised on paper," he writes of the first poem permitted to end the seven years' silence. But poetry ("to hoard unheard; be heard, unheeded") could be only the least and last of his heavy priestly responsibilities. Nineteen poems were all he could produce in his last nine years—fullness to us, but torment pitched past grief to him, who felt himself "time's eunuch, never to beget."

Silence surrounds Rimbaud's silence. Was there torment of the unwritten; haunting of rhythm, of visions; anguish at dying powers, the seventeen years after he abandoned the unendurable literary world? We know only that the need to write continued into his first years of vagabondage; that he wrote:

> Had I not once a youth pleasant, heroic, fabulous enough to write on leaves of gold: too much luck. Through what crime, what error, have I earned my present weakness? You who maintain that some animals sob sorrowfully, that the dead have dreams, try to tell the story of my downfall and my slumber. I no longer know how to speak.*

That on his deathbed, he spoke again like a poet-visionary.

---

* *A Season in Hell.*

Melville's stages to his thirty-year prose silence are clearest. The presage in his famous letter to Hawthorne, as he had to hurry *Moby Dick* to an end:

> I am so pulled hither and thither by circumstances. The calm, the coolness, the silent grass-growing mood in which a man ought always to compose,—that, I fear, can seldom be mine. Dollars damn me. . . . What I feel most moved to write, that is banned,—it will not pay. Yet, altogether, write the *other* way I cannot. So the product is a final hash . . .

Reiterated in *Pierre,* writing "that book whose unfathomable cravings drink his blood . . . When at last the idea obtruded that the wiser and profounder he should grow, the more and the more he lessened his chances for bread."

To be possessed; to have to try final hash; to have one's work met by "drear ignoring"; to be damned by dollars into a Customs House job; to have only weary evenings and Sundays left for writing—

> How bitterly did unreplying Pierre feel in his heart that to most of the great works of humanity, their authors had given not weeks and months, not years and years, but their wholly surrendered and dedicated lives.

Is it not understandable why Melville began to burn work, then ceased to write it, "immolating [it] . . . sealing in a fate subdued"? And turned to occasional poetry, manageable in a time sense, "to nurse through night the ethereal spark." A thirty-year night. He was nearly seventy before he could quit the customs dock and again have full time for writing, start back to prose. "Age, dull tranquilizer," and devastation of "arid years that filed before" to work through. Three years of tryings before he felt capable of beginning *Billy Budd* (the kernel waiting half a century); three years more to his last days (he who had been so fluent), the slow, painful, never satisfied writing and re-writing of it.*

---

*"Entering my eighth decade [I come] into possession of unobstructed leisure . . . just as, in the course of nature, my vigor sensibly declines. What little of

Kin to these years-long silences are the *hidden* silences; work aborted, deferred, denied—hidden by the work which does come to fruition. Hopkins rightfully belongs here; almost certainly William Blake; Jane Austen, Olive Schreiner, Theodore Dreiser, Willa Cather, Franz Kafka; Katherine Anne Porter, many other contemporary writers.

Censorship silences. Deletions, omissions, abandonment of the medium (as with Hardy); paralyzing of capacity (as Dreiser's ten-year stasis on *Jennie Gerhardt* after the storm against *Sister Carrie*). Publishers' censorship, refusing subject matter or treatment as "not suitable" or "no market for." Self-censorship. Religious, political censorship—sometimes spurring inventiveness—most often (read Dostoyevsky's letters) a wearing attrition.

The extreme of this: those writers physically silenced by governments. Isaac Babel, the years of imprisonment, what took place in him with what wanted to be written? Or in Oscar Wilde, who was not permitted even a pencil until the last months of his imprisonment?

Other silences. The truly memorable poem, story, or book, then the writer ceasing to be published.** Was one work all the writers had in them (life too thin for pressure of material, renewal) and the respect for literature too great to repeat themselves? Was it "the knife of the perfectionist attitude in art and life" at their throat? Were the conditions not present for establishing the habits of creativity (a young Colette who lacked a Willy to lock her in her room each day)? or—as instanced over and over—other claims, other responsibilities so writing could not be first? (The writer of a class, sex, color still marginal in literature, and whose coming to written voice at all against complex odds is exhausting achievement.) It is an eloquent commentary that this one-book si-

---

it is left, I husband for certain matters as yet incomplete and which indeed may never be completed." *Billy Budd* never was completed; it was edited from drafts found after Melville's death.

** As Jean Toomer (*Cane*); Henry Roth (*Call It Sleep*); Edith Summers Kelley (*Weeds*).

lence has been true of most black writers; only eleven in the hundred years since 1850 have published novels more than twice.*

There is a prevalent silence I pass by quickly, the absence of creativity where it once had been; the ceasing to create literature, though the books may keep coming out year after year. That suicide of the creative process Hemingway described so accurately in "The Snows of Kilimanjaro":

> He had destroyed his talent himself—by not using it, by betrayals of himself and what he believed in, by drinking so much that he blunted the edge of his perceptions, by laziness, by sloth, by snobbery, by hook and by crook; selling vitality, trading it for security, for comfort.

No, not Scott Fitzgerald. His not a death of creativity, not silence, but what happens when (his words) there is "the sacrifice of talent, in pieces, to preserve its essential value."

Almost unnoted are the foreground silences, *before* the achievement. (Remember when Emerson hailed Whitman's genius, he guessed correctly: "which yet must have had a long *foreground* for such a start.") George Eliot, Joseph Conrad, Isak Dinesen, Sherwood Anderson, Dorothy Richardson, Elizabeth Madox Roberts, A. E. Coppard, Angus Wilson, Joyce Cary—all close to, or in their forties before they became published writers; Lampedusa, Maria Dermout (*The Ten Thousand Things*), Laura Ingalls Wilder, the "children's writer," in their sixties.** Their capacities evident early in the "being one on whom nothing is lost"; in other writers' qualities. Not all struggling and anguished, like Anderson, the foreground years; some needing the immobilization of long illness or loss, or the sudden lifting of responsibility to make writing necessary, make writing possible; others waiting circumstances and encouragement (George Eliot, her Henry Lewes; Laura Wil-

---

* Robert Bone, *The Negro Novel in America,* 1958.

** Some other foreground silences: Elizabeth (Mrs.) Gaskell, Kate Chopin, Cora Sandel, Cyrus Colter, Hortense Calisher.

der, a writer-daughter's insistence that she transmute her storytelling gift onto paper).

Very close to this last grouping are the silences where the lives never came to writing. Among these, the mute inglorious Miltons: those whose waking hours are all struggle for existence; the barely educated; the illiterate; women. Their silence the silence of centuries as to how life was, is, for most of humanity. Traces of their making, of course, in folk song, lullaby, tales, language itself, jokes, maxims, superstitions—but we know nothing of the creators or how it was with them. In the fantasy of Shakespeare born in deepest Africa (as at least one Shakespeare must have been), was the ritual, the oral storytelling a fulfillment? Or was there restlessness, indefinable yearning, a sense of restrictions? Was it as Virginia Woolf in *A Room of One's Own* guesses—about women?

> Genius of a sort must have existed among them, as it existed among the working classes,* but certainly it never got itself onto paper. When, however, one reads of a woman possessed by the devils, of a wise woman selling herbs, or even a remarkable man who had a remarkable mother, then I think we are on the track of a lost novelist, a suppressed poet, or some Emily Brontë who dashed her brains out on the moor, crazed with the torture her gift had put her to.

Rebecca Harding Davis whose work sleeps in the forgotten (herself as a woman of a century ago so close to remaining mute), also guessed about the silent in that time of the twelve-hour-a-day, six-day work week. She writes of the illiterate ironworker in *Life in the Iron Mills* who sculptured great shapes in the slag: "his fierce thirst for beauty, to know it, to create it, to *be* something other than he is—a passion of pain"; Margret Howth in the textile mill:

> There were things in the world, that like herself, were marred, did not understand, were hungry to know. . . . Her

---

* Half of the working classes *are* women.

92

eyes quicker to see than ours, delicate or grand lines in the homeliest things. . . . Everything she saw or touched, nearer, more human than to you or me. These sights and sounds did not come to her common; she never got used to living as other people do.

She never got used to living as other people do. Was that one of the ways it was?

So some of the silences, incomplete listing of the incomplete, where the need and capacity to create were of a high order.

Now, what *is* the work of creation and the circumstances it demands for full functioning—as told in the journals, letters, notes, of the practitioners themselves: Henry James, Katherine Mansfield, André Gide, Virginia Woolf; the letters of Flaubert, Rilke, Joseph Conrad; Thomas Wolfe's *Story of a Novel,* Valéry's *Course in Poetics.* What do they explain of the silences?

"Constant toil is the law of art, as it is of life," says (and demonstrated) Balzac:

> To pass from conception to execution, to produce, to bring the idea to birth, to raise the child laboriously from infancy, to put it nightly to sleep surfeited, to kiss it in the mornings with the hungry heart of a mother, to clean it, to clothe it fifty times over in new garments which it tears and casts away, and yet not revolt against the trials of this agitated life—this unwearying maternal love, this habit of creation—this is execution and its toils.

"Without duties, almost without external communication," Rilke specifies, "unconfined solitude which takes every day like a life, a spaciousness which puts no limit to vision and in the midst of which infinities surround."

Unconfined solitude as Joseph Conrad experienced it:

> For twenty months I wrestled with the Lord for my creation . . . mind and will and conscience engaged to the full, hour after hour, day after day . . . a lonely struggle in a great isolation from the world. I suppose I slept and ate the food put

before me and talked connectedly on suitable occasions, but I was never aware of the even flow of daily life, made easy and noiseless for me by a silent, watchful, tireless affection.

So there is a homely underpinning for it all, the even flow of daily life made easy and noiseless.

"The terrible law of the artist"—says Henry James—"the law of fructification, of fertilization. The old, old lesson of the art of meditation. To woo combinations and inspirations into being by a depth and continuity of attention and meditation."

"That load, that weight, that gnawing conscience," writes Thomas Mann—

> That sea which to drink up, that frightful task . . . The will, the discipline and self-control to shape a sentence or follow out a hard train of thought. From the first rhythmical urge of the inward creative force towards the material, towards casting in shape and form, from that to the thought, the image, the word, the line, what a struggle, what Gethsemane.

Does it become very clear what Melville's Pierre so bitterly remarked on, and what literary history bears out—why most of the great works of humanity have come from lives (able to be) wholly surrendered and dedicated? How else sustain the constant toil, the frightful task, the terrible law, the continuity? Full self: this means full time as and when needed for the work. (That time for which Emily Dickinson withdrew from the world.)

But what if there is not that fullness of time, let alone totality of self? What if the writers, as in some of these silences, must work regularly at something besides their own work—as do nearly all in the arts in the United States today.

I know the theory (kin to "starving in the garret makes great art") that it is this very circumstance which feeds creativity. I know, too, that for the beginning young, for some who have such need, the job can be valuable access to life they would not otherwise know. A few (I think of the doctors, the incomparables: Chekhov and William Carlos Williams) for special reasons sometimes manage both. *But the actuality*

94

*testifies: substantial creative work demands time, and with rare exceptions only full-time workers have achieved it.** Where the claims of creation cannot be primary, the results are atrophy; unfinished work; minor effort and accomplishments; silences. (Desperation which accounts for the mountains of applications to the foundations for grants—undivided time—in the strange bread-line system we have worked out for our artists.)

Twenty years went by on the writing of *Ship of Fools,* while Katherine Anne Porter, who needed only two, was "trying to get to that table, to that typewriter, away from my jobs of teaching and trooping this country and of keeping house." "Your subconscious needed that time to grow the layers of pearl," she was told. Perhaps, perhaps, but I doubt it. Subterranean forces can make you wait, but they are very finicky about the kind of waiting it has to be. Before they will feed the creator back, they must be fed, passionately fed, what needs to be worked on. "We hold up our desire as one places a magnet over a composite dust from which the particle of iron will suddenly jump up," says Paul Valéry. A receptive waiting, that means, not demands which prevent "an undistracted center of being." And when the response comes, availability to work must be immediate. If not used at once, all may vanish as a dream; worse, future creation be endangered—for only the removal and development of the material frees the forces for further work.

There is a life in which all this is documented: Franz Kafka's. For every one entry from his diaries here, there are fifty others

---

*This does not mean that these full-time writers were hermetic or denied themselves social or personal life (think of James, Turgenev, Tolstoy, Balzac, Joyce, Gide, Colette, Yeats, Woolf, etc. etc.); nor did they, except perhaps at the flood, put in as many hours daily as those doing more usual kinds of work. Three to six hours daily have been the norm ("the quiet, patient, generous mornings will bring it") Zola and Trollope are famous last-century examples of the four hours; the *Paris Review* interviews disclose many contemporary ones.

Full-timeness consists not in the actual number of hours at one's desk, but in that writing is one's major profession, practiced habitually, in freed, protected, undistracted time as needed, when it is needed.

that testify as unbearably to the driven stratagems for time, the work lost (to us), the damage to the creative powers (and the body) of having to deny, interrupt, postpone, put aside, let work die.

"I cannot devote myself completely to my writing," Kafka explains (in 1911). "I could not live by literature if only, to begin with, because of the slow maturing of my work and its special character." So he worked as an official in a state insurance agency, and wrote when he could.

> These two can never be reconciled. . . . If I have written something one evening, I am afire the next day in the office and can bring nothing to completion. Outwardly I fulfill my office duties satisfactorily, not my inner duties however, and every unfulfilled inner duty becomes a misfortune that never leaves. What strength it will necessarily drain me of.

1911

> No matter how little the time or how badly I write, I feel approaching the imminent possibility of great moments which could make me capable of anything. But my being does not have sufficient strength to hold this to the next writing time. During the day the visible world helps me; during the night it cuts me to pieces unhindered. . . . In the evening and in the morning, my consciousness of the creative abilities in me then I can encompass. I feel shaken to the core of my being. Calling forth such powers which are then not permitted to function.

. . . which are then not permitted to function . . .

1911

> I finish nothing, because I have no time, and it presses so within me.

1912

> When I begin to write after such a long interval, I draw the words as if out of the empty air. If I capture one, then I have just this one alone, and all the toil must begin anew.

96

1914

> Yesterday for the first time in months, an indisputable ability to do good work. And yet wrote only the first page. Again I realize that everything written down bit by bit rather than all at once in the course of the larger part is inferior, and that the circumstances of my life condemn me to this inferiority.

1915

> My constant attempt by sleeping before dinner to make it possible to continue working [writing] late into the night, senseless. Then at one o'clock can no longer fall asleep at all, the next day at work insupportable, and so I destroy myself.

1917

> Distractedness, weak memory, stupidity. Days passed in futility, powers wasted away in waiting. . . . Always this one principal anguish—if I had gone away in 1911 in full possession of all my powers. Not eaten by the strain of keeping down living forces.

Eaten into tuberculosis. By the time he won through to himself and time for writing, his body could live no more. He was forty-one.

I think of Rilke who said, "If I have any responsibility, I mean and desire it to be responsibility for the deepest and innermost essence of the loved reality [writing] to which I am inseparably bound"; and who also said, "Anything alive that makes demands, arouses in me an infinite capacity to give it its due, the consequences of which completely use me up." These were true with Kafka, too, yet how different their lives. When Rilke wrote that about responsibility, he is explaining why he will not take a job to support his wife and baby, nor live with them (years later will not come to his daughter's wedding nor permit a two-hour honeymoon visit lest it break his solitude where he awaits poetry). The "infinite capacity" is his explanation as to why he cannot even bear to have a dog. Extreme—and justified. He protected his creative powers.

Kafka's, Rilke's "infinite capacity," and all else that has been said here of the needs of creation, illuminate women's silence of centuries. I will not repeat what is in Virginia Woolf's *A Room of One's Own,* but talk of this last century and a half in which women have begun to have voice in literature. (It has been less than that time in Eastern Europe, and not yet, in many parts of the world.)

In the last century, of the women whose achievements endure for us in one way or another,* nearly all never married (Jane Austen, Emily Brontë, Christina Rossetti, Emily Dickinson, Louisa May Alcott, Sarah Orne Jewett) or married late in their thirties (George Eliot, Elizabeth Barrett Browning, Charlotte Brontë, Olive Schreiner). I can think of only four (George Sand, Harriet Beecher Stowe, Helen Hunt Jackson, and Elizabeth Gaskell) who married and had children as young women.** All had servants.

In our century, until very recently, it has not been so different. Most did not marry (Selma Lagerlof, Willa Cather, Ellen Glasgow, Gertrude Stein, Gabriela Mistral, Elizabeth Madox Roberts, Charlotte Mew, Eudora Welty, Marianne Moore) or, if married, have been childless (Edith Wharton, Virginia Woolf, Katherine Mansfield, Dorothy Richardson, H. H. Richardson, Elizabeth Bowen, Isak Dinesen, Katherine Anne Porter, Lillian Hellman, Dorothy Parker). Colette had one child (when she was forty). If I include Sigrid Undset, Kay Boyle, Pearl Buck, Dorothy Canfield Fisher, that will make a small group who had more than one child. All had household help or other special circumstances.

Am I resaying the moldy theory that women have no need, some say no capacity, to create art, because they can "create" babies? And the additional proof is precisely that the few women who have created it are nearly all childless? No.

The power and the need to create, over and beyond reproduction, is native in both women and men. Where the gifted among women (*and men*) have remained mute, or have

---

*"One Out of Twelve" has a more extensive roll of women writers of achievement.

** I would now add a fifth—Kate Chopin—also a foreground silence.

never attained full capacity, it is because of circumstances, inner or outer, which oppose the needs of creation.

Wholly surrendered and dedicated lives; time as needed for the work; totality of self. But women are traditionally trained to place others' needs first, to feel these needs as their own (the "infinite capacity"); their sphere, their satisfaction to be in making it possible for others to use their abilities. This is what Virginia Woolf meant when, already a writer of achievement, she wrote in her diary:

> Father's birthday. He would have been 96, 96, yes, today; and could have been 96, like other people one has known; but mercifully was not. His life would have entirely ended mine. What would have happened? No writing, no books;— inconceivable.

It took family deaths to free more than one woman writer into her own development.* Emily Dickinson freed herself, denying all the duties expected of a woman of her social position except the closest family ones, and she was fortunate to have a sister, and servants, to share those. How much is revealed of the differing circumstances and fate of their own as-great capacities, in the diaries (and lives) of those female bloodkin of great writers: Dorothy Wordsworth, Alice James, Aunt Mary Moody Emerson.

And where there is no servant or relation to assume the responsibilities of daily living? Listen to Katherine Mansfield in the early days of her relationship with John Middleton Murry, when they both dreamed of becoming great writers:**

---

* Among them: George Eliot, Helen Hunt Jackson, Mrs. Gaskell, Kate Chopin, Lady Gregory, Isak Dinesen. Ivy Compton-Burnett finds this the grim reason for the emergence of British women novelists after World War I: ". . . The men were dead, you see, and the women didn't marry so much because there was no one for them to marry, and so they had leisure, and, I think, in a good many cases they had money because their brothers were dead, and all that would tend to writing, wouldn't it, being single, and having some money, and having the time—having no men, you see."

** Already in that changed time when servants were not necessarily a part of the furnishings of almost anyone well educated enough to be making literature.

The house seems to take up so much time. . . . I mean when I have to clean up twice over or wash up extra unnecessary things, I get frightfully impatient and want to be working [writing]. So often this week you and Gordon have been talking while I washed dishes. Well someone's got to wash dishes and get food. Otherwise "there's nothing in the house but eggs to eat." And after you have gone I walk about with a mind full of ghosts of saucepans and primus stoves and "will there be enough to go around?" And you calling, whatever I am doing, writing, "Tig, isn't there going to be tea? It's five o'clock."

I loathe myself today. This woman who superintends you and rushes about slamming doors and slopping water and shouts "You might at least empty the pail and wash out the tea leaves." . . . O Jack, I wish that you would take me in your arms and kiss my hands and my face and every bit of me and say, "It's all right, you darling thing, I understand."

A long way from Conrad's favorable circumstances for creation: the flow of daily life made easy and noiseless.

And, if in addition to the infinite capacity, to the daily responsibilities, there are children?

Balzac, you remember, described creation in terms of motherhood. Yes, in intelligent passionate motherhood there are similarities, and in more than the toil and patience. The calling upon total capacities; the reliving and new using of the past; the comprehensions; the fascination, absorption, intensity. All almost certain death to creation—(so far).

Not because the capacities to create no longer exist, or the need (though for a while, as in any fullness of life, the need may be obscured), but because the circumstances for sustained creation have been almost impossible. The need cannot be first. It can have at best, only part self, part time. (Unless someone else does the nurturing. Read Dorothy Fisher's "Babushka Farnham" in *Fables for Parents*.) More than in any other human relationship, overwhelmingly more, motherhood means being instantly interruptable, responsive, responsible. Children need one *now* (and remember, in our society, the family must often try to be the center for love and health the outside world is not). The very fact that these are

100

real needs, that one feels them as one's own (love, not duty); *that there is no one else responsible for these needs,* give them primacy. It is distraction, not meditation, that becomes habitual; interruption, not continuity, spasmodic, not constant toil. The rest has been said here. Work interrupted, deferred, relinquished, makes blockage—at best, lesser accomplishment. Unused capacities atrophy, cease to be.

When H. H. Richardson, who wrote the Australian classic *Ultima Thule,* was asked why she—whose children, like all her people, were so profoundly written—did not herself have children, she answered: "There are enough women to do the childbearing and childrearing. I know of none who can write my books." I remember thinking rebelliously, yes, and I know of none who can bear and rear my children either. But literary history is on her side. Almost no mothers—as almost no part-time, part-self persons—have created enduring literature . . . so far.

If I talk now quickly of my own silences—almost presumptuous after what has been told here—it is that the individual experience may add.

In the twenty years I bore and reared my children, usually had to work on a paid job as well, the simplest circumstances for creation did not exist. Nevertheless writing, the hope of it, was "the air I breathed, so long as I shall breathe at all." In that hope, there was conscious storing, snatched reading, beginnings of writing, and always "the secret rootlets of reconnaissance."

When the youngest of our four was in school, the beginnings struggled toward endings. This was a time, in Kafka's words, "like a squirrel in a cage: bliss of movement, desperation about constriction, craziness of endurance."

Bliss of movement. A full extended family life; the world of my job (transcriber in a diary-equipment company); and the writing, which I was somehow able to carry around within me through work, through home. Time on the bus, even when I had to stand, was enough; the stolen moments at work, enough; the deep night hours for as long as I could stay awake, after the kids were in bed, after the household tasks were done, sometimes during. It is no accident that the first work I considered publishable began: "I stand here ironing, and what you asked me moves tormented back and forth with the iron."

In such snatches of time I wrote what I did in those years, but there came a time when this triple life was no longer possible. The fifteen hours a daily realities became too much distraction for the writing. I lost craziness of endurance. What might have been, I don't know; but I applied for, and was given, eight months' writing time. There was still full family life, all the household responsibilities, but I did not have to hold an eight-hour job. I had continuity, three full days, sometimes more—and it was in those months I made the mysterious turn and became a writing writer.

Then had to return to the world of work, someone else's work, nine hours, five days a week.

This was the time of festering and congestion. For a few months I was able to shield the writing with which I was so full, against the demands of jobs on which I had to be competent, through the joys and responsibilities and trials of family. For a few months. Always roused by the writing, always denied. "I could not go to write it down. It convulsed and died in me. I will pay."

My work died. What demanded to be written, did not. It seethed, bubbled, clamored, peopled me. At last moved into the hours meant for sleeping. I worked now full time on temporary jobs, a Kelly, a Western Agency girl (girl!), wandering from office to office, always hoping to manage two, three writing months ahead. Eventually there was time.

I had said: always roused by the writing, always denied. Now, like a woman made frigid, I had to learn response, to trust this possibility for fruition that had not been before. Any interruption dazed and silenced me. It took a long while of surrendering to what I was trying to write, of invoking Henry James's "passion, piety, patience," before I was able to re-establish work.

When again I had to leave the writing, I lost consciousness. A time of anesthesia. There was still an automatic noting that did not stop, but it was as if writing had never been. No fever, no congestion, no festering. I ceased being peopled, slept well and dreamlessly, took a "permanent" job. The few pieces that had been published seemed to have vanished like the not-yet-written. I wrote someone, unsent: "So long they fed each other—my life, the writing—; —the writing or hope of it, my life—; but now they begin to destroy." I knew, but did not feel the destruction.

A Ford grant in literature, awarded me on nomination by others, came almost too late. Time granted does not necessarily coincide with time that can be most fully used, as the congested time of fullness would have been. Still, it was two years.

Drowning is not so pitiful as the attempt to rise, says Emily Dickinson. I do not agree, but I know whereof she speaks. For a long time I was that emaciated survivor trembling on the beach, unable to rise and walk. Said differently, I could manage only the feeblest, shallowest growth on that devastated soil. Weeds, to be burned like weeds, or used as compost. When the habits of creation were at last rewon, one book went to the publisher, and I dared to begin my present work. It became my center, engraved on it: "Evil is whatever distracts." (By now had begun a cost to our family life, to my own participation in life as a human being.) I shall not tell the "rest, residue, and remainder" of what I was "leased, demised, and let unto" when once again I had to leave work at the flood to return to the Time-Master, to business-ese and legalese. This most harmful of all my silences has ended, but I am not yet recovered; may still be a one-book silence.

However that will be, we are in a time of more and more hidden and foreground silences, women *and* men. Denied full writing life, more may try to "nurse through night" (that part-time, part-self night) "the ethereal spark," but it seems to me there would almost have had to be "flame on flame" first; and time as needed, afterwards; and enough of the self, the capacities, undamaged for the rebeginnings on the frightful task. I would like to believe this for what has not yet been written into literature. But it cannot reconcile for what is lost by unnatural silences.

1962

103

Personal Statement

(Accompanying an Exhibition of Books and Manuscripts by Writers from the Stanford University Creative Writing Program)

This is about sources, wellsprings, and the enabling gift of circumstances in the eight temporal, infinite, Stanford months when I "made the mysterious turn and became a writing writer." And something of these accompanying scraps, notings, mss. pages.

I did not come to our writing class that late September day in 1955 as the others came. I was a quarter of a century older. I had had no college. I came from that common, everyday, work, mother, eight-hour-daily job, survival (and yes, activist) world seldom the substance of literature.

I came heavy freighted with a lifetime of ever-accumulating material, the sense of unwritten lives which cried to be written. I came from a twenty-year silence "when the simplest circumstances for creation did not exist. . . . Nevertheless there was conscious storing, snatched reading, beginnings of writing, and always the secret rootlets of reconnaissance."

I came as stranger; of the excluded. I came as the exiled homesick come home—*my* home, where literature, writers, writing had centrality, had being. I came to Dick and Ann Scowcroft, the Mirrielees sisters, my to-be first and dearest

From *First Drafts, Last Drafts: Forty Years of the Creative Writing Program at Stanford.* Prepared by William McPheron, with the assistance of Amor Towles (Stanford, Calif.: Stanford University Libraries, 1989), 63–66.

writer friend, Hannah Green; to the hovering presence of Stegner (then on leave), and to unnamed others who embodied that centrality—and remain living sustenance to this day.

I came to circumstanced time.

We met two afternoons a week in the Jones Room, around an oval, an egg-shaped table (shape of new life in creation) encircled by walls solid with books. A writer's library, carefully gleaned, gathered together as if to concentrate for us, incite us to what makes our medium incomparable. The imperishable, the good, side by side with letters, lives, journals of their creators—illuminating, intertwining, the ways of their begetting, the joys . . . labor of their creation.

Encircled, bulwarked so, we practiced writing companionship: read what we had written, listened to each other, talked writing, vivified. Or so it was for me. Enormous had been my morning—with books and notebook in the library, or with the Jones Room books; enormous and yielding would be my late afternoon and evening for I would stay until the last train. When it was possible, I rode from home (San Francisco) with my new friend, Hannah Green, and for the first time had occasion to read aloud, hear in my ears, sounds, rhythms, silences of the written. I read what I had long loved or just come to love: from Verga's *Little Tales of Sicily* to which Hannah had introduced me; all of Cather's "Wagner Matinee," Glaspell's "Jury of Her Peers," Chekhov's "Gusev," "Rothschild's Fiddle," "Ward #6"—among other treasures. And I was in a frenzy, a passion, of starved intense reading, copying; observing, noting, putting together; reremembering; *writing*—in this vast strange freedom of wholly my-own time.

In those circumstanced months, in that writing air, in the comradeship of books and writing human beings; in that freed time (for all that there was still full family life, responsibilities)—in contrast to the years it took for the writing of "I Stand Here Ironing", the first "Hey Sailor, What Ship?"—I came to facility. I made "Hey Sailor" publishable. I wrote all of "O Yes." I began, finished, the first third of "Tell Me a Riddle." Although I did not know it then, I was also gathering, even writing, what would later become substance and actual page after page of *Silences* ("this book was not written, it was harvested")—and comprehensions, lines, paragraphs in other work accomplished the years since.

Little remains of the makings of what came to publication. Here are samplings of the scraps and pages that remain of the loosenings, the wellings just as they came, the practicing of freedom which perhaps made the facility possible; the rounding out and completion of a thought, a story kernel, a noting—where before could only be one word, a scrawl of line, in thieved minutes—to leave some deposit, to affirm that there still lived in me a writer being.

1955–56. Profound earthquake years, presage years— for me, for my country, for our world (therefore also for me). Forty-three years old then, born in 1912 or 1913, I had lived through such periods before, but only now had I time to try to comprehend them, record their impress as they occurred, even try to shape into literature. As I tried in "Oh Yes", "Tell Me a Riddle."

1955–56: Year of writing resurrection for me—yet year of arterial closeness to death and dyings of four of the human beings ineradicably dearest to me: my mother, my father-in-law Avrum, Seevya, and Genya (whose last days of dying are inscribed in "Tell Me a Riddle"). All four of that great vanishing generation whose vision, legacy of belief—in one human race, in infinite human potentiality which never yet had had circumstances to blossom, in the ever-recurring movement of humanity against what degrades and maims—I tried to embed in that novella.

Year for me of overwhelming realization—death-occasioned—of the vulnerability and transcience and dearness of life. World year of escalating nuclear threat—and seeming defeat for the petition movement of millions the earth over to totally disarm; only Picasso's peace dove, created as symbol for us, seemingly remaining.

1955–56: Presage year indeed for our country. Year that began still in the McCarthyite shadow of fear; of pervasive cynical belief that actions with others against wrong were personally suspect, would only end in more grievous wrong; year of proclamation that the young were a "silent generation," future "organization men."

sharks   dragons   los bandidos   the gents   royal esquires   warlords   aces   templars
Apaches   Barts Road runners   Shieks

he hurted me so bad   all my good feeling days is gone
   I done worked & worried & slaved & raised him & he should write

looks like' an accident goin somewhere to happenth

they lives in the old plush

get myself conglomerated

write him a bawlen out letter

sick of this sluggin & tuggin & worryin
               dug up   drug up   beatonh & wore out
fire wagons   slaughter pan

I dont fly fly when they say shoo shoo   I got stubborn wings
he like to collapse
its all I kin do is work not work & worry both
my dumb brat background ntohing to brag off at all
m ake all kinds of oaths & swears
the natural truth
she scorch up some

I dont want that boy to just make a livin   I want him to do some livin

all those testes
           nothing to brag off at all
I'm tellin you the true
nearly killed me graveyard dead
she runnen me crazy   feel like somebody tromping my heart
wear myself to death
just got me down in the dumphouse
in the middle of a bad fix
rhey definly said it
he shoots off to everybody   the policemans   why cant something be did about it
  "I'll blow you in"   they stomped him in the head   jab it off   hes on the needle see
he abrused me   overrejoiced
thats a boy and a half
the mens out of work   just saing it to pass off   thats about the gize
mamma you maulin me
I'M LOOKED DOWN ON   what czn be did about it
loafin his time down
clothes done gone
thoughin it through
a hippy dip

        that is what she do
        we tired of everybody frontin us off
        the policemans
        a real mannerable boy
        get their licks in
        we not animals we peeple
        that wasnt right

Caught in the press of family obligations and without the money to buy books, Olsen got into the practice of copying quotations from library books onto 3 × 5 cards. These, she explains, "I could carry with me for available moments to re-read, ponder, or learn by heart. Yes they have come stained over the years, dog-eared, torn—tacked (as still they sometimes are) over sink or stove during tasks, or over my work desk, or still habitually pulled out to re-read while on the bus or waiting somewhere."

*   In addition to transcribing quotations from canonical authors, Olsen also carefully compiles "evidence of the . . . way language*

Year of the Supreme Court decision against segregation "which generates feelings of inferiority"; of Rosa Parks, Birmingham, Little Rock. Year of the first happenings of the freedom movements against wrong which were to convulse and mark our nation and involve numberless individual lives.

So was burgeoned "O Yes" ("Baptism"). So was begun "Tell Me A Riddle." (Both sourced in the years before as well.)

Other wellsprings fed:

I was again migrating from one world into another— and in more than the twice-a-week commute to Stanford. It had been so with me, unarticulated, in my youthhood when I crossed the tracks to Omaha's academic high school. It was so now with me, as it was happening in my children's lives. I was freshly experiencing, re-experiencing that terrible agony, harm, of having to live in a class/sex/race separating circumscribed time, when those among whom we are born, live, work, those with whom we are most deeply bonded, cannot journey along with us into that other world of books, of more enabling circumstances for use, development of innate capacities.

I was living more and more, too, in the world of written language (some of it consummately used) (though the sound of written language, spoken aloud in class, read to Hannah, my own words spoken to myself while writing, was coming often into my ears).

For years, for nearly a lifetime, in love, in wonder, in envy, I had noted, kept evidence of the *other* consummate way language is, has been, used: the older, more universal oral/ aural—by "ordinary" human beings denied the written form.

---

is, has been used" by America's different cultural groups. Her sensitivity to different modes of speech is evident here on a large blue sheet that records the distinctive words and syntax of black San Francisco diction. This material, gathered together from years of jottings, is integral to the story "O Yes," which is set in a black Baptist church and reflects Olsen's special interest in strains of American English which for racial and class reasons are often excluded from the written medium. Her respect for the integrity of diverse ethnic voices signals the democracy of Olsen's art, which celebrates diversity within its unifying vision of human community. (Exhibition Notes)

On scraps, in notes, in memory—and now, in my Stanford time, typed up, garnered together: remarkable phrasings, expressions, song lines, wisdoms, characterizations heard, spoken, sometimes sung, by unwritten, unwriting others in my life.

I had circumstanced time. I had profoundest need—to encompass, make tangible, visible (I hoped indelible) all the above. So did "O Yes" come to be. So was begun, and one-third finished, "Tell Me a Riddle."

Then—had to return back to that uncircumstanced world of what silences.

❏ Critical Essays

◻ LINDA RAY PRATT ■

The Circumstances of Silence: Literary Representation and Tillie Olsen's Omaha Past

I came to explore the wreck.
The words are purposes.
The words are maps.
I came to see the damage that was done
and the treasures that prevail.
ADRIENNE RICH,
"Diving into the Wreck"

Tillie Olsen's *Silences* addresses "the relationship of circumstances—including class, color, sex; the times, climate into which one is born—to the creation of literature" (xi). Olsen's primary concern is with those conditions that stop women from writing, but implicit in her pursuit of "unnatural silences" is the question of how situations affect *what* one writes. Like Virginia Woolf, Olsen is aware of how difficult it is for a woman to achieve a "totality of self" that can escape such circumstances as "anxieties, shamings," "the leeching of belief," indeed, all the "punitive difference in circumstances, in history" that damage and inhibit the capacity to write

From *The Critical Response to Tillie Olsen,* ed. Kay Hoyle Nelson and Nancy Huse (Westport, Conn.: Greenwood Press, 1994), 229–243.

113

(*Silences* 263, 27). Olsen candidly discusses those things that affected her opportunity to write, but *Silences* does not explore the relationship between her circumstances and what she did write. Many readers presume a connection exists between her fiction and her life, and Olsen has acknowledged that her stories may be in some sense "profoundly autobiographical" and that as a writer she dwells in the past. Most of the story of Olsen's past in the radical Jewish community of Omaha, Nebraska, has not been published before.[1] In a series of interviews about her Omaha years, Olsen recalled her early life and the use she has made of it in the fiction.[2] These accounts illuminate the autobiographical representation in the work, but also significant is what she does not use. Many of the ideological and ethnic circumstances which influenced the young Tillie Lerner are themselves silenced in the literary form.

Olsen's long residency in San Francisco and the general absence of a defined place in much of her work obscure the particulars of her heritage. Readers who know her through "I Stand Here Ironing" are often unaware of the author's Jewish background, and she rejects being categorized as a Jewish writer. Only the couple in "Tell Me a Riddle" are Jewish, and she has said many times that they represent a type and not her particular parents. Few readers associate her with Nebraska and fewer still with the Russian Jewish and socialist community in Omaha. Tillie Lerner grew up in the immigrant working class that settled in north Omaha, a neighborhood once populated by many Jewish businesses and now the center of the city's Black community. The stories in *Tell Me a Riddle* (1961) and her novel of Depression life, *Yonnondio* (1974), draw heavily on her family's life in Omaha but usually without the specifics of a setting or ethnic culture. The Holbrooks in *Yonnondio* are abstractions of the Depression's working-class poor, and the Jewish couple in "Tell Me a Riddle" live in an unnamed city. Yet Olsen grew up in a distinct kind of midwestern Jewish community where "the times, climate into which one is born" composed the often harsh "circumstances" of poverty, bias, and marginalization.

Olsen's belief that the valorizing of the individual self is patriarchal and central to the ethics of capitalism influences her rejection of a self-oriented autobiographical form. Her po-

114

litical belief in one international community of human beings limits the emphasis she is willing to put on ethnic and regional identities. In addition to the conscious role ideologies of politics, gender, and selfhood play in determining form, her responses to the painful nature of her past may also create the need for fictional abstractions and silences. In my interviews with Olsen she frequently returned to two themes: the richness of her radical past in a family of active socialists, and the pain and embarrassment that went with being poor and different, even within one's own ethnic group. The Lerner family story is, in retrospect, representative of a certain kind of Jewish leftwing life among immigrants to the United States. Olsen recognizes her family as a significant type of their generation, but when she was living that life, she often felt a sense of rebellion and alienation. Yet, the intensity of these years makes it her most important subject.

Discussing the autobiographical content of Olsen's work is difficult for her because not writing autobiographically is "what I'm all about" as an author who believes in "one human race without religion." "Should a writer write autobiography is a modern question," she says, noting that earlier authors were not scrutinized for the elements of their life in every piece of fiction they wrote. Yet, she characterizes her story "I Stand Here Ironing" as "close to autobiography," "O Yes" as "profound autobiography," and "Tell Me a Riddle" as "very, very autobiographical." "Autobiography takes many forms," Olsen comments, and explains that often the autobiographical elements in her stories are "probably deeper things" than the details of experiences and places. Her novel *Yonnondio* has some close parallels with her family's history, but she "was not writing an autobiographical novel" when she composed it. "I was not writing an immigrant saga," Olsen has commented in response to questions about the lack of ethnic or religious identity attributed to the novel's fictional Holbrook family. The novel was not "entirely different," however, and "a large part of it was what was in the neighborhood." Two questions I hope to examine are 1) what is the autobiographical experience out of which the author builds this fictional world? and 2) what does it mean for the literature that much of that experience is silenced in the fictional representation?[3]

115

I

Midwestern urban Jewish communities such as the one in Omaha were smaller than their East Coast counterparts and increasingly remote from involvement with radical politics and the labor movement. The socialist beliefs which many Eastern European Jews such as Olsen's parents brought to the Great Plains were perhaps more susceptible to the pressure of acculturation and assimilation in an environment such as Omaha where a tradition of conservative politics, agrarian economics, and a largely homogeneous white Western European population dominated. Though many other Omaha Jews share the same Russian socialist background, the Omaha Jewish community developed westward out of the urban center of the city and into the suburban middle class. This migration out of the urban neighborhoods and up the economic ladder was already underway in the late 1920s when Tillie Lerner was a student at Omaha's Central High.

Working-class socialists such as the Lerners were separated by ideology from the mainstream of the local Jewish community. Socialist Jews often had different economic attitudes and did not participate in the religious life around the synagogues. Radical Jews often rejected religion, and Olsen has described her father as "incorruptibly atheist to the last day of his life" (Rubin 3). Within a Jewish community already smaller and more isolated than those in large urban centers, Olsen's place was further marginalized when she broke with her family's socialism to become a communist. Olsen tried not to embarrass her family with her communism, and she sometimes used aliases in her political work. In school she was aware of painful class differences compounded by being Jewish, working class, immigrant, poor, and female. Tillie Lerner's Omaha background of estrangement and alienation was a painful contradiction to her family's dream of an international society in which the comradeship of humanity transcended the divisions of race, ethnicity, and religion.

Olsen's parents came to the United States at a time when efforts were underway to relocate Jewish immigrants outside the urban areas of the East Coast. Samuel and Ida Lerner had met in Russia but did not begin their family until

116

they settled on a farm near Mead, Nebraska. Samuel was from Odessa; Ida from Minsk. The family memory is that they had first met in Minsk where Samuel had gone to work for the Bund, the Jewish socialist movement organized in Russia in 1897 and devoted to secular Yiddish culture and internationalism.[4] After the failure of the 1905 Revolution in which they had participated, they fled Russian prisons and met again in New York. After working at least through 1907 with the Socialist Party in New York, Samuel made his way to Omaha where other socialist Jews from Minsk and Odessa had already settled.[5]

The family history before 1918 is unclear. For a time the Lerners were tenant farmers in the Mead, Nebraska, area, but Olsen reports that at least one year was spent in Colorado where her father worked in the mines.[6] Olsen remembers that in Mead the children were harassed on their way to school because her father opposed the war and wouldn't buy bonds. *Yonnondio* draws on memories of the farm and mining years. The novel begins in a mining community in Wyoming, but the family moves on to South Dakota where they fail at farming and from there to a packing house city like Omaha. Unlike Anna in the novel, Olsen's mother spoke little English and was isolated in the rural community. The farm years were "terrible for my mother," Olsen said. Her father "loved being on the land," but her mother "had a hunger for a larger life" and desired to leave it. After the move to Omaha Ida Lerner studied English in one of the many night classes that schools such as Kellom Elementary ran for immigrants. Some passages from an exercise her mother wrote in 1924 as part of her English class assignment suggest Ida's own sense of social values, maternal responsibility, and literary bent. The essay, dated December 10, 1924, and addressed to "Dear Teacher" reads in part:

> I am glad to study with ardor but the children wont let me, they go to bed late so it makes me tired, and I cant do my lessons. It is after ten o'clock my head dont work it likes to have rest. But I am in a sad mood I am sitting in the warm house and feel painfull that winter claps in to my heart. I see the old destroyed houses of the people from the old country. I

117

hear the wind blow through them with the disgusting cry
why the poor creatures ignore him, dont protest against him,
that souless wind dont no, that they are helples have no material to repair the houses and no clothes to cover up their
bodies, and so the sharp wind echo cry falls on the window,
and the windows original sing with silver-ball tears seeing all
the poor shivering creatures dressed in rags with frozen fingers and feverish hungry eyes.

Ida Lerner closes this essay with sentiments that begin, "So
as a human being who carries responsibility for action I think
as a duty to the community we shall try to understand each
other." The character of Eva in "Tell Me a Riddle" echoes
many of these sentiments, and she also shares the same sense
of opportunities curtailed by the burdens of childcare. Olsen
used a phrase from her mother's essay in "Tell Me a Riddle"
where Eva's fragmented ruminations include the words, "*As
a human being responsibility.*"

The family probably moved to Omaha no later than
1917. Olsen believes that they initially settled in South
Omaha, the meat packing area of the city, but the first record
of their Omaha residence is at 2512 Caldwell, the family's
permanent home in North Omaha (Omaha *City Directory*,
1918). North Omaha was the section where Omaha's Jews
clustered in the first two decades of the century. South
Omaha, the center of the meat packing industry, was directly
connected by 24th Street to the North Omaha area where the
Lerners lived. Both areas were populated by ethnic and minority groups that migrated to the city to work in packing.
Though not themselves in meat packing, the Lerners lived
among packing house workers in a period of intense labor un-
rest in the industry.

In 1918 Samuel Lerner's occupation was listed in the
City Directory as peddler. In 1920–23 Olsen's father worked
at the Silver Star Confectionery at 1604 North 24th Street, one
of many small Jewish businesses in the area at that time. Olsen's memory of shelling almonds for the candies her father
made appears in some discarded pages of the *Yonnondio*
manuscript where it became Mazie's experience. An unpublished fragment of the manuscript reads as follows:

118

And then Mazie had a "job" for two weeks. Annamae told her about it, for just shelling almonds two blocks away she could get a quarter a day. Bitterly Anna ordered Mazie not to think about it, but then thought of Monday and the insurance man, and the 60¢ made her say yes. It wont hurt the kid, Jim had insisted. So Mazie sat at a high table in a top room filled with steam from the boiling nuts and the oil, her hands in hot water, peeling the almonds. Snap, snap, her fingers seemed independent of her body, red little animals snapping at brown skin.

After the confectionery failed, Sam Lerner worked as a painter and paper hanger.[7]

As socialist Jews, the Lerners built their lives around political circles instead of the synagogue. Sam was active in his union, and both Sam and Ida were active in Workmen's Circles, a national Jewish socialist organization with several chapters in Omaha. The Lerners were founding members of the Omaha Workmen's Circle, Branch 626, in 1920, and also helped found branches in Sioux City, Lincoln, and Des Moines. The Workmen's Circles served as political, social, and cultural centers for Jews whose socialist views and lack of traditional religious beliefs placed them outside the religious community. The Circles provided such traditional services of fraternal organizations as insurance policies, burial benefits, and retirement homes.

As part of the Workmen's Circles the Lerners helped to build Omaha's first Labor Lyceum at 22nd and Clark Streets. After the original labor lyceum was sold for public housing in the 1930s, Olsen's parents helped to build a new Labor Lyceum in 1940 at 31st and Cuming Street. No longer encompassed by small children, Ida Lerner was apparently active in this period, and some Omaha Jews recall her participation in Workmen's Circle activities. Both Sam and Ida spoke at the dedication ceremonies of the new Labor Lyceum which became the center for the district conferences of the Workmen's Circle. Sam Lerner was a president of the Midwest District Committee.

The family's socialist activities were often in support of the labor struggles in the packing houses. Olsen recalls the impact of the packing house strike of 1921–22 on her family, especially her father.[8] By the 1920's the Socialist Party in the midwest had lost most of the members it had before World War I, but Olsen's father continued to be active.[9] He was secretary of the Nebraska Socialist Party and in 1928 was the party's candidate for lieutenant governor of the state. Family life was centered around party activities. On Sundays the children attended the socialist Sunday School and sang of the worker's struggles from the *Socialist Sunday School Song Book*. Their house was a stopping point for prominent socialists, Wobblies, and others on the Left who were traveling through Omaha.

Olsen's memories of her high school years are a mixture of the pleasures of discovering literature and the pain of recognizing her own marginalization. She had both teachers whom she credits with "saving" her and teachers that taught her painful lessons in class differences. Despite her socialist home, Olsen has said that she "didn't really learn about class until I 'crossed the tracks' to Central High School."[10] At Central, the best high school in the state, the curriculum was "college prep" and some of the students were from prominent and wealthy families in Omaha. As children of working-class Jewish immigrants, the Lerners were, she says, "aliens in that school." Olsen remembers the striking contrasts in dress and ways, and that most students carried clean pocket handkerchiefs while the Lerner children had to make do with clean rags. "There were those things that were class differences that I had never encountered first hand," she recalls.

Olsen singled out two teachers who had a strong influence on her—Sara Vore Taylor who taught English and Autumn Davies who taught Civics. Taylor introduced her to Coleridge, De Quincey, and Sir Thomas Browne. "I still have her old stylebook," Olsen says. Taylor was also interested in recent poetry and urged students to go hear Carl Sandburg when he was in Omaha. Davies was "interested in my mind" and wanted Olsen to go to college. Despite occasional trouble with a few teachers because she would not silence her unorthodox and questioning mind, Tillie was praised for the humor column "Central Squeaks" which she wrote in the high school paper under the name "Tillie the Toiler." After the 1934 publication of "The Iron Throat" in *Partisan Review*, the Central

High *Register* published an article on her literary success just six years after graduation. The paper notes that the column "Squeaks" "as run by Tillie was entirely natural and unhampered by rule." The article also noted her recent arrest "at the home of Communist friends" in California and that she was awaiting trial.

Although some of her teachers encouraged her mind, Olsen also recalls the anti-Semitism of others. The difficulty of her position as a Jew was perhaps compounded by also being part of a known radical family and by her own occasionally disruptive classroom behavior. A letter to her in 1934 from her brother Gene gives us an insight into the anti-Semitic climate she found at school. The occasion of the letter from Gene was her arrest in California. At the time of the incident she was receiving her first serious attention as a writer after the publication of "The Iron Throat." Gene's letter expresses his concern that her arrest might make the Omaha papers and give the "anti-semites" a "chance to say 'see what happens to the revolutionary Jew.'" He urges her to think what it would mean to succeed as a writer and imagines a moment of vindication: "It would be the greatest happiness of my life to go to [name of teacher] and throw the book on her desk and say 'look what the revolutionary Jew has done now.'" These sentiments strongly suggest the discrimination the Lerner children felt in school and the desire to prove themselves worthy of their heritage.[11] It also suggests the pressure to vindicate her family through her success as a writer, a need that may enter into Olsen's hesitation in publishing and her silencing of details that would reveal her family to be a major subject.

Olsen's "Tell Me a Riddle" mirrors the Russian Jewish political and intellectual values that Olsen learned at home. "There has been a real eclipsing of the beliefs of Jews of this generation," she has observed, but they were people who saw their lives as committed to the liberation of an international human community. Some members of the Omaha Jewish community characterized the Russian socialist Jews as "a kind of intelligentsia," but as the community changed, those Jews who remained socialist and communist were less influential and less visible to the broader community.

Olsen broke with the family's socialism when she

joined the Young Communist League in 1931, a decision her parents could not approve. Although her parents were not happy with her decision, she says her decision to join the YCL "was not a rebellion against my home. My decision to join the YCL was rooted absolutely out of the beliefs in our house." Her break with her parents' views paralleled in many ways the splits taking place in the Socialist Party during the early days of the American Communist Party.[12] The decline of the Socialist Party after World War I may have contributed to the younger generation's interest in communism. From the early 1920s communists and communist laborites had groups in Omaha, and some former socialists had aligned themselves with them (W. Pratt, "Socialism on the Northern Plains" 27–29). Tillie's case was not unlike that of others whose parents had been socialists in the 1900–1919 period but the children grew up to be communists in the 1924–1939 period. Despite the unhappiness of her family at her decision, Olsen recalls her father saying to her mother, "Well, she didn't join the capitalist class." "My mother would have said, 'Never join the floggers against the flogged.' She always taught us that."

Because her family, well known as socialists in the community, disapproved of her communist affiliation, Olsen sometimes used aliases in her political work. The front page story of the Feb. 6, 1932 *Omaha Bee-News* features photographs of a "peaceful and small" crowd of about 100 members of the Omaha Council of the Unemployed marching to present their demands to Acting Mayor Arthur Westergard. Tillie Olsen identified herself as the woman speaker in one of the pictures under the name of "Theta Larimore, 2023 Burt Street," who is quoted as "shouting" "What becomes of the women who lose their jobs? Save their respectability." In 1934 when she was arrested in California she apparently used the name "Teresa Landale." After joining the YCL she worked in packing houses and factories in Kansas City and St. Joseph, Missouri. In Kansas City she was arrested for leafleting and jailed for five months. After she was released she returned to Omaha to recover her health, but by late 1932 Tillie Lerner left Omaha, first to Faribault, Minnesota, where she began writing *Yonnondio,* and then to California where she lives today.

The Lerner family history in Omaha ends in the late

1940s except for one sister who lived in Omaha until the 1980s. In the housing shortage after World War II Sam and Ida Lerner sold their home on Caldwell Street and moved to the Washington, D.C., area where Tillie's brother Harry lives. Tillie's mother died in January 1956, and her father died in a Workmen's Circle retirement home in Media, Pennsylvania, in February 1974.

II

The details of Olsen's family life and the identifying of incidents and characters that appear in her fiction give us an insight to how the work is autobiographical. Two points stand out: the extensive degree to which the work draws on family experience, and the centrality of the early period of her life to her fictional imagination. *Yonnondio* sets a pattern that reappears throughout much of her work. Here the plot recasts experiences of her own family, the mother and child characters reflecting memories of her mother and herself, but the family as a whole is generalized to represent a type. Olsen commented that she identified with Mazie but that Mazie was "not a reader" and Tillie was. Mazie was also not "freaky in the same sense that I was freaky." Mazie's response to the evening star and her school were the kinds of "deeper things" about the character that were autobiographical. Olsen's comment suggests that specific traits of Mazie were different but that Mazie's emotional responses are the "deeper" autobiographical part. Yet specific personal experiences and persons from her youth also appear in the novel. Mr. Caldwell, the farmer in the novel who wants to give the child some books, was, according to Olsen, mainly based on Dr. Alfred Jefferson, one of several socialists the family knew. Jefferson was a physician who "loved talking to my mother and was good to me. He was interested that we read." The character of Jeff, "the little Negro boy" who hears a humming in his head "that would blend into music" (*Yonnondio* 91), was based on Jeff Crawford, the son of Suris and Mattie Crawford, the Black family who were neighbors to the Lerners on Caldwell Street, and whose daughter, Joe Eva, was Tillie's close girlhood friend. According to the *City Directory*, Suris Crawford worked as a butcher at Armours. The story "O Yes" in *Tell Me a Riddle* also reflects the friendship between the two families.

Olsen's memory of the city in *Yonnondio* is that she merged details from Omaha, Kansas City, and St. Joseph, all places where she worked briefly in meat packing. The details of the city, unnamed in the novel except that the father says the family may "go to Omaha—get on at the slaughterhouse," closely parallel the geography of South Omaha. Like the unnamed city in the novel, Omaha lies just west of the Missouri River on a series of bluffs with the packing plants in a shallow valley. The viaduct in the novel which the workers cross going to the packinghouse is like the Q Street viaduct which connects the ethnic neighborhoods on the bluffs to the packing houses and stock yards in the valley. The Armours plant is described in the novel as "way down, like a hog, a great hulk of a building wallowed. A—R—M—O—U—R—S gray letters shrieked" (85). Photographs of the Omaha area from the 1930s and 1940s show a massive packing house in the center of the district with "Armours" spelled in large letters across the wall. In *Yonnondio* "the children can lie on their bellies near the edge of the cliff and watch the trains and freights, the glittering railroad tracks, the broken bottles dumped below, the rubbish moving on the littered belly of the river" (61–62). The bluffs on the eastern edge of Omaha overlook the river, and a railroad track runs beside the river. Though the old meat packing district in Kansas City also was near the river, the placement of bluffs, factories, and streets in the novel all fit the topography of Omaha. Olsen's fictional intent seems to be that the Holbrooks and the city where they live function generically, but the mass of detail in the family history and the setting suggests that the fictional representation is also specific. The fictionalizing obliterates the ethnic, regional, and political details that would locate the story in a more defined historical context.

The story "O Yes" also draws on Olsen's childhood friendship with the Black child next door, but here she combines it with similar incidents in the lives of her own children. The story tells of two twelve-year-old girls, one white and one Black, whose friendship dissolves when they reach the age at which race and class consciousness begin to divide school children. Olsen says that "the story is fiction, but it is rooted in the real." The names of popular musicians date the story from her children's youth, but the memories of the Black church come from Olsen's own girlhood. In the story the white child is shocked at the intensity of the emotion in the Black church. "That sound and the church" in Olsen's mind were Calvary Baptist Church, located in Omaha at 25th and Hamilton Streets between 1901–1923, where she sometimes went to hear the music on summer nights. She used this material as the recitation in Alva's mind in the story. The Black church, she remembers, was "a certain kind of community where you could let things out."

Olsen has repeatedly stated that Eva and David in "Tell Me a Riddle" are not specifically her parents, but the history of Sam and Ida Lerner, socialists from Russia in 1905, parents of six children, active in the union, selling their house and retiring to a Workmen's Circle home, suggests how deeply rooted this story is in the lives of her parents. Many other Russian Jews of their generation came to the United States after the 1905 Revolution, but numerous details specific to her family fit the fictional characters. David and Eva have been married forty-seven years, and in 1956 when Olsen's mother died, her parents, who apparently had been united in Nebraska sometime between 1908 and 1910, had been together approximately forty-seven years. David and Eva have six living children, as did the Lerners. Like Sam Lerner, David was "an official" who had helped organize and run the Workmen's Circles. At one point when David is trying to convince Eva to sell the house, he tells her about the reading circles in the retirement home, and she says, "And forty years ago when the children were morsels and there was a Circle, did you stay home with them once so I could go?," an apparent reference to the Workman's Circle. Some of Eva's words are Olsen's mother's, as we have seen in the essay written by Ida. Olsen told me that the episode in *Yonnondio* in which Anna takes time from her laundry to teach her children how to blow bubbles with a green onion is based on a memory of her mother. This memory reappears in "Tell Me a Riddle" when Vivi recalls how Eva, also while washing clothes, taught her how to blow bubbles:

Washing sweaters: Ma, I'll never forget, one of those days so nice you washed clothes outside; one of the first spring days it must have been. The bubbles just danced while you scrubbed, and we chased after, and you stopped to show us how to blow our own bubbles with green onion stalks.

Looking at the text from the background of Olsen's Omaha life suggests that family and personal experiences are the crucial ground of her fiction. Yet much of the ethnic and radical past that she remembers so vividly and emotionally in interviews is distanced or dropped in the fiction. In *Yonnondio* the "unlimn'd" who "disappear" and fade from "the cities, farms, factories" fade within the novel whose epigram promises to recall them. As abstractions of the Depression poor, the Holbrooks lack history, community, and beliefs, all of which were integral to the way of life among packing town families. "Tell Me a Riddle" reflects the Russian past before David and Eva's immigration but does not reflect the fifty years of ongoing political commitment in her parents' lives. Like the Holbrooks, David and Eva stand for a type within a generation but just what "type" can never be clear when characters lose so much context. These characters dramatize the pathos of lives constrained by poverty, of women whose energies are depleted by child care and housework, but the rich texture of a place, a heritage, and active beliefs that have historically given substance to immigrant culture, including the Lerner family of Omaha, are largely absent.

III

Olsen's decision to create characters who represent in the abstract the experiences of many fulfills her ideological and artistic principles, but her writing is most powerful when it escapes the generic and becomes culturally specific. The brilliant clarity given David and Eva's Jewish language and the poignancy of the lost youth in Russia contrast sharply with the featureless pathos of the Holbrooks. The closer Olsen writes to autobiography, the finer her work, as the weaknesses in "Requa" may also illustrate. The autobiographical background also suggests that family life is her essential subject. Paradoxically, however, her art often silences much of the richness in her imaginative sources. If the early years appear to be a major touchstone for her imagination, her often painful recollections in the interviews suggest that Omaha is where the silencing began. In those early years Olsen learned the lessons of discrimination on the basis of class, ethnicity, and gender. Olsen remembers both the strength she found in a socialist home and the marginalization she felt as a poor Jew who was also radical, female, and literary. Her tentative place in the wider community was underscored when her decision to join the Communist Party created anger and embarrassment at home. Those "circumstances" described in *Silences* that "blight" and damage the young woman writer match those she felt "in the vulnerable girl years" growing up in Omaha. *Silences* gives us "the barest of indications as to vulnerabilities, balks, blights; reasons for lessenings and silencings" that affect the young woman who hopes to write:

> Anxieties, shamings. "Hidden injuries of class." Prevailing attitudes toward our people as "lower class," "losers," (they just didn't have it); contempt for their lives and the work they do . . . . the blood struggle for means: . . . . class—economic circumstance; problems of being in the first generation of one's family to come to writing (263–64).

If these are the circumstances that silence creativity, it may also follow that the artist may wish to silence the silencers, may, indeed, have to silence them in order to write at all. When I asked about the power the past holds for her, Olsen said, "I certainly still dwell in that world in my writing."

Like Adrienne Rich's speaker, Olsen's stories "circle silently/about the wreck" amid "the evidence of damage," "back to this scene" (Rich 24). The self that speaks, the artist in the woman, must counter that which silences. The particular eloquence of Olsen's work is in her portraits of women who survive with enough intact to be themselves in a world that does not open for them. In "I Stand Here Ironing" the mother explains what she did and could not do to protect her vulnerable daughter, Emily, a sensitive and artistic child "of depression, of war, of fear." Though the past "will never total," the mother believes that in Emily "there is still enough left to live by" (*Riddle* 20–21). Perhaps this story can be seen as a metaphor for Olsen's own mothering of her artistic self, one without the "totality of self" that may exist where the past was full of love and wisdom, but one with "enough left" to build on what was strong and spoke of survival.

And like the young Omaha woman who used aliases when she did her communist work, Olsen's fiction functions like an alias, too. Names are changed and events reformed, sometimes to universalize the specific; sometimes to protect herself and her family from the scrutiny that accompanies overt autobiography; and sometimes, perhaps, to distance the anguish of being marginalized by the surrounding world. The pain of being viewed as a radical in one's own ethnic community, as a troublesome Jew at school, and as a disappointment in one's own family may well leave one haunted by the past but unable to embrace it, remembering all the places and faces, and yet unwilling to speak their names.

☐ *Notes* ■

1. Deborah Rosenfelt's "From the Thirties: Tillie Olsen and Radical Tradition" examines her radical past after Olsen had moved to California.

2. Personal interview December 30, 1990. This essay is based largely on a set of interviews and correspondence that began in the fall of 1987 and continued through 1991. In addition to telephone interviews, the two longest of which occurred on February 13, 1988, and Dec. 30, 1990, Olsen provided a number of newspaper clippings, family letters, manuscript fragments, and miscellaneous documents from her past. I wish to express my gratitude to Olsen for her generosity in sharing her memories and allowing me to use these materials. An earlier sketch of the Lerner family was published locally as "Tillie Olsen's Omaha Heritage: A History Becomes Literature" in *Memories of the Jewish Midwest: Journal of the Nebraska Jewish Historical Society* (Fall 1989), 1–16.

3. Most of the criticism on autobiographical novels defines the genre from male-centered works such as *David Copperfield*. More useful to me were works on women's autobiography, especially

Sidonie Smith's *A Poetics of Women's Autobiography,* and the essays in Shari Benstock's *The Private Self* and Estelle C. Jelinek's *Women's Autobiography.*

4. Olsen has discussed her understanding of the Bund and "what I feel is *my* Yiddishkeit, my Jewish heritage" in the interview article by Rubin. See also Howe, *World of Our Fathers,* 17.

5. Carol Gendler's M.A. thesis, "The Jews of Omaha," University of Nebraska–Omaha (1986), is the most extensive local history. See also *Our Story: Recollections of Omaha's Early Jewish Community 1885–1925,* eds. Jonathan Rosenbaum and Patricia O'Conner-Seger, with Carol Gendler, for personal accounts, including several of immigrants from Minsk and Odessa.

6. All six of the Lerner children were born in Nebraska and attended Omaha's Central High. The first four (Tillie was the second in order) were apparently born on the farm, the last two in Omaha, though Tillie remains uncertain exactly where and when she was born. Previously published accounts that give a specific date, usually January 14, 1913, are inaccurate, according to Olsen, who unsuccessfully researched her birth date a few years ago when she applied for a passport.

7. The City Directory lists his occupation as "painter" beginning in 1925.

8. The strike was part of a nationwide effort that ended in the breakup of the union in South Omaha. For details, see William C. Pratt, "'Union Maids' in Omaha Labor History, 1887–1945."

9. See William C. Pratt, "Socialism on the Northern Plains, 1900–1924," for a detailed account of the Party at this time.

10. Zelenka, n.p. In *Silences* Olsen calls Central High her "first College-of-Contrast" (vii).

11. Another brother, Harry, was active in the Workmen's Circle. In 1940 he was Secretary of the Omaha Workmen's Circle, Branch 690E, and wrote an editorial for the *Labor Lyceum Journal* honoring the dedication of the new Labor Lyceum. The editorial is entitled, "Shall Youth Be Away?" and urges his generation to join the Workmen's Circles and learn to appreciate what it had meant to the parents. I wish to thank Mrs. Morris Fellman of Omaha for making this booklet available to me.

12. Minnesota author Meridel Le Sueur is another case of children of well known socialist parents who joined the Communist Party in the 1920's. Both Le Sueur and "Tillie Lerner" signed

the "Call for an American Writers' Congress" in 1935. See Linda Ray Pratt, "Woman Writer in the CP," for details of Le Sueur's CP involvement.

☐ Works Cited ■

Benstock, Shari, ed. *The Private Self: Theory and Practice of Women's Autobiographical Writings.* Chapel Hill: U of North Carolina P, 1988.

Gendler, Carol. "The Jews of Omaha." University of Nebraska–Omaha, 1968.

Howe, Irving. *World of Our Fathers.* New York: Harcourt Brace, 1976.

Jelinek, Estelle C., ed. *Women's Autobiography.* Bloomington: Indiana University Press, 1980.

Olsen, Tillie. *Silences.* New York. Delacorte Press, 1978.

———. *Tell Me a Riddle.* New York: Dell, 1961.

———. *Yonnondio: From the Thirties.* New York: Dell, 1974.

Pratt, Linda Ray. "Tillie Olsen's Omaha Heritage: A History Becomes Literature." *Memories of the Jewish Midwest: A Journal of the Nebraska Jewish Historical Society* (Fall 1989): 1–16.

———. "Woman Writer in the CP: The Case of Meridel Le Sueur." *Women's Studies* 14 (1988): 247–64.

Pratt, William C. "Socialism on the Northern Plains, 1900–1924." *South Dakota History.* 18 (Summer 1988): 1–35.

———. " 'Union Maids' in Omaha Labor History, 1887–1945." In *Perspectives: Women in Nebraska History.* Lincoln: Nebraska Department of Education and Nebraska State Council for the Social Studies, 1984, 202–03.

Rich, Adrienne, *Diving into the Wreck.* New York: Norton, 1973.

Rosenbaum, Jonathan, and Patricia O'Conner-Seger, eds., with Carol Gendler. *Our Story: Recollections of Omaha's Early Jewish Community 1885–1925,* Omaha Section of the National Council of Jewish Women, 1981.

Rosenfelt, Deborah. "From the Thirties: Tillie Olsen and Radical Tradition." *Feminist Studies* 7 (Fall 1981): 371–406.

Rubin, Naomi. "A Riddle of History for the Future." *Sojourner* (June 1983): 3–4, 18.

Smith, Sidonie. *A Poetics of Women's Autobiography: Marginality and the Fictions of Self Representation.* Bloomington: Indiana University Press, 1987.

Zelenka, Julia. "Old Neighborhood Stays With Her." Omaha *World Herald.* August 5, 1980.

☐ DEBORAH SILVERTON ROSENFELT ■

From the Thirties: Tillie Olsen and the Radical Tradition

This paper focuses on Tillie Olsen's experience as a woman, a writer, and an activist in the Old Left of the 1930s. It grew out of my view of Olsen's life and art as an important link between that earlier radical tradition and contemporary feminist culture. This perspective, of course, is only one lens through which to look at her life and art, magnifying certain details and diminishing others. In dwelling on Olsen's political activities and in placing her work in the context of a "socialist feminist" literary tradition, I have, as Olsen herself has pointed out to me, given insufficient weight to two poles of her life and art. On the one hand, there was the dailiness of her life, characterized most of the time less by political activism or participation in the leftist literary milieu than by the day-to-day struggles of a first-generation, working-class mother simply to raise and support a family—the kind of silencing that takes priority in all of her own writings. On the other hand, there was her sense of affinity as an artist with traditions of American and world literature that lie outside the "socialist feminist" literary tradition as I have defined it.

The latter point, especially, needs clarification. Obviously, literary traditions are not demarcated by clear boundaries. Some works of literature, by virtue of their art and scope, transcend the immediate filiations of their authors to become

From *Feminist Studies* 7, no. 3 (Fall 1981): 371–406.

part of a "great tradition" of their own—not in an idealistic sense, but as models which inspire and challenge later writers, regardless of their political commitments. Olsen's work is part of this "great tradition," both in its sources and in its craft. Then too, in some eras of intense political activity, such as the thirties or the sixties, writers whose essential concerns are not explicitly political or whose work takes other directions when the era has ended may be temporarily drawn into a leftist political milieu. Edna St. Vincent Millay, Katherine Anne Porter, Mary McCarthy, and Dorothy Parker were among the women writers associated, in the thirties, with the Left; in our own era, writers like Adrienne Rich and Susan Griffin—close to Olsen both as friends and as artists—initially shared connections and visions with the New Left, subsequently articulating values and world views partly in opposition to it.

Yet the definition of a "socialist feminist" tradition is, I think, legitimate and useful, for it does identify writers who, like Olsen, shared a certain kind of consciousness, an engagement with the political issues of their day, and an involvement in a progressive political and cultural movement. It also enables us to examine the connections between the radical cultural traditions of the past and those our own era is creating, questioning that earlier heritage when necessary, but acknowledging also the extent to which we as contemporary feminists are its heirs.[1]

I could not have written this paper without Tillie Olsen's assistance, although its emphasis, its structure, and any errors in fact and interpretation are my responsibility. Over the past two years, Olsen has granted me access to some of her personal papers—journals, letters, and unpublished manuscripts. Both she and her husband, Jack Olsen, have been generous in sharing their recollections of life in the thirties. In fall 1980, Olsen responded with a detailed critique to an earlier version of this paper.[2] Some of her comments called for a simple correction of factual inaccuracies; some questioned my interpretations of her experience. The paper in its present form incorporated many, although not all, of her suggestions for revision.

This paper, then, is part of an ongoing dialogue about issues that matter very much to both Tillie Olsen and myself:

134

the relationship of writing to political commitment: the "circumstances"—a favorite Olsen word—of class and sex and their effect on sustained creative activity, literary or political; and the strengths and weaknesses of the radical cultural tradition in this country.

. . .

Tillie Olsen's fiction and essays have been widely acknowledged as major contributions to American literature and criticism. Her work has been particularly valued by contemporary feminists, for it has contributed significantly to the task of reclaiming women's achievements and interpreting their lives. In 1961, she published the collection of four stories, *Tell Me a Riddle* (Philadelphia: J. B. Lippincott), each story focusing on the relationships between family members or friends; each revealing the injuries inflicted by poverty, racism, and the patriarchal order; each celebrating the endurance of human love and will. In 1974, she published *Yonnondio: From the Thirties* (New York: Delacorte Press/Seymour Lawrence), the first section of a novel about a working-class family, told mostly from the point of view of the daughter, Mazie. Begun in the thirties, then put away, this novel was finally revised forty years later "in arduous partnership" with "that long ago young writer."[3] In 1978, she published her collected essays in *Silences* (New York: Delacorte Press/Seymour Lawrence), a sustained prose poem about the silences that befall writers and those who would be writers—especially, although not exclusively, women; especially, although not exclusively those who must also struggle for sheer survival. In addition to being a gifted writer and critic, Olsen is also a teacher who has helped to democratize the literary canon by calling attention to the works of Third World writers, working-class writers, and women.

Olsen's importance to contemporary women who read and write or who write about literature is widely acknowledged. Yet although her work has been vital for feminists today, and although one article does discuss her background in some depth,[4] few of Olsen's contemporary admirers realize the extent to which her consciousness, vision, and choice of sub-

ject are rooted in an earlier heritage of social struggle—the
communist Old Left of the thirties and the tradition of radical
political thought and action, mostly socialist and anarchist,
that dominated the Left in the teens and twenties. Not that
we can explain the eloquence of her work in terms of its sociopolitical origins, not even that left-wing politics and culture
were the single most important influences on it, but that its
informing consciousness, its profound understanding of class
and sex and race as shaping influences on people's lives,
owes much to that earlier tradition. Olsen's work, in fact, may
be seen as part of a literary lineage so far unacknowledged
by most contemporary critics: a socialist feminist literary
tradition.

Critics such as Ellen Moers and Elaine Showalter have
identified a literary tradition of women writers who read one
another's work, corresponded with one another about everything from domestic irritations to the major issues of the day,
and looked to one another for strength, encouragement, and
insight.[5] Literary historians like Walter Rideout and Daniel
Aaron have traced the outlines of a radical literary tradition in
America, composed of two waves of twentieth-century writers
influenced by socialism in the early years, by communism in
the thirties, who had in common "an attempt to express a predominantly Marxist view toward society."[6] At the intersections
of these larger traditions is a line of women writers, associated
with the American Left, who unite a class consciousness and
a feminist consciousness in their lives and creative work,
who are concerned with the material circumstances of people's lives, who articulate the experiences and grievances of
women and of other oppressed groups—workers, national minorities, the colonized and the exploited—and who speak out
of a defining commitment to social change.

In fiction this tradition extends from turn of the century socialists like Charlotte Perkins Gilman, Vida Scudder,
and Susan Glaspell, through such thirties Old Left women
as Meridel Le Sueur, Tess Slesinger, Josephine Herbst, Grace
Lumpkin, and Ruth McKenney, to contemporary writers with
early ties to the civil rights and antiwar movements and the
New Left: Marge Piercy, Grace Paley, Alice Walker, and others. Although the specific political affiliations of these writers

136

have varied from era to era and from individual to individual, the questions they raise have been surprisingly consistent. These range from basic questions about how to survive economically to more complex ones, such as how to understand the connections and contradictions between women's struggles and those struggles based on other categories and issues, or how to find a measure of emotional and sexual fulfillment in a world where egalitarian relationships are more ideal than real. Sometimes as in Gilman's *Herland,* published serially in *The Forerunner* in the midteens, or Piercy's *Woman on the Edge of Time,* these writers try to imagine socialist feminist utopias. More often, as with the women writers associated with the Left, especially the Communist party, in the 1930s, their work constitutes a sharp critique of the present. Sometimes, as in Agnes Smedley's *Daughter of Earth,* Slesinger's *The Unpossessed,* Piercy's *Small Changes,* much of Alice Walker's fiction, and, implicitly Olsen's *Tell Me a Riddle,* that critique includes a sharp look from a woman's point of view at the sexual politics of daily life in the political milieus with which these authors were associated.

Olsen's relationship to her political milieu in the 1930s most concerns me here, for this paper is not so much a literary analysis of Olsen's work as it is a study of her experience in the Left in the years when she first began to write for publication. I will first give a brief overview of Olsen's background and life in those years, focusing on the roots of both her political commitment and her creative work, and then identify a series of central contradictions inherent in her experience. In thus imposing a paradigmatic order on Olsen's individual experience, I have tried, not always successfully, to maintain a balance between fidelity to the idiosyncracies of the individual life and the identification of patterns applicable to the experience of other women artists in leftist movements then and now.

Tillie Olsen's parents, Samuel and Ida Lerner, were involved in the 1905 revolution in Russia, fleeing to the United States when it failed and settling in Nebraska. Her father, in addition to working at a variety of jobs, including farming, paperhanging, and packing house work, became state secretary of the

Nebraska Socialist Party, running in the midtwenties as the socialist candidate for the state representative from his district. Tillie Lerner, second oldest of six children in this depression-poor family, dropped out of high school in Omaha after the eleventh grade to go to work—although, as she is careful to remind people who today take their degrees for granted, this means that she went further in school than most of the women of her generation. Given the radical political climate of her home, it is not surprising that she too would have become active, first writing skits and musicals for the Young People's Socialist League, and subsequently, at seventeen, joining the Young Communist League (YCL), the youth organization of the Communist party. During most of her mid and late teens, she worked at a variety of jobs, took increasing responsibility as a political organizer, and continued to lead an ardent inner literary and intellectual life, in spite of the interruption of her formal schooling. In the draft of a letter to Philip Rahv, editor of the *Partisan Review,* apparently in response to his request for biographical information, she later drew a swift self-portrait:

> Father state secretary Socialist party for years.
> Education, old revolutionary pamphlets, laying around house, (including liberators), and YCL.
> Jailbird—"violating handbill ordinance"
> Occupations: Tie presser, hack writer . . . , model, housemaid, ice cream packer, book clerk.

To this catalogue of occupations she might have added packing house work, waitressing, and working as a punch-press operator.

Although essentially accurate, this self-portrait does reflect some irony, some self-consciousness in the delineation of the pure working-class artist educated only in revolutionary literature and the "school of life." In fact, even as a young woman, Olsen was an eager reader, regularly visiting the public library and second-hand bookstores in Omaha. She recalls today that she was determined to read everything in the fiction category in the library, making it almost through the M's. She also borrowed books from the socialist doctor who took care of the family and from the Radcliffe graduate for whom she worked for several months as a mother's helper. Olsen's earliest journal, written when she was sixteen, in addition to recording the more predictable emotions, events, and relationships of adolescence, shows a familiarity with an extraordinary variety of literature—popular fiction, the nineteenth-century romantics, contemporary poets ranging from Carl Sandberg to Edna St. Vincent Millay. Although remarkably eclectic, her reading was predisposed toward what she calls "the larger tradition of social concern"—American populists like Walt Whitman; European social critics like Ibsen, Hugo, the early Lawrence, and especially Katherine Mansfield; black writers like W. E. B. DuBois and Langston Hughes; American women realists like Elizabeth Madox Roberts, Willa Cather, and Ellen Glasgow; as well as leftists like Upton Sinclair, John Dos Passos, Mike Gold, Guy Endore; and socialist feminists like Olive Schreiner, whose *Story of An African Farm* she refers to in the journal as "incredibly *my* book," and Agnes Smedley, whose *Daughter of Earth* she would later bring to the attention of the Feminist Press and a new generation of readers.

As she explains in her notes to The Feminist Press edition of Rebecca Harding Davis's *Life in the Iron Mills* (1972), she first read that work in a volume of bound *Atlantic Monthly's* bought in an Omaha junkshop when she was fifteen. Davis's work, she writes, said to her: "Literature can be made out of the lives of despised people," and "You, too, must write." Olsen's journals indicate that from a very early age, perhaps even before she read *Life in the Iron Mills,* she consciously and carefully apprenticed herself to the craft of writing. Her early journal is filled with resolutions for a future as a writer, expressions of despair at her own inarticulateness, and frequent humorous deprecations of her own attempts at poetic prose: "Phooey—I was just being literary."

Several passages show her grappling too with the critical and social issues raised by the journals of the Left:

> I read the *Modern Quarterly* today, and all the while I was thinking—Christ, how ignorant, how stupid I am. Paragraphs I had to read over, names as unknown to me as Uranus to

man; ideas that were untrodden, undiscovered roads to me; words that might have been Hindu, so unintelligible they seemed . . . But there was an article substantiating my what I thought insane conclusions about the future of art.

She does not elaborate on her "insane conclusions" but the *Modern Quarterly* at the time was a nonsectarian Marxist journal, with a manifesto that, in Daniel Aaron's words, "denied the distinction between intellectual and worker and between pure art and propaganda and committed the magazine to Socialism." Its editor, V. G. Calverton, boasted that he printed "almost every left wing liberal and radical who had artistic aspirations";[7] the several references to the magazine scattered through Olsen's journal indicate that she was a regular reader, as she had been even earlier of *The Liberator*, the eclectically socialist journal of art and politics edited by Max Eastman. In another passage, the sixteen-year-old Olsen urges herself to take a stand on an almost comical array of global issues—issues, however that would continue to occupy her throughout her life:

Have been reading Nietszche & *Modern Quarterly*. I must write out, clearly and concisely, my ideas on things. I vacillate so easily. And I am so—so sloppy in my mental thinking. What are my *true* opinions, for instance, on socialism, what life should be, the future of literature, true art, the relation between the sexes, where are we going. . . . Yes, I must write it out, simply so I will *know*, not flounder around like a flying fish, neither in air or in water.

Later: That's quite simple to say, but there are so few things one can be sure and definite about—so often I am pulled both ways—& I can't have a single clear cut opinion. There are so few things I have deep, unalterable convictions about.

The clear opinions and deep convictions would come a year later through her disciplined work and study in the Young Communist League. Her own writings before that time— some stories and many poems—are not on the whole political. The poems I examined, some interspersed in her journals, some typed drafts, tend to be romantic, lyrical, full of the pain of lost or unrequited love, the anguish of loneliness, and the mysteries of nature, especially the winds and snows of the Nebraska winters. Several express deep love and affection for a female friend, and one describes a bond with her younger sister. Olsen says that there were other poems, now lost, on political themes like the execution of Sacco and Vanzetti in 1927. Mostly, though, these early poems are the effusions of an intense, imaginative young woman as influenced by the romantic traditions of nineteenth-century poetry and its twentieth-century practitioners like Millay as by the "larger tradition of social concern."

Olsen's decision to join the YCL in 1931 was a turning point; for the next year and a half she dedicated much of her energy to political work. She was sent from Omaha to Kansas City, where she attended the party school for several weeks, formed close ties to political comrades like the working-class women Fern Pierce and "Red" Allen, whom she helped to support by working in a tie factory, and became involved in an unhappy relationship with a party organizer. It was during this time that she was sent to the Argentine Jail for passing out leaflets to packing house workers. She was already sick at the time, having contracted pleurisy from working in front of an open window at the tie factory with a steam radiator in front of it; in jail, she became extremely ill and in 1932 was sent back to Omaha.

During this time, her poems begin to acquire different subjects, a different quality. They still focus on personal experience and emotion, including the anguish of an abortion or miscarriage and the bitterness of misplaced or betrayed love. But now she sometimes interweaves political metaphors to express emotional states. One such poem begins with the speaker sitting "hunched by the window,/watching the snow trail down without lightness." The poem goes on:

> The branches of trees writhe like wounded animals,
> like small frightened bears the buds curve their backs to the
> > white onslaught,
> and I think of what a Wobbly told me of his third degree,
> no violent tortures, but exquisitely, civilized,

141

a gloved palm lightly striking his cheek,
in a few minutes it was a hammer of wind pounding nails of
    hail,
in fifteen a sledge, in twenty, mountains rearing against his
    cheek . . .
Somehow, seeing the constant minute blow of the snow on
    the branches,
and their shudder, this story falters into my mind,
with some deeper, untranslatable meaning behind it,
something I can not learn.

The untranslatable meaning finally has something to do with
the

wisdom
of covering the dead, the decaying,
the swell and stir of the past, the leaves of old hope, with
    inexorable snow,
Of stripping bare and essential the illusions of leaves,
leaves that were moved by any wind.

This poem uses the landscape in a traditional way as a
mirror for the speaker's state of mind, bleak but resolute, from
which she can draw a lesson for living, but it complicates the
natural imagery by attributing to a snowfall the implacable,
impersonal characteristics of the professional interrogator—
an analogy accessible only to someone with a certain kind of
political experience and sympathy. The analogy doesn't quite
work, because ultimately the inexorable snow has something
redeeming in it, as the political interrogation does not; yet the
parallel between the speaker and the Wobbly, both of whom
must remain firm under onslaught, gives the poem a social as
well as a natural dimension and suggests that its writer was
struggling for both personal and political reasons to discipline
the chaos of her emotions.

During this period of intense political organizing, Olsen
began to have the "deep, unalterable convictions" she had earlier wished for, and she took herself to task for the relative
absence of a political dimension in most of her earlier work:

142

> The rich things I could have said are unsaid, what I did write anyone could have written. There is no Great God Dough, terrible and harassing, in my poems, nothing of the common hysteria of 300 girls every 4:30 in the factory, none of the bitter humiliation of scorching a tie; the fear of being late, of ironing a wrinkle in, the nightmare of the kids at home to be fed and clothed, the rebelliousness, the tiptoe expectation and searching, the bodily nausea and weariness . . . yet this was my youth.[8]

Late in 1932, Olsen moved to Faribault, Minnesota, a period of retreat from political and survival work to allow her recovery time from the illness that by now had become incipient tuberculosis. It was there at nineteen that she began to write *Yonnondio,* the novel that for the first time would give full expression to "the rich things" in her own and her family's experience. She became pregnant in the same month that she started writing, and bore a daughter before her twentieth birthday. In 1933, she moved to California, continuing her connection with the YCL in Stockton, Los Angeles, and San Francisco. She also continued to write—poems and reportage and more of the novel that would become *Yonnondio.* In 1936 she began to live with her comrade in the YCL, Jack Olsen, whom she eventually married; in the years that followed, she bore three more daughters and worked at a variety of jobs to help support them. Gradually she stopped writing fiction, concentrating on raising the children and working, but remained an activist into the forties, organizing work related to war relief for the Congress of Industrial Organizations (CIO), serving as president of the California CIO's Women's Auxiliary, writing a column for *People's World,* and working in nonleftist and nonunion organizations related to childcare and education, including the Parent-Teacher Association. During the late forties and fifties, she and her family endured the soul-destroying harassment typically directed at leftists and thousands of suspected leftists during that period. It was not until the midfifties that Olsen began writing again, her style less polemic, more controlled, her vision deepened by the years, her consciousness still profoundly political. In the years that followed, she produced the works which most of us know her for today: the stories in *Tell Me a Riddle; Yonnondio,* finally published in 1974, polished and organized, but not substantially rewritten; and the essays gathered and expanded in *Silences.*

As Elinor Langer has remarked, when Olsen began to write again in the fifties, it was not as a woman who had lived her life as an artist but as an artist who had lived her life as a woman.[9] Yet in those turbulent years of the early to midthirties, Olsen lived fully as artist, as activist, as worker, and as woman/wife/mother, though often suffering from the conflicting demands, always having to give primacy to one part of her being at the expense of another.[10] In examining the political contexts of Olsen's life in the Left in the thirties, I will consider the ways her participation both limited and nurtured her as a woman and an artist. I will focus on three basic contradictions confronting her as an activist, a writer, and a woman in the Left in those years.

First, the Left required great commitments of time and energy for political work, on the whole valuing action over thought, deed over word; yet it also validated the study and production of literature and art, providing a first exposure to literature for many working-class people, fostering an appreciation of a wide range of socially conscious literature, and offering important outlets for publication and literary exchange. Second, although much left-wing criticism, especially by Communist Party writers, was narrowly prescriptive about the kind of literature contemporary writers should be producing, it also inspired—along with the times themselves—a social consciousness in writers that deepened their art. Third, for a woman in the thirties, the Left was a profoundly masculinist world in many of its human relationships, in the orientation of its literature, and even in the language used to articulate its cultural criticism; simultaneously, the Left gave serious attention to women's issues, valued women's contributions to public as well as to private life, and generated an important body of theory on the Woman Question.

The first contradiction, of course, affected both male and female writer-activists on the Left. Then as now, the central

144

problem for an activist trying to be a writer was simply finding the time to write. In the section of *Silences* called "Silences— its Varieties," Olsen has a brief entry labeled *Involvement* un- der the larger heading, "Political Silences": "When political involvement takes priority, though the need and love for writ- ing go on. Every freedom movement has, and has had, its roll of writers participating at the price of their writing" (9). Olsen has spoken little of these silences compared with the fullness of her analysis of other kinds of silences—not those freely chosen, but those imposed by the burdens of poverty, racial discrimination, female roles. Partly this disproportion exists because, in her own life, and the lives of so many others, the compelling necessity to work for pay—the circumstance of class, and the all-consuming responsibilities of homemaking and motherhood—the circumstance of gender, clearly *have* been the major silencers, and if I do not speak of them at length here, it is because Olsen herself has done so, fully and eloquently. Partly also, I suspect, she has not wanted to be misread as encouraging a withdrawal from political activism for the sake of "art" or self-fulfillment. Yet this little passage could well allude to her own dilemma in the thirties.

The dilemma, as she points out now, was sharper for her as a working-class woman and a "grass roots" activist in- volved in daily workplace struggles than for those profession- als who were already recognized as writers, who participated in the movement primarily by writing, and whose activity as writers was sometimes even supported by federally funded projects like the Works Projects Administration. Except for the interlude in 1932 in Faribault and another withdrawal from political activity in Los Angeles in 1935, another "good writing year," Olsen's political work came first throughout the early and midthirties—along with the burdens of survival work and, increasingly, domestic work; and it required the ex- penditure of time and energy such work always demands. As a member of the YCL in the Midwest, she wrote and distributed leaflets in the packing houses, helped organize demonstra- tions, walked in picket lines, attended classes and meetings, and wrote and directed political plays and skits. In high school, she had written a prize-winning humor column called "Squeaks"; in the YCL, she recalls, she was able to use her particular kind of humor and punning to great effect with the living audiences who came to the league's performances.

The nature of Olsen's commitment in the early thirties emerges with particular clarity in a letter she received from a fellow YCL organizer and close friend, as she recuperated from her illness in Omaha, ostensibly on leave for two months from league duties. The letter praises her growth as an organizer, but reprimands her for being "too introspective." It is full of friendly advice and firm pressure:

> Read. Read things that will really be of some help to you. The Daily Worker every day . . . the Young Worker. All the new pamphlets . . . and really constructive books. . . . You'll have time to now, and you've got to write skits and plays for the League. This you can do for the League, and it will be a great help . . . have only one thing in mind—recovery, and work in the League, and if you pull thru, and are working in the League again in a few months, I will say that as a Communist you have had your test.

The letter concludes by asking her how the play is coming, and urging her to rush it as soon as possible, then adds a postscript: "How about a song for the song-writing contest?"

Reflecting on this letter in her journal, Olsen attributes to its author "full understanding of what it means to me to leave now." She goes on to condemn herself for "the paths I have worn of inefficiency, procrastination, idle planning, lack of perseverance," adding, "Only in my League work did these disappear, I have that to thank for my reconditioning." She expresses her wish to write in a more disciplined way, but adds: "I must abolish word victories . . . let me feel nothing till I have had action—without action feeling and thot are disease. . . ." The point is not, then, that insensitive and rigid communist bureaucrats imposed unreasonable demands on party members, but rather that rank-and-file communists made these demands on themselves, because they believed so deeply in the liberating possibilities of socialism; the necessity for disciplined, organized action; and the reality of the revolutionary process, in which their participation was essential. The times themselves instilled a sense of urgency and possibility: a depression at home, with all its concomitant anguishes of hunger, poverty, unemployment; the rise of fascism in Europe with its threat of world war; the example of a successful revolution in the Soviet Union and the feeling of connection with the revolutionary movements there and in other countries, such as China. Like many progressive people, Olsen felt herself to be part of a valid, necessary, and global movement to remake the world on a more just and humane model. If the Left in those years, especially the circles in which Olsen moved, tended to value action over thought, deed over word, there were good reasons.

Olsen's comments today about the author of this letter and her other movement friends suggest both the depth of her commitment to them and the feelings of difference she sometimes experienced as an aspiring writer. What becomes clear in her comments is that for her, political work with such women was a matter of class loyalty. She could not, then or later, leave the "ordinary" people to lead a "literary" life.

> They were my dearest friends, but how could they know what so much of my writing self was about? They thought of writing in the terms in which they knew it. They had become readers, like so many working class kids in the movement, but there was so much that fed me as far as my medium was concerned that was closed to them. They read the way women read today coming into the women's movement who don't have literary background—reading for what it says about their lives, or what it doesn't say. And they loved certain writings because of truths, understandings, affirmations, that they found in them. . . . It was not a time that my writing self could be first. . . . We believed that we were going to change the world, and it looked as if it was possible. It was just after Hindenberg turned over power to Hitler—and the enormity of the struggle demanded to stop what might result from that was just beginning to be evident. . . . And I did so love my comrades. They were all blossoming so. These were the same kind of people I'd gone to school with, who had quit, as was common in my generation, around the eighth grade . . . whose development had seemed stopped, though I had known such inherent capacity in them. Now I was seeing that

147

evidence, verification of what was latent in the working class. It's hard to leave something like that.

For Olsen, then, the relationship between the intellectual and the working class was far more than an academic question, for she herself belonged to one world by birth and commitment and was drawn to the other by her gift and love for language and literature. Both the "intellectual" activities of reading and writing and the struggles of working people to improve the quality of their lives were essential to her. The problem was how to combine them. "These next months," she wrote in her Faribault journal, at last with some free time before her,

> I shall only care about my sick body—to be a good Bolshevik I need health first. Let my mind stagnate further, let my heart swell with neurotic emotions that lie clawing inside like a splinter—afterwards, the movement will clean that out. First, a strong body. . . . I don't know what it is in me, but I must write too. It is like creating white hot irons in me & then pulling them out . . . so slowly, oh so slowly.

In beginning to write *Yonnondio,* Olsen hoped to link her writing and her political commitment. But the chaotic years that followed—the moving back and forth, the caring and working for her family, and the political tasks—gave her little opportunity for sustained literary work. Her most intense political involvement during these years centered around the San Francisco Maritime strike of 1934, which spread from San Francisco up and down the Western Seaboard to become the first important general strike of the era. She helped put out the Longshoremen's publication, the *Waterfront Worker,* did errands and relief work, and got arrested for "vagrancy" while visiting the apartment of some of the YCL members involved in the strike, going to jail for the second time.

Passages from her journal in these years include frustration at the amount of time required for housework and political work, agonized self-criticisms at not being able to write regularly in a more disciplined way, sometimes anger at the necessity to write specifically pieces on demand, often guilt

148

because no matter what the choice of labor, something is always left undone:

> Struggled all day on the Labor Defender article. Tore it up in
> disgust. It is the end for me of things like that to write—I
> can't do it—it kills me. . . . Why should I loathe myself—why
> the guilt . . .

All the writing that Olsen did publish in the 1930s
came out in 1934. That year two poems were published in the
Daily Worker and reprinted in *The Partisan*. One was based
on a letter in the *New Masses* by a Mexican-American woman
from Texas, detailing the horrors of work in the garment industry sweatshops of the Southwest, and the other celebrated
the spirit of the Austrian socialists killed by the Dollfus government.[11] "The Iron Throat," the first chapter of *Yonnondio,*
was published the same year in *The Partisan Review,*[12] as
were "The Strike" and "Thousand-Dollar Vagrant," two essays
based on her involvement in the San Francisco dock strike.[13]
In "The Strike," one of the best pieces of reportage in an era
noted for excellence in that genre, the conflict between her
"writer self" and her activist self emerges strongly, here transformed into rhetorical strategy. The essay, in the published
version, begins:

> Do not ask me to write of the strike and the terror. I am not
> on a battlefield, and the increasing stench and smoke sting
> the eyes so it is impossible to turn them back into the past.
> You leave me only this night to drop the bloody garment of
> Todays, to cleave through the gigantic events that have
> crashed one upon the other, to the first beginning. If I could
> go away for a while, if there were time and quiet, perhaps I
> could do it. All that has happened might resolve into order and
> sequence, fall into neat patterns of words. I could stumble
> back into the past and slowly, painfully rear the structure in
> all its towering magnificence, so that the beauty and heroism,
> the terror and significance of those days, would enter your
> heart and sear it forever with the vision.[14]

Toward the end of the essay, the writer explains that she
was not on the literal battlefield herself, but in headquarters,

typing, "making a metallic little pattern of sound in the air, because that is all I can do, because that is all I am supposed to do." The conclusion is another apology for her incapacity to do justice to the magnitude of the strike:

> Forgive me that the words are feverish and blurred. You see, if I had time I could go away. But I write this on a battlefield. The rest, the General Strike, the terror, and arrests and jail, the songs in the night, must be written some other time, must be written later. . . . But there is so much happening now. . . .[15]

The conflict here is partly between her role as a writer, in this case a reporter doing her job, and her guilt at not being on the real battlefield herself—between the word and the deed. But more important is the conflict between two kinds of writing: the quick, fervent, impressionistic report from the arena of struggle, and the leisured, carefully structured and sustained rendering of the "beauty and heroism, the terror and significance" of those days—a rendering that, ironically, would require for its full development a withdrawal from the struggle.

For a committed leftist in the thirties, political action, with all its demands on time and energy, had to take priority over intellectual work, yet the atmosphere on the Left did value and nurture literature in a variety of ways. Olsen would have been a reader in any case, but her friends in the YCL in Kansas City were among the many working-class people inspired by the movement to read broadly for the first time. And Olsen's own reading, eclectic though it was, was to some extent guided, extended, and informed by left-wing intellectual mentors such as the critics of *The Liberator,* the *New Masses,* and the *Modern Quarterly.* She recalls today that the Left

> was enriching in the sense that . . . in the movement people were reading like mad. There was as in any movement a looking for your ancestors, your predecessors. . . .
>
> There was a burst of black writers. . . . I knew about W. E. B. DuBois before, but because the movement was so conscious of race, of color, we were reading all the black writers, books

150

> like Arna Bontemps' *Black Thunder;* Langston Hughes. We read Ting Ling, we read Lu Hsun, we read the literature of protest that was beginning to be written in English out of South Africa; we read B. Traven; writers from every country. The thirties was a rich, an international, period. . . . And from whatever country or color this was considered to be part of our literature.

Being part of the Left milieu, then, gave Olsen, a working-class woman from Omaha, a sense of belonging to an international intellectual as well as political community.

The literary establishment of the Left was receptive to and supportive of the efforts of new, young writers like Olsen. The Communist party sponsored the development of cultural associations called the John Reed Clubs, established specifically to encourage young, unknown writers and artists.[16] And there were outlets for publication like the *New Masses* and the various organs of the local John Reed Clubs, including the *Partisan Review* in New York and *The Partisan* in San Francisco, in both of which Olsen published. Her work was well received and much admired. Joseph North, a respected Left critic, compared her ability to portray working-class life in "The Iron Throat" favorably to Tess Slesinger's rendering of the East Coast intelligentsia in her first novel, *The Unpossessed* (1934).[17] Robert Cantwell praised "The Iron Throat" in *The New Republic* as "a work of early genius."[18] A number of editors and publishers sought her out after its publication, and eventually she made arrangements with Bennett Cerf at Random House for the publication of *Yonnondio* on its completion, although at the time she could not be reached because she was in jail for her participation in the dock strike, becoming something of a cause célèbre. In New York, Heywood Broun chaired a protest meeting over her arrest, irritating her and her jailed comrades who had not published anything and were therefore not getting all this national attention.

After her release from jail, she visited Lincoln Steffens and Ella Winter, who had invited her to their home in Carmel, California. This was her first experience, she recalls now, with that kind of urbane, sophisticated literary atmosphere. Steffens encouraged her to write the other essay associated with the strike, "Thousand-Dollar Vagrant," which describes her arrest in deliberately tough, colloquial language. The following year, she was invited to attend the American Writers Congress in New York, where she marched in a parade side by side with Mike Gold and James T. Farrell, Nelson Algren and Richard Wright, and where she was one of a very few women to address the assembly, which included most of the major writers of the day.[19] A drawing of her, a cartooned profile of a lean, intense young woman, was one of a few portraits of American women writers to appear among the myriad renderings of male literary personages in the May 7, 1935, issue of *New Masses* that reported on the congress.[20]

Clearly, though Olsen's involvement in the Left as an activist, coupled with the other demands on her worker-mother life, took time, energy, and commitment that might in another milieu and another era have gone into her writing, and although her closest friends in the midwestern movement did not always understand her literary aspirations, the atmosphere of the Left as a whole did encourage her. The Left provided networks and organs for intellectual and literary exchange, gave her a sense of being part of an international community of writers and activists engaged in the same revolutionary endeavor, and recognized and valued her talent.

The second contradiction I will consider is closely related to the first and third; in using it as a bridge between them, I will turn first to the way in which Left critical theory validated and supported Olsen's subject and vision before suggesting how some of its tenets ran counter to and perhaps impeded the development of her particular artistic gift.

Literary criticism flourished on the Left in the thirties, and writers like Gold, editor of the *New Masses* and one of the most influential of Communist party critics, and Farrell, a leading critic and writer for the increasingly independent *Partisan Review*, as well as a novelist, hotly debated such issues as the role of the artist in revolutionary struggle, the applications of Marxist thought to American literature, and the proper nature and functions of literature in a revolutionary movement.[21] As Olsen's early journals indicate, she followed such discussions with intense interest. There was much in the

152

spirit even of the more dogmatic, party-oriented criticism to encourage her own writing.

Left critical theory accorded an honored place to the committed writer, the writer capable of expressing the struggles and aspirations of working-class people or of recording the decline of capitalism. Critical debates often centered on the best literary modes for accomplishing this purpose. The dominant critical theory on the communist Left in the early thirties was proletarian realism, a theory which even nonsectarian leftists eventually viewed as far too limited. Nevertheless, its basic premise—that fiction should show the sufferings and struggles and essential dignity of working-class people under capitalism and allow readers to see the details of their lives and work—encouraged young working-class writers like Olsen to write of their own experiences and confirmed her early perception that art can be based on the lives of "despised people." This theory told writers that their own writing could and should be a form of action in itself; art was to be a weapon in the class struggle.[22]

All of Olsen's published writing during the early thirties is consistent with this view of the functions of literature. Her developing craft now had an explicitly political content which grew out of her own experience and was confirmed by major voices in the Left literary milieu. All of it expresses outrage at the exploitation of the working class and a fierce faith in the transformative power of the coming revolution. One need only compare the poem, "I Want You Women up North to Know,"[23] with the passage from her poetry cited earlier to see that the growing clarity of her literary and political convictions gave her work a scope and an assuredness that it had lacked earlier.

This poem juxtaposes the desperate situation of Mexican-American women workers and the families they struggle unsuccessfully to support with that of the "women up north" who consume the products of their labor. As Selma Burkom and Margaret Williams have noted, the poem faithfully constructs the details of their daily lives while its central metaphor "transforms the women themselves . . . into the clothing they embroider—*they* become the product of their labor."[24] The poem is artful as well as polemical; its free-verse form is deliberately experimental, its subtler ironies woven into the fabric of diction and metaphor, its structure tight, its portraits clearly individuated. On one level, it is metapoetry, that is, poetry *about* art, for it specifically contrasts its own purpose and vision—to document the realities of these women's lives and to offer a Marxist interpretation of the causes of and solutions to their suffering—with the consciousness of the "bourgeois poet" who would find in the movement of their hands *only* a source of aesthetic pleasure.

On the other hand, the polemicism of the poem, especially the didactic interpolations of the speaker, represented a kind of writing that Olsen herself gradually rejected. The same issues arise in her work on *Yonnondio,* her most important literary effort during the thirties. In the rest of this paper I will focus on that novel, for its evolution reveals with special clarity the contradictory nature of Olsen's experience in the Left.

Olsen's earliest journals, before she joined the YCL, speak of her wish to write about her family and people like them. After her year and a half of intense involvement, she begins to do so in a serious, disciplined way, writing in her Faribault journal as she works on the early chapters: "O Mazie & Will & Ben. At last I write out all that has festered in me so long—the horror of being a working-class child—& the heroism, all the respect they deserve." Familiarity with the political and critical theory of the Left combined with and applied to her own experience gave her the coherent world view, the depth of consciousness, and the faith in her working-class subject essential to a sustained work of fiction.

Set in the 1920s, the novel's lyrical prose traces the Holbrook family's desperate struggle for survival over a two-and-a-half-year period, first in a Wyoming mining town, then on a farm in the Dakotas, finally in a Midwest city—Omaha, perhaps—reeking with the smell of the slaughterhouses. In *Yonnondio,* as in Olsen's later work, the most powerful theme is the tension between human capacity and creativity—the drive to know, to assert, to create, which Olsen sees as innate in human life—and the social forces and institutions that repress and distort that capacity. Olsen's understanding of those social forces and institutions clearly owes a great deal to her

154

tutelage in the Left. The struggles of her central characters dramatize the ravages of capitalism on the lives of working people—miners, small farmers, packing house workers, and their families—who barely make enough to survive no matter how hard they work, and who have not yet learned to seek control over the conditions of their workplaces or the quality of their lives.

Unfortunately for all of us, she never finished the novel. Its title, taken from the title of a Whitman poem, is a Native American word meaning "lament for the lost"; it is an elegy, I think, not only for the Holbrooks, but also for Olsen's own words lost between the midthirties and late fifties, for the incompleteness of the novel itself. The demands on Olsen already discussed would have been reason enough for her not having completed the novel in those hectic years; what she wrote, after all, she wrote before she was twenty-five, in the interstices of her activist-worker-mother life. Yet I suspect that she was wrestling with at least one other problem that made completion difficult. For although Olsen's immersion in the theory and political practice of the Marxist Left and her exposure to its literature and criticism gave her a sense of the importance of her subject and strengthened the novel's social analysis, the dominant tenets of proletarian realism also required a structure, scope, resolution, and political explicitness in some ways at odds with the particular nature of her developing craft.

What we have today is only the beginning of the novel that was to have been. In Olsen's initial plan, Jim Holbrook was to have become involved in a strike in the packing houses, a strike that would draw out the inner strength and courage of his wife Anna, politicize the older children as well, and involve some of the women in the packing plant as strike leaders in this essential collective action. Embittered by the length of the strike and its lack of clear initial success, humiliated by his inability to support his family, Jim Holbrook was finally to have abandoned them. Anna was to die trying to give herself an abortion. Will and Mazie were to go West to the Imperial Valley in California, where they would themselves become organizers. Mazie was to grow up to become an artist, a writer who could tell the experiences of her people, her mother especially living in her memory. In Mazie's achievement, political consciousness and personal creativity were to coalesce.

The original design for the novel would have incorporated most of the major themes of radical fiction at that time. Walter Rideout's study, *The Radical Novel in the United States, 1900–1954,* classifies proletarian novels of the thirties into four types: the strike novel, the novel of conversion to communism, the bottom dog novel, and the novel documenting the decay of the middle class. He also mentions certain typical subthemes: anti-Semitism, black-and-white relationships, episodes in American history, and the life of the communist organizer.[25] *Yonnondio* would have been both a strike novel and a novel of political conversion, and it would have touched on relationships between whites and people of color and on the life of the communist organizer. It would have fulfilled also a major tenet of proletarian realism—that proletarian fiction should demonstrate revolutionary optimism, including elements predicting the inevitable fall of capitalism and the rise of the working class to power.

Proletarian fiction, in other words, was supposed to show not only the sufferings of working-class people, but also their triumphs. When Meridel Le Sueur, for example, published an account of the helpless sufferings of poor women in 1932, she was attacked by Whittaker Chambers in the *New Masses,* in a note appended to Le Sueur's article, for her "defeatist attitude" and "non-revolutionary spirit."[26] "There *is* horror and drabness in the Worker's life, and we will portray it," wrote Mike Gold in the *New Masses* in 1930, in an article defining proletarian realism, "but we know this is not the last word; we know . . . that not pessimism, but revolutionary elan will sweep this mess out of the world forever."[27]

Olsen, too, wanted to incorporate this optimism, indeed, it was central to her initial conception of the novel.

> Characters [she writes in her journal when she was beginning *Yonnondio*]. Wonderful characters. Hard, bitter, & strong. O communism—how you come to those of whom I will write is more incredible beautiful than manna. You wipe

the sweat from us, you fill our bellies, you let us walk and
think like humans.

She immediately cautions herself, "Not to be so rhetorical or
figurative or whatever it is"—a struggle against didactic rheto-
ric that would characterize her work on the novel itself. Olsen
maintained throughout her work on *Yonnondio* in the thirties
her commitment to show the transformative power of Communism—her commitment, that is, to "revolutionary optimism,"
but as her craft developed she felt less and less satisfied with
telling about the coming revolution—and more and more concerned with *showing* how people come to class consciousness
in "an earned way, a bone way." She gradually rejected the
political explicitness that alone was enough to win praise for
literary work in the more sectarian Left criticism, but she had
a hard time incorporating the essential vision of systematic
social change in other ways.

The "revolutionary elan" in the opening chapters of
Yonnondio still partakes of the didacticism she ultimately rejected. It comes less through the events or characterizations
than from the voice of the omniscient narrator, who in the first
five chapters provides both political analysis and revolutionary
prophecy. In the first chapter, this voice comments on the life
of thirteen-year-old Andy Kvaternick, on his first day in the
mines:

> Breathe and lift your face to the night, Andy Kvaternick. Try-
> ing so vainly . . . to purge your bosom of the coal dust. Your
> father had dreams. You too, like all boys, had dreams—vague
> dreams of freedom and light. . . . The earth will take those
> too. . . .
>
> Someday the bowels will grow monstrous and swollen
> with these old tired dreams, swell and break, and strong fists
> batter the fat bellies, and skeletons of starved children batter
> them. . . . (14)

In the second chapter, the voice becomes ironic as it comments on a scene where women wait at the mouth of a mine

for word of their men after an accident. Like "I Want the Women up North To Know," this passage attacks the modernist aesthetic, which elevates a concern for form over a concern for subject, yet it also argues that Olsen's subject itself is worthy of the transformations of enduring art.

> And could you not make a cameo of this and pin it onto your aesthetic hearts? So sharp it is, so clear, so classic. The shattered dusk, the mountain of culm, the tipple; clean line, bare beauty. . . .

> Surely it is classical enough for you—the Greek marble of the women, the simple, flowing lines of sorrow, carved so rigid and eternal. (30)

And the voice goes on to prophesy revolution against the companies and the system they represent: "Please issue a statement: quick, or they start to batter through with the fists of strike, with the pickax of revolution" (31).

In chapter 5, we hear the voice of the revolutionary prophet twice. The first passage comments on the life of young Jim Tracy, Jim Holbrook's codigger in a sewer, who quits when the contractor insists that two men must do the amount of digging previously done by several. Here, the voice is at first scathingly satiric, pointing out how Tracy will be victimized by his own naive belief in the shibboleths of American culture—"the bull about freedomofopportunity," and predicting Tracy's inevitable descent into the hell of unemployment, hunger, cold, vagrancy, prison, death; damned forever for his apostasy to "God Job." The passage concludes with an apology to Jim, in which the narrator speaks with the collective "we" of the revolutionists:

> I'm sorry, Jim Tracy, sorry as hell we weren't stronger and could get to you in time and show you that kind of individual revolt was no good, kid, no good at all, you had to bide your time and take it till there were enough of you to fight it all together on the job, and bide your time, and take it till the day millions of fists clamped in yours, and you could wipe out the

158

whole thing, and a human could be a human for the first time on earth. (79)

This is the voice that concludes the chapter, too, as Jim Holbrook sits in the kitchen holding his daughter Mazie after Anna has had a miscarriage, bitterly condemning himself for not seeing her illness, bitterly aware that he has no access to the food and medicine and care the doctor has prescribed for Anna and Baby Bess:

> No, he could speak no more. And as he sat there in the kitchen with Mazie against his heart . . . the things in his mind so vast and formless, so terrible and bitter, cannot be spoken, will never be spoken—till the day that hands will find a way to speak this: hands. (95)

In these interpolations, Olsen was deliberately experimenting with the form of the novel, not unlike Dos Passos, whom she had earlier read. Rachel Blau DuPlessis suggests that Olsen has appropriated certain modernist techniques here to turn dialectically against modernism.[28] On the other hand, the prophetic irony of these passages, the imagery of hands and fists uniting in revolution, characterize much of the writing of the leftists during this period; this is the tone and imagery that appear at the conclusion of Olsen's two published poems and that predominate in "The Strike." In any case, these passages add a dimension of "revolutionary elan" not present in the early events of the novel itself. The narrator sees more, knows more, than the characters, about the causes of and remedies for their suffering, and the voice is the device used to incorporate that knowledge into the novel.

Olsen's correspondence indicates that she was aware of a disjunction between that voice and the increasingly more lyric, less didactic tone and texture of the whole. In March 1935, John Strachey, whom she had met in Carmel and to whom she had sent the first three chapters of *Yonnondio* for evaluation and advice, wrote to her in Venice, California: "As to advice, personally I like both your styles of writing, and I am in favor of having the interpolations in the book." Their "agit-prop" quality was increasingly at odds with the direction in which Olsen's art was growing. It was developing gradually away from the didacticism that made the incorporation of "revolutionary elan" relatively easy and toward a more lyrical, less explicit mode, at its best when lingering on the details of daily life and work, exploring the interactions between individual growth, personality, and social environment, and laying bare the ruptures and reconciliations of family life. As the novel progressed, as the characters acquired a life and being of their own, Olsen, I think, found herself unable to document the political vision of social revolution as authentically and nonrhetorically as she was able to portray the ravages of circumstance on families and individuals and the redeeming moments between them. She did not want to write didactically. She wanted to write a politically informed novel that would also be great art. The problem is that the subtlety and painstaking craft of her evolving style did not lend themselves readily to a work of epic scope, and she was increasingly unwilling to rely on shortcuts like the narrative interpolations to tell rather than show political context and change. In any case, she had trouble extending the novel in its intended direction. In a note on its progress from sometime in the midthirties, she writes: "Now it seems to me the whole revolutionary part belongs in another novel . . . and I can't put out one of those 800 page tomes."

I think that there was a tension, too, between two themes: the awakening class consciousness that was the central drama of her time, and her other essential theme, the portrait of the artist as a young girl—not an inevitable conflict based on inconsistent possibilities, for Olsen's own experience embraced both processes, but a writing tension, based on the difficulty of merging the two themes in a cohesive fictive structure. Yet the more "individualistic," subjective, and domestic concerns—the intellectual and psychological development of the young girl, the complicated familial relationships, the lyrical vision of regeneration through love between mother and child—would not have been acceptable to Olsen or the critical establishment of the Left without the projected Marxian resolution that showed working-class people taking power collectively over their own lives. In other words, Olsen had so fully internalized the Left's vision of what proletarian litera-

160

ture could and should do to show the coming of a new society that she did not even consider then the possibility of a less epic and for her, more feasible structure. Nor could she be content simply to accord centrality to the familial interactions and the stubborn growth of human potential in that unpromising soil, leaving the tensions between human aspiration and social oppression unresolved. So *Yonnondio* remained unfinished, but the struggle to write fiction at once political and nonpolemical was an essential apprenticeship for the writer who in her maturity produced *Tell Me a Riddle*.

The concerns I have called, for lack of better terms, more "subjective" and "domestic," grew to a great extent out of Olsen's experience as a woman and a mother. Thus, my second and third contradictions overlap, for as we shall see there was little in Left literary criticism that would have validated the centrality of these concerns, except insofar as they touched on class rather than gender. The rest of this paper, then, will be concerned with the third contradiction: between the fact that the world of the Left, like the larger society it both challenged and partook of, was essentially androcentric and masculinist, yet that it also demonstrated, more than any other sector of American society, a consistent concern for women's issues.

The painful and sometimes wry anecdotes of women writers like Josephine Herbst, Meridel Le Sueur, and others amply testify to the sexual politics of life in the literary Left. For example, Herbst writes to Katherine Anne Porter about the "gentle stay-in-your-place, which may or may not be the home," she received from her husband, John Herrmann, when she wished to join him at a "talk fest" with Mike Gold, Edmund Wilson, Malcolm Cowley, and others: "I told Mister Herrmann that as long as the gents had bourgeois reactions to women they would probably never rise very high in their revolutionary conversations, but said remarks rolled off like water."[29] Olsen herself remembers that at the American Writers Congress, James Farrell informed her that she and another attractive young woman present were "the two flowers there," compared with the other "old bags."

Because she was not really a part of the literary circles of the Left, their sexual politics had less impact on Olsen than

161

on writers who were more involved, like Herbst and Le Sueur. If for Herbst it was her gender that prevented her from moving freely in the heady circles of the literary Left, for Olsen it was more the depth of her own class loyalties to the rank and file. The sexism she experienced in her daily life mostly reflected the structure of gender-role assignments in society as a whole, although she does recall some incidents peculiar to life on the Left, such as the pressure on YCL women to make themselves available at parties as dancing partners especially to black and Mexican-American men, whether the women wanted to dance or not. As a writer, though, Olsen was keenly aware of the male dominance of Left literature and criticism and the relative absence of women's subjects and concerns.

If one examines the composition of the editorial boards of Left magazines of culture and criticism, one finds that the mastheads are largely male; in 1935, one woman wrote to the *New Masses* complaining at the underrepresentation of women writers,[30] although a few women writers, like Herbst and Le Sueur, were regular contributors. The numerical dominance of men in the literary Left paralleled the omnipresence of a worker-figure in literature and criticism who almost by definition was male; proletarian prose and criticism tended to flex their muscles with a particularly masculinist pride. Here, for example, is a passage from Gold's famous *New Masses* editorial, "Go Left, Young Writers," written in 1929:

> A new writer has been appearing; a wild youth of about twenty-two, the son of working-class parents, who himself works in the lumber camps, coal mines, and steel mills, harvest fields and mountain camps of America. . . . He writes in jets of exasperated feeling and has not time to polish his work. . . . He lacks self-confidence but writes because he must—and because he has a real talent.[31]

An even more pronounced masculinism prevails in Gold's "America Needs a Critic," published in *New Masses* in 1926:

> Send us a critic. Send a giant who can shame our writers back to their task of civilizing America. Send a soldier who has studied history. Send a strong poet who loves the masses,

and their future. . . . Send one who is not a pompous liberal, but a man of the street. . . . Send us a man fit to stand up to skyscrapers. . . . Send no saint. Send an artist. Send a scientist. Send a Bolshevik. Send a man.[32]

Gold's worst insult to a writer was that he was a pansy, his art, effeminate.[33] Gold, of course, was an extreme example of working-class male chauvinism, but he was not atypical. Even as late as 1969, when Joseph North edited an anthology of *New Masses* pieces, masculinity predominates. North's Prologue praises the *New Masses* for capturing the essence of American life in its portrayals of the industrial proletariat, in its emphasis on the "day of a workingman," that of a miner, a locomotive engineer, a weaver. "Its men," he said, "its writers and artists understood this kind of a life existed."[34] In spite of his once-favorable notice of Tillie Lerner's work, he does not mention its women.

When women writers on the Left did write about explicitly female subjects from a woman's perspective, they were sometimes criticized outright, sometimes ignored. Le Sueur has remembered that she was criticized for writing in a lyrical, emotive style about sexuality and the reproductive process.[35] I have already noted Chambers's attack on her for writing about the conditions of women on the breadlines without building in a revolutionary dialectic. Elinor Langer, having worked for several years on a biography of Herbst, believes that one of the reasons Herbst's impressive trilogy of novels failed to win her the recognition she deserved was that she was a woman and the central experience in two of the three novels is that of female characters.[36] Not that the scorn or neglect of male Left critics was reserved exclusively for women writers. The more dogmatic of them viewed any literature concerned primarily with domestic and psychological subjects as suspect. One novel focusing on the experience and perceptions of a child of the working classes, Henry Roth's *Call It Sleep* (1935), which Olsen read and admired during the later stages of her work on *Yonnondio,* was one of the more intricate, imaginative works in the proletarian genre. Yet the *New Masses* dismissed it in a paragraph, concluding, "It is a pity that so many young writers drawn from the proletariat can make no better use of their working class experience than as material for introspective and febrile novels."[37]

In writing *Yonnondio,* Olsen was consciously writing class literature from a woman's point of view, incorporating a dimension that she saw ignored and neglected in the works of most contemporary male leftists. All of Olsen's work, in fact, testifies to her concern for women, her vision of their double oppression if they are poor or women of color, her affirmation of their creative potential, her sense of the deepest, most intractable contradiction of all: the unparalleled satisfaction and fulfillment combined with the overwhelming all-consuming burden of motherhood. Indeed, her writings about mothering, about the complex, painful, and redemptive interactions between mother and child, have helped a new generation of women writers to treat that subject with a fullness and honesty never before possible in American literature.

In *Yonnondio,* Anna as mother wants for her children what she can no longer dream for herself: the freedom to live fully what is best in them; to the extent that the circumstances of their lives prevent this, her love is also her despair. Anna has a special kinship with her oldest daughter, Mazie, in whom her own intelligence and early hunger for knowledge are reincarnated. Mirroring each other's dreams and capacities, the two mirror also the anguish of women confronting daily the poverty of their class and the assigned burdens of their sex. At times they protect one another—Anna, Mazie's access to books, to literature; Mazie, Anna's physical well-being, she herself becoming temporarily mother when Anna lies unconscious after a miscarriage. Mazie's painful sensitivity—the sensitivity of the potential artist—makes her as a child deeply susceptible to both the beauty and ugliness around her; overcome at times by the ugliness, it is to her mother that she turns for renewal. For example, one of the gentlest, most healing of *Yonnondio*'s passages is the interlude of peace when Anna and Mazie pause from gathering dandelion greens, and Anna is transported by the spring and river wind to a forgetful peace, different from her usual "mother look," the "mother alertness . . . in her bounded body" (120). Absently, she sings fragments of song and strokes Mazie's body:

> The fingers stroked, spun a web, cocooned Mazie into happiness and intactness and selfness. Soft wove the bliss round hurt and fear and want and shame—the old worn fragile bliss, a new frail selfness bliss, healing, transforming. Up from the grasses, from the earth, from the broad tree trunk at their back, latent life streamed and seeded. (119)

The transformation here is not the political conversion that was to have taken place later, but one based on human love, on the capacity to respond to beauty, and on the premise of a regenerative life cycle of which mother and daughter are a part.

To be sure, Olsen wanted to weave this emphasis on "selfness," and this image of a regenerative life cycle that prefigures, but does not itself constitute, social and economic regeneration into a larger structure that would incorporate both personal and political transformation. Yet the hope *Yonnondio* offers most persuasively, through its characterizations, its images and events, and its present conclusion, is less a vision of political and economic revolution than an assertion that the drive to love and achieve and create will survive somehow in spite of the social forces arraigned against it, because each new human being is born with it afresh.

It is with this "humanistic" rather than "Marxist" optimism that the novel now ends. In the midst of a stifling heat wave, Baby Bess suddenly realizes her own ability to have an effect on the world when she makes the connection between her manipulations of the lid of a jam jar and the noise it produces, so that her random motions become, for the first time, purposeful: "Bang, slam, whack. Release, grab, slam, bang, bang. Centuries of human drive work in her; human ecstasy of achievement; a satisfaction deep and fundamental as sex: *I can do, I use my power; I! I!*" (153). And her mother and sister and brothers laugh, in spite of the awesome heat, the rising dust storms. Then for the first time the family listens to the radio on a borrowed set, and Mazie is awed at the magic, *"transparent meshes of sound, far sound, human and stellar, pulsing, pulsing"* (153). This moment of empowerment and connection *is* linked to the revolutionary vision, and Anna's final, "The air's changin', Jim. I see for it [the heat wave] to end tomorrow, at least get tolerable" (154), certainly hints at the possibility for greater change. Still, there is a great gulf between socialist revolution and the temporary individualized relief of this final passage. Yet the end seems right; indeed, today, the novel hardly seems unfinished, because it offers in its conclusion the affirmation most fully embedded in the texture of the novel as a whole: an affirmation of human will, familial love, and, at least in the child not yet deadened and brutalized by the struggle for sheer survival and the corrupt influence of social institutions, the drive toward achievement and creation.

To say this is not to diminish the power of *Yonnondio* as an indictment of society; Olsen makes it clear that the Holbrooks do not merely suffer—they are oppressed, in quite specific ways, as a working-class family in a capitalist system. The whole fabric of the book deals with how poverty, exploitation, and what today we would call sexism combine to extinguish gradually the very qualities Olsen values most. The loss of creative capacity is not, as Wordsworth would have it, the inevitable price of growing up, but rather the price of growing up in a society *like this one*.

In according that creative capacity especially to women and children, as in detailing the impact of social circumstance on the dailiness of family life, Olsen added a significant dimension to the largely masculine and public world of the proletarian novel. Women's work in preserving and nurturing that creative capacity in the young is shown in *Yonnondio* to be an essential precondition to social change.

Although in this regard, Olsen's work was deliberately oppositional to the androcentrism of the Left literary milieu, and although the tenets of proletarian criticism would not have validated this feminist and humanist dimension without the projected Marxian resolution, Olsen's affiliation with the Left undoubtedly encouraged and informed her writings about women in at least two ways.

First, there was the fact that in spite of the sexism of the Left milieu, the existence of serious analysis of women's status and roles meant that, in Olsen's circles at least, women's capacities were recognized and supported, however inconsis-

166

tently, and women's grievances were recognized as real. It is certainly true, as Olsen recalls today, that on "those things that come particularly to the fore through consciousness-raising, having to do with sexuality, with rape, and most of all with what I call maintenance of life, the bearing and rearing of the young," the circles of the Left were little better than those of society as a whole—in spite of a body of theory on housework and the frequent bandying about of Lenin's observations on its degrading nature. And Olsen is in accord with Peggy Dennis, married for years to party leader Eugene Dennis, on the "explicit, deliberate and reprehensible sexism" of the party's leadership.[38] Yet Olsen also knew party women who brought their own husbands up for trial on charges of male chauvinism, one of them herself a party activist whose husband refused to help with childcare; he was removed from his leadership position when her charges were upheld. She remembers seeing women in the party, women like herself, grow in their capacities and rise to positions of leadership; she herself helped set up, after much debate about the pros and cons of autonomous women's formations, a separate Women's Division of the Warehouse Union to which Jack Olsen belonged, establishing thereby a whole secondary leadership of women. This process of women's coming to strength and voice was to have been central to *Yonnondio,* and if, paradoxically, her own activism in the Left helped prevent her from finishing the novel, her experience in that milieu nevertheless gave her, too, a sense of confidence and worth essential to both her political work and her writing.

She wanted, moreover, to pay tribute to, to memorialize, the women she knew on the Left: women like her YCL comrades and especially immigrant women like her own mother—strong women, political women, but sometimes also women defeated by their long existence in a patriarchal world. Sometime in 1938 she wrote in her journal:

> To write the history of that whole generation of exiled revo-
> lutionaries, the kurelians and croations, the bundists and the
> poles; and the women, the foreign women, the mothers of six
> and seven . . . the housewives whose Zetkin and Curie and

> Bronte hearts went into kitchen and laundries and the patching of old socks; and those who did not speak the language of their children, who had no bridge . . . to make themselves understood.

Tell Me a Riddle is dedicated to two such women, and its central character, Eva, is a vividly drawn composite of several; Eva, a passionate socialist organizer and orator in her youth, who is silenced by years of poverty and tending to others' needs, only to find her voice and vision again when she is dying. The publications of the Left in the thirties are full of tributes to women like Mother Bloor, Clara Zetkin, Krupskaya; in a way, *Yonnondio* and *Tell Me a Riddle* are both extensions and demystifications of such portrayals, renderings of the essentially heroic lives which circumstances did not allow to blossom into public deeds, art, and fame.

Second, the theoretical analysis of crucial aspects of women's experience was encouraged by articles, lectures, party publications devoted solely to women's issues, and study groups on the Woman Question. Olsen herself taught a class on the Woman Question at YCL headquarters on San Francisco's Haight Street. A self-styled feminist even then, she had read not only Marxist theory, but also works from the suffragist movement like the *History of Woman Suffrage* and the *Woman's Bible,* and she invited suffragists to her class to talk about their own experiences in the nineteenth-century woman's movement, establishing a sense of the history and continuity of women's struggles.

Theory about the Woman Question undoubtedly helped to shape her own thinking about women's issues. Communist Party theory on women, like its practice, certainly had weaknesses. Most arose from the fact that gender was not identified as a fundamental social category like class. Thus, working-class women could be viewed as suffering essentially the same oppressions as their husbands, directly if they were workers, by extension if they were wives. Consequently, they would presumably benefit from the same measures. Analysis tended to focus on women in the paid labor force; and although housework did receive a substantial amount of critical attention, few analysts, except perhaps in special women's columns

168

or special women's publications like the *Woman Worker,* suggested seriously that men should share equal responsibility for it, although many argued—not strongly enough, according to Olsen—for its collectivization.[39]

The socialist writers of the earlier years of the century tended to be fuller in their analyses of sexuality and "life styles" than the Communist party in the thirties, which generally avoided such discussions, failing to link political revolution and sexual freedom as Agnes Smedley had at the close of the twenties. *Yonnondio* is far more reticent than *Daughter of Earth* on this subject. Although it includes the painfully explicit rape of wife by husband, and although it is better than a history book at raising issues of women's health, *Yonnondio* is largely silent about women's sexuality per se—even though this is a topic which Olsen speaks of freely in her early poems and sometimes in her journals. That silence may well have something to do with the rather puritanical and conservative attitudes of the Communist party on sexuality throughout the 1930s.[40]

Still, in no other segment of American society at that time were there such extensive discussions about the sources of women's oppression and the means for alleviating it. A recent article by Robert Shaffer, "Women and the Communist Party, USA, 1930–1940," provides a useful summary of the nature of women's status and roles in the Communist party, its theory about the oppression of women, its publications and organizations designed to counteract such oppression, its involvement in mass work among women and around women's issues, and its views on the family and sexuality. He concludes that "despite its important weaknesses, the CP's work among women in the 1930s was sufficiently extensive, consistent, and theoretically valuable to be considered an important part of the struggle for women's liberation in the United States."[41]

Shaffer discusses two books by communist women published in the 1930s that were important contributions to the analysis of women's issues. The first, by Grace Hutchins, focused on *Women Who Work*—that is, women in the paid work force; according to Shaffer, it underplays male chauvinism and sometimes blames women for their own oppression, but it also scrupulously documents the conditions of working women and formulates important demands to better them. The second book, written in 1939 by Mary Inman, takes a position reflecting the less sectarian consciousness of the Popular Front Years. Inman argues that all women are oppressed, not just working-class women, and that one of the symptoms of this oppression is their isolation in their homes; that working-class men sometimes oppress their wives; and that housework must be viewed as productive labor—positions rejected by the party's East Coast leadership, but supported in the West, where *People's World* was published and read. She also discusses how girls are conditioned to a "manufactured femininity" by childrearing practices and the mass media.[42] Inman eventually left the party over the controversy her book engendered, but clearly the ideas it expressed had some currency and support in Left Circles at least on the West Coast.

In many ways, *Yonnondio* anticipates in fiction Inman's theoretical formulations. The conditioning of children to accept limiting sex roles is an important theme in *Yonnondio*. One thinks, for example, of the children's games that so cruelly inhibit the preadolescent Mazie, or of the favorite text— "the Movies, selected"—of twelve-year-old Jinella, who with Mazie as partner plays a vamp from *Sheik of Araby, Broken Blossoms, Slave of Love, She Stopped at Nothing, The Fast Life*, and *The Easiest Way* (127–28), her imaginative capacity absurdly channeled by her exposure to these films, her only escape from her real life as Gertrude Skolnick. Even Anna, full of her own repressed longings, imparts the lessons of sex roles to her children. "Boys get to do that," she tells Benjy wistfully, talking of travel by trains and boats, "not girls" (113). And when Mazie asks her, "Why is it always me that has to help? How come Will gets to play?" Anna can only answer, "Willie's a boy" (142). Olsen, then, suggests throughout *Yonnondio* that both women and men are circumstanced to certain social roles, and that these roles, while placing impossible burdens of responsibility on working-class men, constrict the lives of women in particularly damaging ways.

Olsen understands and portrays the double oppression of working-class women in other ways as well. Anna's spirit is almost broken by her physical illness—"woman troubles"— connected with pregnancy and childbirth and compounded by inadequate medical care. Her apparent apathy and incompetence make her a target of her husband's rage; he strikes out at and violates her because he has no other accessible target for his frustrations and fears, until her miscarriage forces him to a pained awareness and reawakened love. Few other American novels, perhaps none outside the radical tradition of which *Yonnondio* is a part, reveal so starkly the destructive interactions of class and sex under patriarchal capitalism.

In *Yonnondio,* as in Olsen's other work, the family itself has a contradictory function, at once a source of strength and love, and a battleground between women and men in a system exploiting both. This, of course, is a profoundly Marxian vision; it was Marx and Engels who wrote in the *Communist Manifesto:* "The bourgeois clap-trap about the family and education, about the hallowed relation of parent and child, becomes all the more disgusting, the more, by the action of Modern Industry, all family ties among the proletarians are torn asunder."[43] The vision of the family in *Yonnondio* is formed both by Olsen's own experience and by her familiarity from childhood on with socialist ideas.

Another aspect of that vision is Olsen's treatment of the relationship between housework and paid labor in *Yonnondio.* One of the novel's crucial structural principles is the juxtaposition of men's (and women's) work in the paid labor force and women's work in the home—especially in the final chapter, which shifts back and forth between Anna's canning at home, as she tends to the demands of her older children and juggles Baby Bess on her hip, and the hellish speedup of the packing plant where Jim works. The overwhelming heat, prelude to the great droughts and dust storms of the thirties, becomes a common bond of suffering. There is nothing redeeming about the brutal and exploitative labor at the plant; Anna at least is engaged in production of goods the family will use and in caring for children whom she loves through her exhaustion. Olsen makes it clear that both forms of work are essential, and that the degrading conditions of both have the same systemic causes. If she is finally unable in *Yonnondio* to suggest a systemic solution, her instincts were perhaps more historically accurate than those of other Marxists writing in the same period.

Yonnondio, of course, is far more than ideology translated into fiction. Olsen wrote from what she had lived, what she had seen, at last incorporating "the common hysteria" of factory work, the bodily nausea and weariness, along with the incessant demands of work in the home. But her understanding of those events, the nature of her protest, although in many ways going beyond Communist party theory and practice of the early thirties, could only have been deepened by the very presence in her milieu of theory and controversy on the Woman Question.[44]

On the whole, in spite of the Left's demands on her time and energies, the prescriptiveness of its more dogmatic criticism, and the androcentrism or outright sexism of many of its spokesmen, there is no doubt but that Olsen's Marxian perspective and experience ultimately enriched her literature. In a talk in 1974 at Emerson College, in Boston, explaining some of the reasons why she is a "slow" writer, she discussed without using the terminology of the Left the differences between her own concerns and what a Marxist would identify as bourgeois ideology:

> My vision is very different from that of most writers. . . . I
> don't think in terms of quests for identity to explain human
> motivation and behavior. I feel that in a world where class,
> race, and sex are so determining, that that has little reality.
> What matters to me is the kind of soil *out* of which people
> have to grow, and the kind of climate around them; circum-
> stances are the primary key and not the personal quest for
> identity. . . . I want to write what will help change that which
> is harmful for human beings in our time.[45]

In the fifties, partly out of a spirit of opposition to the McCarthy era, and blessed with increased time as the children grew up and there were temporary respites from financial need, Olsen began to do the work that gave us the serenely beautiful but still politically impassioned stories of the *Tell Me a Riddle* volume. Olsen's enduring insistence that literature must confront the material realities of people's lives as shaping circumstances, that the very categories of class and race and sex constitute the fabric of reality as we live it, and that literature has an obligation to deepen consciousness and facilitate social change are part of her—and our—inheritance from the radical tradition.

☐ *Notes* ∎

1. To my knowledge, the connections between the contemporary women's movement and the Old Left have never been sufficiently explored, although its roots in the civil rights movement and the New Left are well documented, as in Sara Evans's *Personal Politics: The Roots of Women's Liberation in the Civil Rights Movement and the New Left* (New York: Random House, 1979). It would be interesting, for example, to look at the number of feminist leaders and spokeswomen with family or other personal ties to the Old Left.

2. The earlier version of this article was delivered at a session on Women Writers of the Left at the National Women's Studies Association convention in Bloomington, Indiana, June 1980. Olsen's comments on that version were made mostly during an eight-hour tape-recorded conversation in Fall 1980. I have quoted extensively from that discussion as well as from earlier interviews, without attempting to distinguish between them.

3. "Tillie Olsen," "A Note About This Book," *Yonnondio: From the Thirties* (New York: Dell, 1975), p. 158. All references are to this edition, and page numbers will be supplied in parentheses in the text.

4. Selma Burkom and Margaret Williams, "De-Riddling Tillie Olsen's Writings," *San Jose Studies* 2 (1976): 65–83. In spite of some inaccuracies, this important study is the best source of biographical and bibliographic information on Olsen outside of her own writings.

5. Ellen Moers, *Literary Women* (New York: Doubleday, 1976); and Elaine Showalter, *A Literature of Their Own: British Women Novelists from Brontë to Lessing* (Princeton, N.J.: Princeton University Press, 1977).

6. Walter B. Rideout, *The Radical Novel in the United States, 1900–1954* (New York: Hill and Wang, 1956), p. 3; and Daniel Aaron, *Writers on the Left* (New York: Harcourt, Brace & World, 1961).

7. Aaron, *Writers on the Left*, pp. 336–37.

173

8. From an unmailed letter to Harriet Monroe, apparently intended as a cover letter for poems Olsen was planning to submit for publication in Monroe's influential *Poetry: A Magazine of Verse*.

9. From Elinor Langer's transcription of her introduction to a talk given by Olsen at a Reed College symposium in Portland, Oregon, in Fall, 1978.

10. In "Divided Against Herself: The Life Lived and the Life Suppressed," *Moving On* (April–May 1980): 15–20, 23, I explored the theme of the "buried life" in women's literature, as it appears in the work of leftist feminist writers like Olsen and Agnes Smedley. In "Tell Me a Riddle," the buried life is Eva's engaged, articulate, political self, whereas in Smedley's *Daughter of Earth,* it is the maternal, domestic self. Both works testify to the pain of denying part of one's being, and both condemn the society that does not allow women to be whole.

11. Burkom and Williams reprint these poems in their article "De-Riddling Tillie Olsen"; "I Want You Women up North to Know," pp. 67–69, and "There Is a Lesson," p. 70.

12. Tillie Lerner, "The Iron Throat," *Partisan Review* 1 (April–May 1934): 3–9.

13. Tillie Lerner, "Thousand-Dollar Vagrant," *New Republic* 80 (29 August 1934): 67–69; and "The Strike," *Partisan Review* 1 (September–October 1934): 3–9, reprinted in *Years of Protest: A Collection of American Writings of the 1930s,* ed. Jack Salzman (New York: Pegasus, 1967), pp. 138–44.

14. Salzman, ed., *Years of Protest,* p. 138.

15. Ibid., p. 144.

16. One of the best accounts of the importance of these clubs for young writers, in spite of his ultimate disillusionment with the Communist party, is Richard Wright's 1944 essay printed in *The God That Failed,* ed. Richard H. Crossman (New York: Harper, 1950).

17. This is Olsen's recollection: I did not locate the actual source.

18. Cited in Burkom and Williams, "De-Riddling Tillie Olsen," p. 71.

19. Among those who signed the call to the conference and/ or attended were Nelson Algren, Kenneth Burke, Theodore Dreiser, Waldo Frank, Joseph Freeman, Granville Hicks, Langston Hughes, Edwin Seaver, and Nathaniel West.

20. Langer mentions this drawing in her talk at Reed College cited above. Olsen has a copy of the cartoon in her files, and Salzman includes it with twenty others in *Years of Protest,* p. 307.

21. The selections in Salzman's chapter on "The Social Muse," in *Years of Protest,* pp. 231–307, are well chosen to represent various positions in this debate.

22. Rideout's discussion of the efforts of the Left to define the "proletarian novel" is particularly helpful and more detailed than I can be here; see *Radical Novel in the United States,* especially pp. 165–70.

23. Printed in *Feminist Studies,* 7, no. 3 (Fall 1981).

24. Burkom and Williams, "De-Riddling Tillie Olsen," p. 69.

25. Rideout, *Radical Novel in the United States,* pp. 171–98. In only three of the many novels Rideout discusses do female characters play a major role: those by Josephine Herbst.

26. From an unpublished paper by Elaine Hedges, "Meridel Le Sueur in the Thirties," first presented at the Modern Language Association Convention in San Francisco, December 1978.

27. Mike Gold, "Proletarian Realism," reprinted in *Mike Gold: A Literary Anthology,* ed. Michael Folsom (New York: International Publishers, 1972), p. 207.

28. Rachel Blau DuPlessis, in an editorial comment on this paper.

29. Elinor Langer, "'The Ruins of Memory': Josephine Herbst in the 1930s," unpublished; also in Langer, "If In Fact I Have Found a Heroine . . . ," *Mother Jones* 6 (May 1981), 43. Meridel Le Sueur has mentioned similar episodes in talks at a conference on women writers at the Women's Building in Los Angeles in 1972 and at the National Women's Studies Association Conference in Lawrence, Kansas, 1979.

30. Robert Shaffer, "Women and Communist Party, USA, 1930–1940," *Socialist Review* 45 (May–June 1979): 93, note. I am indebted to Shaffer's article throughout the final section of this paper.

31. Folsom, ed., *Mike Gold,* p. 188.

32. Ibid., p. 139.

33. See, for example, Gold's "Wilder: Prophet of the Genteel Christ," in Salzman's *Years of Protest,* pp. 233–38.

34. Joseph North, *New Masses: An Anthology of the Rebel Thirties* (New York: International Publishers, 1969), p. 24.

35. Meridel Le Sueur, in talks cited above and personal conversations with her on those occasions; also see Hedges, "Meridel Le Sueur in the Thirties," p. 7.

36. Langer, "The Ruins of Memory," p. 16.

37. In Rideout, *Radical Novel in the United States,* p. 189.

38. Peggy Dennis, *The Autobiography of an American Communist: A Personal View of a Political Life, 1925–1975* (Berkeley, Calif.: Creative Arts Books, 1977), p. 294.

39. Shaffer, "Women and the Communist Party," pp. 94–96.

40. Ibid., especially pp. 104–107.

41. Ibid., p. 10.

42. Ibid., pp. 83–87. I am also grateful to historian Sherna Gluck for discussing Inman's work and the controversy surrounding it with me.

43. This version is from Barbara Sinclair Deckard's *The Women's Movement: Political, Socioeconomic, and Psychological Issues,* 2d ed. (New York: Harper & Row, 1979), p. 234.

44. Olsen's concern with the Woman Question continued into the forties. She authored for a few months in 1946 a women's column in *People's World,* writing articles like "Wartime Gains of Women in Industry," and "Politically Active Mothers—One View," which argued like Inman that motherhood should be considered political work. Also in the forties she participated actively in some of the organizations targeted by the Communist party for mass work on what the party considered to be women's issues—health and education—work related also, of course, to her own deepest concerns.

45. From a tape transcription in Olsen's files.

☐ ELAINE NEIL ORR ■

A Feminist
Spiritual Vision

I am serious about the images I make.
MIRIAM SCHAPIRO,
"Notes from a Conversation
on Art, Feminism, and Work"

The last step in this process is to leave God. I take this to
mean, in religious terms, that we have to leave the Lord
in order to find God in our brothers and sisters. We have
to give up obedience to find solidarity. We have to give
up relationships of domination, even if our role in them is
the servant's role. We have to overcome the master-
servant relationship and become one with our brothers
and sisters. . . .
That would be a major step in the direction we have to
travel. I think what we need in order to take that step is a
new language, and feminists (both male and female) are
working hard today to develop a language that says
more clearly what it amounts to and means to leave God
for God's sake.
And so . . . I ask God to make me quit of God for God's
sake. And with that I would like to close.
DOROTHEE SOELLE,
The Strength of the Weak

If spiritual Being begins in life experience, we are in the process of disclosing the truth, the light, and the way. Human
beings are then responsible for all that is in us to be. We leave
the God of dominion, power, and priority, for divinity that is
on the journey, among the people. Dorothee Soelle, German

From *Tillie Olsen and a Feminist Spiritual Vision* (Jackson, Miss.: University Press of Mississippi, 1987), 167–183.

feminist theologian, says we can no longer use sentences like "Christ is the Son of God" as a departure for theology. She suggests that sentences derived from human experience, like "Mrs. Schmidt has been waiting for seventeen months for an 8-by-12 foot room in a nursing home," are more promising beginnings for religious understandings. Such a sentence, she says, "can lead us somewhere" in contemplating the nature of God.[1]

Tillie Olsen's narrative and poetic texts "can lead us somewhere" in our search for truth, light, and way. Moments within the texts (words, images, metaphors) and the span of the stories themselves confront us with news of a world in which people struggle for identity and purpose. Emerging language patterns (like life/miracle/flower) are the writer's means of evoking in readers a comprehension like her own. The otherness we confront in Olsen is the depth of her longing and faith arising from abused and despised life. For readers instilled with a theological sense of our helplessness and God's supreme power, the notion that human care and community may be the locus for the world's and divine's recreation is alien indeed.

Reading Olsen with a religious interest, we come to ask why it is that for so long we have needed God to be separate from us. Why have we needed to deny change and to fear a humane world? Why do we prefer destruction, and why do we use God as a reason for it? In a vision of life that supposes the expansion of Being in human becoming, we begin to wonder why it has been assumed that divinity is diminished in human contexts. In other words, reading a woman writer like Tillie Olsen religiously accomplishes a major task in the present work of feminist theologians. It allows us to make "the mysterious turn" to an entirely different way of thinking about holiness and redemption, about beauty and salvation. Olsen's body of work is a source of new thinking about what matters in the intertwined realms of physical and spiritual life, about what efforts are lasting.

A Metaphorical Rendering

From the perspective of Olsen's latest period, we can fruitfully reflect upon a metaphorical pattern that has developed

through her writing, communicating a vision of human transformation.[2] It is telling that the metaphors are mixed, drawn
from nature and human manufacture. Using the *journey* or
quest motif, Olsen pictures the human search for a viable
place to be, an environment or home in which one may grow
and *blossom*. Inheriting an abused and broken world, people
search the past and their environment to discover what in-
heritances may nurture life. The yields of the search, like the
members of the community, are *threads of a whole* to be woven or *pieced* together in a pattern of humane coexistence.
Thus, full human being, like a quilt or a mosaic, is envisioned
as a coherent and patterned search for truths faithful to human needs and visions and leading to actions that elicit mutual well-being and wholeness. Like Nelle Morton, who writes
in a different mode, Tillie Olsen shows that "the journey is
home."[3] Not ends but beginnings and makings are the goal.
The way is the negotiated, not pure way of being faithful in
relationship. Movements toward human unfolding and being
cast light on the journey, disclosing what is essential and true
"for human beings in our time."[4] Faithfulness to one's own
time and circumstance, not allegiance to distant worlds, is the
calling echoed in Olsen's literature.

JOURNEYING

To journey at one's will is an expression of freedom. At the
same time, journeying may be a quest for freedom. The literary use of journeying as a leitmotif for human dreams and
visions is standard. As reflected in a contemporary anthology
such as *Myths and Motifs in Literature,* the journey or quest
motif in Western literature has largely been concerned with
the individual (almost always male) and "his hopes to find the
Self" through "a slow process forward to a final goal (heaven)
along a linear movement of time."[5]

Recently, feminist scholars have begun to identify
trends and patterns in the female quest, as reflected in literature by women. One such study is Carol Christ's *Diving Deep
and Surfacing: Women Writers on Spiritual Quest.*[6] Christ
suggests the often communal nature of women's quests and
the grounding of women's struggle in the historical reality of
their traditional voicelessness. The pattern she discovers in

women's texts, however, is by and large a radical break with the past and a mystical, futuristic naming of a new reality.

Houston A. Baker's *The Journey Back: Issues in Black Literature and Criticism* may offer a better parallel for understanding Olsen's use of the metaphor: "The black writer, having attempted the journey, preserves details of his voyage in that most manifest and coherent of all cultural systems—language. Through his [sic] work we are allowed to witness, if not the trip itself, at least a representation of the voyage that provides some view of our emergence."[7] For Baker, the writer makes an "effort at return," which then leads to emergence. Journeys in a literature like Olsen's are the re-presentation of historical quests, which in turn spark new worlds and imaginative voyages. Out of people's past comes the way of journeying in the present. Language, then, is a kind of map, a rendering of valleys and highways, of crossroads and destinations.

A book like Nelle Morton's *The Journey Is Home* is a language map for feminist scholars. It records the way women have come in recent years (to self and other understanding and truth) and charts paths for their continued journeying. In the process of Morton's own use of the image in relation to women's lives, new or different meanings emerge. While we journey politically, historically, and geographically, we also journey spiritually. In a note at the end of her book, she writes, "Maybe 'journey' is not so much a journey ahead, or a journey into space, but a journey into presence. The farthest place on earth is a journey into the presence of the nearest person to you."[8] These sentences are evocative for literary criticism. The reading journey is one into presence, into the presence of characters and of their world, where we learn as much about ourselves as about the peopled text.

Olsen's reconstructionist vision shares a basic impulse expressed by Carol Christ in the conclusion to her book, the impulse toward integration. Olsen's use of journeying expands the possibilities for understanding the human quest by an integration of past and future, self and other, male and female. Depicting in her first fiction the quest for a better life, in later stories Olsen uses the journey to illuminate her characters' communal struggles for understanding and for a sense of meaningful participation in life.

180

A journey bridges the first two settings of *Yonnondio*. Though there are other brief episodes of happiness in the novel, this scene (Chapter 3) is uniquely joyful, marked by singing and bodies in relationship: "Willie slumbered against Mazie's shoulder. Ben drowsily had his head in her lap, staring into the depthless transparent green above. . . . 'Roses love nightwinds, violets love dew, angels in heaven, know I love you.' Their voices were slow curving rhythms, slow curving sounds. Voices, rising and twining, beauty curving on rainbows of quiet sound" (38). Throughout the chapter, the emphasis is less on the passage from place to place than on the community created by the travel. The family's bodily support of one another is imagized in the twining voices. The passage suggests an understanding of human bondedness and the possibility of human cooperation.

Mazie is infused with feelings of expansion: "[She] stood up, her hands on the wagon seat, screaming with delight. The wind came over her body with a great rush of freedom" (35). A range of nature images—snow, wind, rainbow, sunshine—points to the characters' anticipation and wonder as they travel. The girl, in particular, senses the flow of life's energies and intuits her connection with the vast possibilities of the new geography.

Joyous, exhilarating, the journey is portrayed from Mazie's perspective as a wondrous moment, for Anna it is a hallmark of the future: "with bright eyes [she] folded and unfolded memories of past years—plans for the years to come" (38). The family's search is for work, home, schooling, for identity and connection. In their moving, the Holbrooks express their dearest hopes: "A new life . . . in the spring" (38). Thus the journey is metaphoric of the desire for opportunity and renewal. They hope not merely for survival, but for beginning and building: "lovely things to keep, brass lamps, bright tablecloths, vines over the doors, and roses twining" (38). Things of material beauty suggest a sense of permanence and belonging, where children can ponder questions and invite their souls to wander, where relationships that offer sustenance for life can be fostered.

In the Holbrooks' journeying, two human quests are metaphorically intertwined: one, the necessary quest for sustaining work, a living wage, and the other, the desire to begin anew, to find a life of meaning characterized by mutual caring and abundant yields. As the journey for work is described, certain characteristics of the human quest for meaning are suggested. Mazie experiences release, boundlessness, and contentment as they travel. Furthermore, the journey is characterized by solidarity, by human community and interdependence. Mazie helps her father when the wheels are stuck, and Anna shelters the children bodily when it snows.

In the story of Whitey, the journeying metaphor reflects the hopes of the past. The sailor once felt connected to others in his work because they shared "the brotherhood." What was good for one was good for all. Now that the camaraderie has disintegrated, he struggles to sustain meaning in his life. He is like a wrecked vessel, no longer able to make himself "feel good" because the adventure and community his travels once embodied are no longer intact. Without the community he once knew, the journeying of his present is empty.

The steerage ship of Eva's story connects her past journey for political freedom with her present quest for self-identity. A former embarkment, made in desperation, now signifies the way Eva must travel to gain a sense of herself and of the belief that has given her life meaning. What she discovers is an unshakable faith in human beings. Though her present journey is singular, it gains its meaning from the movement of thousands toward freedom and dignity. We might understand the journey's conclusion to signify Olsen's own faith. Searching for meaning, Eva finds that the quester (herself) finds meaning by sharing with others the same struggle for freedom. She (and Olsen) embody the truth that the "purpose" of freedom is to create it for others."[9] Thus, Eva's spiritual search suggests that to understand the journey of one's life is to see it in the context of movements larger than oneself.

As readers, we journey into Eva's world. Reading fosters journeying into another's presence. In "Tell Me a Riddle," we are invited into Eva's human heart, to learn of her understandings, pains, and hopes. The result is an expansion of our own journeying. Meeting another on her way, we have made a detour on our own. Thus we might say that reading fictive worlds teaches sympathy born out of interruption. Practicing a willed suspension of our own world, we enter the otherness of a new world, thinking and feeling as another. Journeys are thus intertwined, and we carry in our minds the crossed paths of self and other.

While Eva's personal hope is symbolized by the socialist dream, Stevie's journey begins at the personal level and expands toward a vision of universal quest through imagistic association with animal and plant worlds and the significant relations of this life. The longer light of spring, accompanying the boy's quest for a place and for the knowledge that he is connected with others by love, points to the metaphysical depth of the story. Through the settings of junkyard and cemetery, journeying becomes a metaphor not only for the living but for the hopes of the dead, whose memory sparks the present search for meaning and for a feeling of continuity.

The journeys of Olsen's characters are marked by struggle and community. Employing the quest as a leitmotif of American literature, the writer revitalizes its metaphoric potential by offering an unlikely set of vehicles: the poor, minorities, women, and children. The incoherent chantings of an old Jewish immigrant woman, the vision of an eight-year-old girl or a fourteen-year-old boy, the desires of a poverty-stricken woman, balancing a baby on her hip, a union sailor, reeling drunk, whose quest he no longer understands: these are the people whose journeying Olsen depicts as the essential human quest for freedom, place, and meaning. She makes us feel the desire "for mattering" from their perspectives and shows the springs of hope flowing, almost miraculously, from their lives. These questers come in groups, struggling together as family: mother/daughter, husband/wife, friend/friend. The black church in "O Yes" is emblematic of communal journeying, where everyone is brought along: the old, the sick, the infant.

In her notes, Olsen has written, "In the human being is an irrepressible desire for freedom that breaks out century after century."[10] In her fiction she shows that desire to be not merely for freedom *from* want, hunger, and fear, but freedom *for* fulfillment, expression, and community. Using women's, children's, and working-class perspectives, Olsen transforms the vision of human longing from solitary to community quest-ing. Through the lens of domestic needs, limitations, and promises, Olsen suggests that the movement toward freedom is most genuine and realistically promising as an inclusive journey that begins where people are the weakest and least fortunate.

In *Silences,* Olsen writes of "the unnatural thwarting of what struggles to come into being, but cannot" (6), suggesting that the human quest is the journey into Being, into authentic and expressive selfhood. When she writes of the desire for "spaciousness that puts no limit to vision" (102), she evokes for us an image of creativity in geographical terms. Imagina-tive work needs room without a roof. The journeys inward and outward reflect similar truths. Movement, change, and pos-sibility are core human needs that are also liberations. In the modern world, many take for granted the sense of expansive-ness gained in travel. But in sympathy with people who are denied journeying, as today black South Africans (and others) are and as Olsen's people are, we may remember the power of the journey to express the human movement into holiness.

BLOSSOMING

The flower—witness Emerson's rhodora—is a symbol of beauty and fulfillment as well as vulnerability, the time of blossoming the apex of the plant's development and the glory of its existence. To speak of human blossoming is to suggest the natural beauty of our selves, even more, abundance and future fruition. Olsen's use of the image is prophetic, suggest-ing the condition of life as it should be, not as it is. In the world of her characters, the hope of blossoming is slim; parents wit-ness the atrophy of children's talents because the world gar-den denies them the nourishment that might help them grow and flourish. For now, "the time is drought or blight or infes-tation." [11] But if the "subterranean forces" are fed, if the "root-lets of reconnaissance" are showered, "the mysterious turn" may occur, and a time of blossoming be ushered in. [12] Like other organic images literarily employed, blossoming suggests cycles of growth, bounty, and return, pointing to the interrelationships of seed, soil, and flower, of child, environment, and future yield. While the metaphor has often been used, Olsen's employment of it in contexts of depletion, exhaustion, and death offers new insights.

Alice Walker's use of organic imagery may be used as an interpretive grid for Olsen. Writing about art and women, Walker uses the imagery of seed and flower: "And so our mothers and grandmothers have, more often than not anonymously, handed on the creative spark, the seed of the flower they themselves never hoped to see."[13] In the next paragraphs she offers her mother's gardens as the source of the imagery:

> Whatever she planted grew as if by magic, and her fame as a grower of flowers spread over three counties. Because of her creativity with her flowers, even my memories of poverty are seen through a screen of blooms. . .
>
> I notice that it is only when my mother is working in her flowers that she is radiant, . . . involved in work her soul must have.[14]

The connection Walker makes between her mother's work and her soul, between art and deep human need, suggests an understanding of the organic/spiritual connection as more than a literary device. The connection is rooted in human being. The work of hands feeds the spirit, blending body and soul in radiance.

The singular moment of repose experienced by Mazie and Anna in *Yonnondio* follows their discovery of catalpa blossoms "scattered in the green." The flowers' fragrance and beauty transport Anna back to her childhood, making it possible for her to abandon the worried present and feel for a moment with her daughter the wonder of the universe: "Up from the grasses, from the earth, from the broad tree trunk at their back, latent life streamed and seeded. The air and self shone boundless. Absently, her mother stroked; stroked unfolding, wingedness, boundlessness" (119). The description combines images drawn from flower and butterfly. Petals and wing "unfold," flowers "seed," and the butterfly's compass is "boundless." The girl, like the budded flower, contains within the capacity to come to fruition. Here and elsewhere in Olsen's writing, blossoming signifies the potential for wholeness and holiness in human beings.

At the close of the story "I Stand Here Ironing," the blossoming metaphor is the mother's way of expressing her daughter's capacity. Reflecting her hopes and fears, the protagonist pleads, "Let her be. So all that is in her will not bloom—but in how many does it?" (20–21). Earlier she thought of the girl's gift for pantomime as too often "clogged and clotted," not "used and growing" (19). In this story, the association of flower and girl yields ambivalent meanings. She may not grow at all, she may grow but never come to fulfillment, or she may blossom fully, like Anna's catalpa.

The mother's fear and her negative expression of the metaphor—"so all that is in her will not bloom"—is reflected in Olsen's essay about her mother's death. Describing her mother's life, Olsen writes of "that common everyday nightmare of hardship, limitation, longing; of baffling struggle to raise six children in a world hostile to human unfolding."[15] The allusion to the metaphor is slight but recognizable: human unfolding is an image drawn from nature. It is the normal condition in favorable circumstances where, like flowers, children may grow and blossom. But because our world unnaturally limits potential in children by preferring war and destruction to creativity, the blossoms of humanity wither prematurely or never come to flower at all. Some may be skeptical of the seemingly romantic view that most children are born with vast creative potential. From Olsen's perspective, what is unbelievable is the bomb, mass indifference, wholesale destruction. In a deep hearing of her literary voice, we perceive how twisted is the "truth" of greed, competition, and slaughter that directs so much human behavior.

Reading a passage from the last pages of *Yonnondio*, cognizant of Olsen's continued use of the metaphor in later work, we are able to see blossoming and its denial as a metaphorical lens for human potential and what threatens it:

Bang!

> Bess who has been fingering a fruit-jar lid—absently, heedlessly drops it—aimlessly groping across the table, reclaims it again. Lightning in her brain. She releases, grabs, releases, grabs. I can do. Bang! I did that. I can do. I! . . . That noise! In triumphant, astounded joy she clashes the lid down. Bang, slam, whack. . . . human ecstasy of achievement; . . . *I can do. I use my powers. I! I!* Wilder, madder, happier the bangs [153].

Against the family's poverty and the story's preoccupation with losses and limitations, the brief episode of unfolding human potential is a reminder of the latent powers in human life. Like the unfolding of one petal, the first lesson is only the beginning of the blossom. But in her environment, will Bess continue to flower? Coming back to the story from Olsen's later fiction and the probing question of the unnamed mother in "I Stand Here Ironing," the reader is undoubtedly led to ask the question.

When in later addresses or talks, Olsen refers to "fullness of life," "thwarting of the human," or "the sense of one's *unused powers*," the blossoming metaphor from her first fiction is evoked.[16] Expression, creativity, and purposeful action are the human values to which Olsen gives imagistic expression in terms of the flower's full maturation and glory. In "Tell Me a Riddle," Eva's speech evokes the metaphor when she, dying, pleads with David: "So strong for what? To rot not grow?"

Olsen gives interpretation to her metaphors in many of her unpublished texts. In personal notes, she writes of "[t]he irrepressible little ones in whom all the art qualities are . . . germinal." But experience has taught her that often family circumstances, more than potential, determine what one will become. In children, she sees "the passion for language, for imitation, make-believe acting, deft use of the body, love of rhythm, music."[17] As a seed whose germination and growth depend almost entirely on favorable conditions, the child whose potential is miraculously given at birth, depends on a world of encouragement and means if he or she is to grow in health. The "word" of the human infant spoken into the world is an act of divine faith. Our faithfulness or unfaithfulness lies in our human response to that word.

In language reflective of Eva's, Olsen uses the organic image for cosmic questioning: "Has it always been this: this world of winter, only breaking on the new life toward the longer light, the warmth, the blossoming"?[18] If the world is a great seed, the light is the morality of valuing each human being, and warmth, the sustenance of human caring.

The miraculous rebirth of dead objects in "Requa" makes it possible to believe in the resurrection of human potentials. Even dirt has a life wish, and junk desires the holiness of being made useful. Through Stevie's eyes, we see beauty in rust patterns and the mystery of decay. All about are living clues to the cycles of death and rebirth that turn the universe. Seeing his own worth reflected in his uncle's face, Steve learns a central lesson of life: others need caring for, too. Reciprocating Wes's attention reflects Stevie's most difficult journey into another's presence; his blossoming is intimated by his unfolding from isolation and reaching out to others. Thus his story expands our sense of the religious dimension of human flowering, since the moral principles of shared responsibility and mutual enhancement are the truths that elicit Stevie's own resurrection.

In portraits of human struggle, Olsen shows some, like Eva and Whitey, who know the feelings of waste and untapped potential. Others, like Emily, Carol, Jeannie, and Steve, seem to span our lives and pose a question that waits for the reader's reply. How might those whose lives are still before them bring their gifts to bear on the world and find their paths of righteousness?

PIECING

Repairing, patching, and sewing, work that women have traditionally performed in the home, are all piecing activities. Piece goods are materials purchased by the yard to be patterned, cut, and sewn, especially into garments. But any creativity that combines parts into a whole may be understood metaphorically as piecing. Olsen's use of the image brings a

188

historically female sphere of work to consciousness as a perspective for viewing human activity and values. The metaphor
implies reconstruction, since in Olsen's world, the characters
seldom piece new goods but rather sort through discards and
make something new from something old.

The quilt is a most salient work of piecing. Colorful and
patterned, it symbolizes not only the human ingenuity that
creates something of use out of something old, but as a finished product, it suggests an eye for the beauty and harmoni-
ous design that characterize human creativity. While all of
these meanings are suggested in Olsen's employment of the
metaphor, more dramatically, she suggests a morality of re-
appropriation: choosing from the past usable patterns for life
in the modern present.

Miriam Schapiro, a contemporary artist, expresses a
similar morality and evokes the imagery of piecing in describing her own movement to feminist consciousness in her work:
"The new work was different from anything I had done before.
I worked on canvas, using fabric. I wanted to explore and express a part of my life which I had always dismissed—my
homemaking, my nesting. I wanted to validate the traditional
activities of women, to connect myself with the unknown
women artists who made quilts, who had done the invisible
'women's work' of civilization."[19] Schapiro's collage style is
drawn from the historical work of foremothers (including their
quilting) and seeks to integrate the values of their traditional
lives with her current feminist perspectives. Using more than
one medium and fabrics and objects out of women's traditional contexts, Schapiro's "piecing" on canvas is like Olsen's
in word.

Olsen warns against the danger of glorifying one aspect
of women's work (homemaking) or overemphasizing one creative expression of women (like needlework), while not encouraging women in different ways of making art. Schapiro's
use of a piecing style seems important, however, in that it
gives her a female tradition and allows her to claim a part of
herself that she had not expressed before (the caring angel).
Olsen's use of the metaphor in word and image appears, as it
does with Schapiro, to grow out of her experience in female
contexts, though she expands it in her universal vision.

In the second chapter of *Yonnondio,* as the family works desperately to gain the necessary money for moving, we are given this narrative depiction of Anna's participation: "Somehow to skimp off of everything that had long ago been skimped on, somehow to find more necessities the body can do easiest without. The old quilt will make coats for Mazie and Ben, Will can wear Mazie's old one. This poverty's arithmetic for Anna" (26). The gift Anna brings to a limited situation is her ability to create something of use out of what she has, to divide and multiply fragments. The quilt, already something made of fragments and leftovers, can be remade as two coats, a girl's coat can be converted into a boy's.

Children, like their parents, learn the art of making something out of scraps and leftovers:

> On the dump there is Jinella's tent, Jinella's mansion, Jinella's roadhouse, Jinella's pagan island, Jinella's palace, whatever Jinella wills it to be that day. Flattened tin cans, the labels torn off to show the flashing silver, are strung between beads and buttons to make the shimmering, showy entrance curtains. Here sometimes, . . . Mazie is admitted—*if* she brings something for the gunny sack. The gunny sack . . . stuffed with "properties": blond wood-shaving curls, moldering hats, raggy teddies, torn lace curtains (for trains and wedding dresses), fringes, tassels, stubs of lipstick, wrecks of high-heeled shoes and boots, lavish jewelry. (127)

Like an artist or a "bricoleur," Jinella determines the name of what she creates, as she strings tin cans, beads, and buttons to form a chain curtain, brings together the worn old toy and lady's lipstick stub to form her treasure, or turns a bit of lace into a bride's veil.[20] She is a namer of her world—mansion, palace, roadhouse—and by naming creates her reality. Through Jinella's cunning, if desperate, imagining, Olsen points to the unique human ability to make and create. Furthermore, the writer uses the girl's piecing to reflect the value of cast-off junk, still recognizable to the discerning eye.

The piecing imagery of the *Yonnondio* passages is evoked in "O Yes" by a description of voices raised together in song. The passage reminds us of the Holbrooks' intertwined voices as they journeyed to the farm. In "O Yes," the young protagonist ponders: "If it were a record she would play it over and over, . . . to untwine the intertwined voices, to search how the many rhythms rock apart and yet are one glad rhythm" (50). Twining is an action of lapping and turning, yet it brings separate, even disparate, pieces together and suggests the intention of combining. The pieces intertwined may be characteristically the same, as a rope or chain, or they may, as voices, be different. What is pieced together in "O Yes," through song, sermon, and scripture, is a message, a plea by the black community for ultimate justice on earth as well as in heaven.

The "spinning" preacher's voice elicits in Carol's mind a tapestry of childhood games: "Tag. Thump of the volleyball. Ecstasy of the jump rope" (52). In Carol's thought, words and images are combined that will in the end remind her of her allegiances and responsibilities. The twining voices, singing of justice and humanity, metaphorize Carol's moral situation: she must choose from the past what will direct her future. Similarly, Alva's dream is drawn from pieces or fragments of experience: her own pregnancy, loneliness and poverty; the diminutive guide who leads her to paradise with parade stick and motorcycle; the convey line and the damned souls. Furthermore, in an interview Olsen has remarked that her writing of the passage came about as a combination of stories she had heard from black women.[21] Thus, the writer's method reflects her characters', and vice versa: choosing images and thoughts from the past and weaving them into a coherent, if also paradoxical, narrative for understanding life.

In "Tell Me a Riddle," we are told of Eva's "one social duty . . . the boxes of old clothes left with her, as with the life-practiced eye for finding what is still wearable within the worn . . . she scans and sorts—this for rag or rummage, that for mending and cleaning, and this for sending away." Eva's sorting is reminiscent of Anna's piecing, looking for what can be remade or used again. Looking through the old clothes, Eva's sorting reflects not only the artistry of Anna's novel use of an older object, but also a sense of human interconnectedness. When she looks through the clothes for what can still be used, she reflects the human moral choice to bring need into alignment with resource. From this perspective, we conclude politically and religiously that an imbalance or nonalignment of goods and people is evil, and that in regaining the original holiness/wholeness and promise of the universe, we are responsible to right such imbalance.

Stevie's rebirth is elicited by sustained use of piecing imagery. Acts leading to wholeness—bringing parts together, teaching a skill, meeting human needs—are the seeds of holiness. Because individual human wholeness cannot be fully and timelessly achieved, the human community must impart wholeness, offering the individual a place in the pattern of life. Moving from the domestic sphere to the contexts of industry and technological waste, Olsen universalizes the metaphor, making clear her vision of redemption as the historical and material reconstruction of beauty and health out of waste and brokenness.

The metaphor of piecing contributes to the moral vision Olsen describes in her interviews and talks. Her first sentence is structurally parallel with Anna's thought (what can be saved, what cannot) in these remarks: "Our situation . . . is: what do we keep, what do we discard. What is going backward, what narrows us, limits us, makes us too liable to hatreds, bigotries, closing off, not recognizing what the central enemy is, where our allies lie, where our common humanity lies."[22]

Olsen's view of intergenerational responsibility may also be interpreted in terms of "piecing." She understands that the dreams and struggles of revolutionaries form the basis, indeed are the beginnings, of our present struggle, knowledge, and hope.[23] Like Will's coat converted from Mazie's, such an attitude suggests that we inherit possibilities and hopes from the previous generation. Our task is to sort, discard, and piece, to find what is fitting for a life of commitment to human unfolding, and out of our inheritance, to weave a garment for today.

Women have long been needleworkers. They have designed their art for beauty and warmth. Piecing images, Olsen is a word worker, a designer of life in fiction, poetry, and report. Like earlier women workers, she starts with what is needed. Her vision of truth and beauty begins with the essentials: voice, place, affirmation, warmth, light, way.

A MOSAIC OF MEANINGS

Journeying, blossoming, and piecing together suggest the vision evoked by Olsen's writing. Each elicits a matrix of meanings that can be used effectively as an interpretive grid for reading Olsen's stories. Viewed together, their meanings offer a way of understanding three central and interwoven concepts in Olsen's writing, and "lead us somewhere" in religious ponderings: journeying suggests the struggle for place, identity, and community engaging all humanity, while blossoming reflects the hope for each individual—and for the whole earth—to attain fulfillment and to become whole. The piecing metaphor points to a new spirituality wherein individual and community gain grace and freedom through patterns of life that are mutually enhancing. Faithfully sorting from the past what is usable for a new earth, a new humanity, and a new sense of divinity, we gain the transcendence of Spirit as the miraculous power that makes things new.

Together, the metaphors evoke a set of meanings. All point to human desires for coherence, pattern, continuity, fullness, and connection. All suggest a sense of intergenerational responsibility. The roots of future generations are planted today, and the direction and resources of the present generation were yielded from the past. Human responsibility flows both ways—toward root and blossom—past and future. The dead are not lost as long as we struggle in their name, and bondage to time is overcome in faithful telling of the dreams that inspirit us.

The metaphors imply moving, direction, and purpose. They are historical images connecting resource and yield, nature and creativity. Earth and human, ancestor and grandchild, material and intellect, male and female are bound in imagistic visions. And in each, the desire for "more" compels human action. Olsen's metaphors reflect her own representative hope for her characters and suggest the ultimate vision inspiring her fiction: a universe in which we act as though human quests are the very matter of truth and where no person, no hope, is ultimately lost.

Wholeness is holiness, the words describe an existence in which no part is broken, impaired, injured, or useless. Rather, every element, resource, action, decision, person is remembered and integrated.

The vision offered by the metaphors sustains the actual and often despairing struggles of the characters and thus is a lens for a liberation theology, which begins where people today struggle for bread, civil rights, and freedom of expression. To integrate the seeming conflict between vision and historical reality, Olsen draws her images as a paradox: beauty is created from seeming ugliness, the hope for a new life is born out of degradation and despair, the "pieces" that may mold a better world come from fragmented lives of hurt and disease, even from the graves of our ancestors.

Conclusion

The miraculous is not, for Olsen, the extraordinary, but the ordinary: birth, small acts of kindness forged in darkness and loss, learning, art, songs of faith, moments of meditation, creativity in all of its forms. Everyday life is the miracle she limns and celebrates.

The morality her writing elicits transcends all human-made divisions and depends upon the possibility that people can become essentially caring. Olsen's stories and prose offer an understanding of what is right as what enhances human growth and potential. Thus, her vision points to experience and need as the legislators of morality. In our reading, we have called the powers of life and sustenance (in traditional language, God) the encouraging presence of love evolving with humanity in the quest for fulfillment and beauty. Human responsibility, then, is for nothing less than the co-creation of the world. In such a vision of possibility, all actions have ultimate potential because they make us who we are; they give us identity and purpose.

It is only a step from Olsen's moral understanding to her prophetic vision. Mutual love and care will not only make possible more abundant living individually but will redeem the struggles of generations before who have striven for a more humane and beneficent universe, transforming all human losses into an expansive pattern of living, which we continue with our own lives. Thus are we participants in the ongoing struggle of humanity *and of God* to be free and committed, independent and yet bound in relation to those things that concern Being most deeply.

Critical to the religious awareness Olsen's writing offers are the characters, settings, dilemmas, themes, and metaphors drawn from and reflecting historical female experience in domestic spheres. For example, while socialist Jewish men often broke radically with traditional religious practice and the sacred spaces and texts of orthodox religious understanding, Jewish women were never full participants in that religious life. Like most American women of the same period, turn-of-the-century Jewish women attracted to new ideologies still largely maintained their life activities in the spheres of action and with the values they had traditionally inhabited and sustained. The sacred space of Olsen's foremothers, like the stories they wrote with their lives, were primarily, though never exclusively, domestic.

Bringing to light the essential values and ethics of women's caretaking as well as the hindrances, encumbrances, and silences of mothering, Olsen's fiction—insofar as we interpret its implications for understanding the depth dimension of human life—gives critical voice to a religious consciousness arising out of women's historical experience. Its criticism of religion is a criticism of traditional, male-dominated religions, and its prophetic vision of blossoming life reveals a spiritual understanding that has long undergirded and empowered women: the belief that making life possible is a holy activity. The feminist bent of Olsen's world attitude simply extends that belief to women's own lives. It is also holy to nurture oneself and to ask for encouragement from others that one may experience one's own fulfillment.

We may, as Olsen's writing imagines, hear the voices of truth, like Mazie, in the wind, or, as Alva does, receive a divine message from a child. Some still need another to speak for them because they cannot yet speak for themselves. But Tillie Olsen's vision is for a world in which we ourselves—men and women—are born in our own voices, as we search for truths that may redeem us in our own stories of faith.

Olsen is one writer who has told her truth. Other women writers—voices out of Africa, Latin America, Eastern Europe, and elsewhere—are telling their stories. We have much to learn from them of truth, journey, spirit, and way. In the past we have feared this plenitude, preferring instead one text, one truth, one way (all male authored in our Western Jewish and Christian traditions). It is time to read new stories and old stories newly told. It is time for the truth in women's lives to find hearing and voice. Why do we fear expansiveness, Tillie Olsen's literature asks. What small God binds our hands and mouths, fearing human talents? Mysteries remain; Olsen's world offers no new idols. Instead her vision frees us to imagine our lives as if our living mattered, as if our care leads to care and our hope to hope. Every life is a potential text for understanding the depths of human longing and possibility, and human actions undertaken in the Spirit of Holiness are the hope of our salvation.

☐ Notes ■

1. Dorothee Soelle, *The Strength of the Weak: Toward a Christian Feminist Identity,* trans. Robert and Rita Kimber (Philadelphia: Philadelphia Press, 1984), p. 91.

2. Page references to Olsen's books given in the remainder of the chapter are to the editions noted in the bibliography. The Olsen entries in this casebook's bibliography correspond to the editions Orr uses.

3. The phrase is the title of Morton's recent book.

4. Olsen's phrase.

5. *Myths and Motifs in Literature,* ed. David J. Burrows, Frederick R. Lapides, and John T. Showcross (New York: The Free Press, 1973), p. 135.

6. Christ does not suggest a monolithic understanding of women's questing but carefully asserts that she is describing "*a* common pattern" in women's literature. Christ, *Diving Deep and Surfacing* (Boston: Beacon Press, 1980).

7. Houston A. Baker, *The Journey Back: Issues in Black Literature and Criticism* (Chicago: University of Chicago Press, 1980), p. 1.

8. Nelle Morton, *The Journey Is Home* (Boston: Beacon Press, 1985), p. 227.

9. Bernard Malamud, *The Fixer,* quoted in James Cone, *God of the Oppressed* (New York: The Seabury Press, 1975), p. 147.

10. From Olsen's personal files, written in the seventies or early eighties.

11. Olsen, *Silences,* p. 6.

12. Olsen's phrases, used in the first chapter of *Silences,* where she speaks of her own experience.

13. Alice Walker, *In Search of Our Mothers' Gardens* (San Diego: Harcourt Brace Jovanovich, Publishers, 1983), p. 240.

14. Ibid., p. 241.

15. Olsen, "Dream-Vision," p. 261.

16. These phrases come from notes or transcriptions of talks in Olsen's personal files.

17. From Olsen's personal files.

18. From Olsen's personal files.

19. Miriam Schapiro, "Notes from a Conversation on Art, Feminism, and Work," in *Working It Out,* ed. Sara Ruddick and Pamela Daniels (New York: Pantheon Books, 1977), p. 296.

20. In French, a "bricoleur" is a Jack of all trades, a professional do-it-yourself person. Claude Levi-Strauss uses the concept of "bricolage" to describe the human process of creativity and coming to knowledge that is practiced by one who, with limited resources, puts things together in novel ways. See "The Science of the Concrete" in *The Savage Mind* (Chicago: The University of Chicago Press, 1966), pp. 16–33.

21. Tillie Olsen, telephone interview with the author, July 1984.

22. Tillie Olsen. Quoted by Naomi Rubin, "A Riddle of History for the Future," *Sojourner* (July 1983): 4.

23. Rubin makes this point in her summary introduction of Olsen in "Riddle of History."

☐ JOANNE TRAUTMANN BANKS ■

Death
Labors

> We shall not cease from exploration
> And the end of all our exploring
> Will be to arrive where we started
> And know the place for the first time.
> T. S. ELIOT,
> "Little Gidding"*

They look so different on the page, these two seemingly similar stories.[1] Tolstoy's paragraphs are long, his sentences complete and declarative, his words richly abundant. His page is
filled in. In contrast, Olsen works with empty space as if it
were as important an element as language. Many of her sentences are fragments, italicized, parenthetical. These are not
only styles of writing for Tolstoy and Olsen; they are also, as I
hope to show, styles of living for their main characters. It is
the deepest irony that in order to die well, the characters must
reconstitute—even repudiate—the very styles that the authors
have used so brilliantly.

It is all, finally, a matter of identity. Can these two
people, Olsen's old woman[2] and Tolstoy's Ivan Ilych (or can
any of us, for that matter), die as they (or we) have lived? Can
they carry into the last scene of their lives' dramas the same
roles, the same selves, that they have built with such energy
in the preceding acts? Tolstoy and Olsen say "no." The people
who go to meet death in these stories are not the people who

From *Literature and Medicine* 9 (1990): 162–171.

*Excerpt from "Little Gidding" in *Four Quartets*, copyright © 1943 by T. S.
Eliot and renewed 1971 by Esme Valerie Eliot, reprinted by permission of
Harcourt Brace Jovanovich, Inc.

existed before their illnesses intervened. Cancer has challenged every dimension of their lives.

Before her cancer, the old woman in "Riddle" had largely based her identity on her service to others, rather than on her own primary needs. The field theory psychologists, who believe that one's personhood can be explained as the focus of one's relationships, would probably find her a clear instance of their concepts.[3] As Olsen develops her, however, the elements of her identity are loosely connected. There are significant spaces between them. There is a literal one, for instance, in her geographical identity. The early part of her life was spent in revolutionary Russia; all the rest, in America. Metaphorically, the experience in America is separated by a vast space from her intellectual, political life in Russia. Even apparently intimate spaces are wide. To her daughter's statement that the mother lived all her life *for* people, she replies, "'Not *with*'" (italics mine). The spaces are not precisely voids, any more than the spaces between Olsen's paragraphs mark major hiatuses. Some sort of meaning inheres in them. But, like Rosencrantz and Guildenstern in Tom Stoppard's play of that name about Hamlet, the old woman has perhaps not been the main character in her own drama. She has had to work out her identity in the parentheses, as it were, between other people's utterances. She has found her self in life's interstices.

The same phenomenon can be described in terms of space's correlative, time. There was never time in the old woman's life to finish a project in the way she would have preferred, seldom time even to finish reading a story by her favorite, Chekhov, let alone live a life of the mind. She believes that all her life she has been *"forced to move to the rhythms of others,"*[4] and thus there are major discontinuities in her experience of her self.

"Discontinuity"—that's Olsen's term. In her study of the barriers to creativity, she suggests that discontinuity is a pattern imposed on women's lives.[5] In context, it's clear that she means women whose lives are defined for many of their adult years by maternal exigencies and the Sisyphean tasks of daily housekeeping. She cites the old woman in "Riddle" as an instance. In her case, the discontinuities and spaces are the inevitable consequences of having so many children to raise

200

in a condition of constant poverty, and with a passionate husband (she grants that his desires are the "most beguiling" interruption of them all). She is an "outsider" not only because of her gender and her class, but also because of her Jewishness.[6] Even within that tradition, she is an outsider, an atheist who spits on religion's conventions as oppressive. Outsiders prowl the circle of society, taking on such identities as they have in opposition and at great cost to creativity.

Then comes the cancer. When the disease is doing its initial damage, the old woman does not, of course, know about it—at least in the usual sense of "knowing." She knows in terms of D. H. Lawrence's fleshly knowing.[7] Her body has a consciousness of sorts, and it immediately begins to communicate with her mind: in concert they prepare to die. For instance, there is good reason to blame the agitation she feels on outside causes, namely, her husband's insistence that they sell the house where she feels comfortable and move to a retirement community. But she wonders "if the tumult was outside, or in her." She "knows" she has cancer. It "knocks" on "the great ear pressed inside." Because of its insistence, she begins to explore her life and to rebuild the identity she will need in the near and urgent future.

But "explore" implies cognitive acuity, and the old woman's disease eventually attacks that function. Early on, as is common in age, her recent memories fade in favor of those from long ago, and finally she expresses herself only in isolated snippets. It would seem that in a grotesque extension of her lifelong habits, her identity in the final days lies scattered around her, as if—in a phrase of Yeats from another context entirely—"the centre cannot hold" ("The Second Coming"). And yet she *is* exploring. "'No pills, let me feel what I feel.'" Even in neurological disarray, the old woman has the power she needs.

Significantly, her given name is not revealed until now, when the story is nearly over. She has always been "Ma" or one of a series of insulting epithets hurled by her husband in their mutual game of bitterness—"Mrs. Unpleasant," "Mrs. Excited Over Nothing," "Mrs. Word Miser." Her name is Eva.

Eva's job, her last one, is to recollect herself. She accepts this position without question. It is what she must do before she can die meaningfully. Her method will be to undo, to reverse in some ways, and to balance the style by which she has lived thus far. That is, she will fill in some of the gaps in space and time that have prevented her from having a solid self. She will attempt to connect the prose of her life as a beleaguered mother and wife with the poetry that somehow still fuels her.[8]

At her core there is solitude. But it is not, she discovers, the same thing as emptiness. In fact, at this stage of her life, she relishes it, refusing to give it up by moving to a communal life, even creating it artificially, if necessary, by turning off her hearing aid. She senses that from the silence will come the identity she needs: "in the reconciled solitude, to journey to herself." Eva moves, instinctively Olsen seems to suggest, to the ocean's edge, there to look "toward the shore that nurtured life as it first crawled toward consciousness the millions of years ago." Eva is herself engaged in seeking her beginnings.

Soon the necessary data come. Though they come in scraps, they also come in torrents—words from beloved books and speeches, music from her idealistic youth. Her husband is shocked; she has not spoken of these things for decades. Hiding in the body of this frail, embittered, and normally silent woman is the young girl with noble dreams for humankind. She has survived all this time in the memory cells. At this point, Olsen introduces a poetic image for a scientific truth: it seems to Eva's husband that "for seventy years she had hidden a tape recorder, infinitely microscopic, within her, that it had coiled infinite mile on mile, trapping every song, every melody, every word read, heard, and spoken." The memories are so intense that they are almost real presences for Eva in her deteriorating but (or therefore?) receptive state. She is reunited in this sense with her girlhood friend and mentor, the aristocratic rebel Lisa, for whom, because she is a follower of Tolstoy, knowledge is holy and to be shared among all classes.

If times and spaces have thereby been reconnected for Eva, the achievement has been bought at a terrible price. This woman, whose hands were always busy with a child, now can scarcely bear to touch one. In Sylvia Plath's memorable image from "Three Women," a baby's cries are "hooks that catch and grate like cats." Eva's grandchildren are vessels of vitality, from which she knows she must detach herself. The full context of a phrase already quoted is: "Somewhere coherence, transport, meaning. If they would but leave her in the air now stilled of clamor, in the reconciled solitude, to journey to herself." One grandchild entreats her to tell him a riddle, but she is not playful. She has not time for life's inherent ambiguities. Her task requires that she leave even her husband. As he listens to the "tape recorder" of her past, he hears nothing of their springtime love or their joyful hours as a family. For him, it is the moment of bitterest grief. By her last day, Eva has left present time entirely. She is now ready to enter the final turnstile, as she must, alone.

It would be wrong to conclude that Ivan Ilych has the simpler task just because for most of his life he has a more secure sense of self. I am inclined to think, as a matter of fact, that constructing an identity from scraps is easier than dismantling a rigid one. But the latter is precisely what Ivan Ilych must do if he is to die in peace.

His problem has its origins, as Eva's did, in the literary choices made by the author. It is almost as if a certain style of dying is irrevocably linked with certain aesthetic conventions. Olsen's organization and rhythms are basically lyrical;[9] her point of view, essentially a post-Jamesian center of consciousness, wherein the world is only as real as an individual's perception of it. The poetic subjectivity extends to her title, which begs for multiple interpretations. Tolstoy works within a very different mode. He has the advantages, and the limitations, of a linear, realistic style. From the bluntly explicit title on, he and his readers assume some truthful correspondence between what he describes and the world as we agree to see it. His voice is the one long known in narrative theory as *omniscient*. Because Tolstoy's talent and insight persuade readers that he deserves to declare such a perspective on human events, the narrator speaks with great authority. This powerful presence has philosophical consequences for Ivan Ilych. Consider, for instance, the finality that sounds in this famous sentence: "Ivan Ilych's life had been most simple and most ordinary and therefore most terrible." Like realists before and after him, Tolstoy takes the nature of society as his arena. He also practices satire as an extension of both his social interests and his omniscient stance. That is, the satire results from his looking closely at institutions such as the family, law, and medicine, and judging them wittily on the basis of firmly held values. A story that will end as powerfully as any in literature begins hilariously as a satirical look at the behavior of self-centered "mourners," who see Ivan Ilych's death solely in terms of its interruption of their own affairs.

Ivan Ilych's life style partakes of Tolstoy's literary stances, and, with one necessary exception,[10] might even be seen as a parody of them. True, Ivan Ilych is not a purveyor of satire among his friends (at least so far as we know), but he has the satirist's smug certainty that his or her values are the proper ones from which others depart at their peril. He thus tells himself the story of his own life omnisciently without ever questioning his assumptions. Furthermore, he is firmly anchored in society's abundant details, and this too is a parallel with Tolstoy's style. If Eva is an outsider, Ivan Ilych is clearly an insider, living in the public world of power. "Think: If Tolstoy had been born a woman," muses Olsen in *Silences*.[11] Socially created realities are for Ivan Ilych the only realities. He derives his identity from the opinions of others of his rank and time.

Ivan Ilych has not so much lived his life as built a résumé. His professional credentials are impeccable. He has accepted the ladder as a metaphor for success, and he has moved up it at regular intervals, ending pleasantly above the midpoint of the judicial bureaucracy. He is, in Willy Loman's pitiful phrase from *Death of a Salesman*, not only liked, but well liked, chiefly because he conducts his relationships with propriety and decorum (two terms that are very important to him). When he furnishes a house, he chooses those items that will make him appear to be rich; it has nothing whatever of the personal about it. But neither has his personal life. In his youth, his sexual relationships were conducted "with clean hands, in clean linen, with French phrases." When it is time to marry, he chooses a woman whose background will look good, as it were, on his résumé under the biographical details section. That the marriage turns hostile distresses him chiefly because of his wife's "coarse" demands for attention. He has had a few setbacks, but in his opinion everything has gone on the whole very satisfactorily indeed, and the evidence indicates that the second half of his life should be even better.

He has allowed no space for major contingencies. His illness nearly breaks him in two, so rigid has he become. In contrast, Eva bends like a bamboo tree in the wind. She accepts her coming death far more easily and sets to work on what must be done. For Ivan Ilych, disease is a gross impropriety against which he rages ineffectually for much of the story.

At the same time, his anger serves as a powerful corrosive that begins little by little to weaken the false girders of his life. I need not repeat the phases of his torment and terror. They have in fact been given a kind of renewed fame among medical educators by virtue of their being a nearly perfect example of Kübler-Ross's stages of dying.[12] But it is important to my argument to note that the process involves the tearing down of almost all his previously held tenets. That moving *up* and *on,* for instance, is the only criterion for success. Is he now a failure, and his life meaningless, because he is horizontal? That cleanliness in bodily functions somehow mysteriously insures the social order. Now that he must be helped with his excretions, has all turned to shameful chaos? That professional people ought always to affect indifference to their clients. Since the doctors he consults do not listen to him, what does that say about his years in the law? That a certain aloofness in human relationships, even in marriage, maintains decorum. Why will not his friends and his family comfort him? That a gentleman does not ask too many questions about life. Do gentlemen, then, live in basic and mutually supportive deceit, especially as regards the absolute fact of one's death? Perhaps most insidious of all: that he is a man, when inside he is a little boy crying out to be pitied. Ivan Ilych has "to live thus all alone on the brink of an abyss."

Of course, there is the pain. The pain is ghastly and ought not to be paraphrased, even if that were possible. But just as *Ivan Ilych* prefigured Kübler-Ross, so does the story demonstrate what many clinically experienced philosophers and theologians have said about the distinction between physical agony (pain) and mental agony (suffering). Suffering is the worse torture. If suffering can be reduced, pain can be endured. If life has been meaningful, death can be likewise.

As part of his attempt to understand, Ivan Ilych takes a journey that is at one point similar to Eva's. Both return to their youth for substance—Eva to connect with what she already feels to be good and true, Ivan Ilych to understand his child self for the first time. To be sure, his early venture into childhood memories elicits one of the most poignant passages in the story. Thinking of the well-known syllogism that ends "therefore Caius is mortal," Ivan Ilych refuses to accept that *he* is mortal. Caius is abstract logic. But he, Ivan Ilych, had once been a little boy called Vanya with a mamma and a papa and a beloved striped ball. Little Vanya cannot die!

Near the end, he returns more often to his childhood, savoring what we would now call Proustian sensations. Life, he concludes, was better and more vital then. In fact, the closer he comes to his beginnings, and the farther he gets from death, the more real he feels. That may be fear speaking, but it leads to another conclusion that carries more conviction: his entire life has been lived in false rectitude except for those "scarcely perceptible attempts to struggle against what was considered good by the most highly placed people." They alone had been real. This awareness is hardly freeing. In fact, with this insight, he has reached the bottom of his despair. Immediately, his pain multiplies tenfold. Ivan Ilych had come as far as he can alone.

But why is he so isolated? Where, in particular, are the doctors and the nurses? Part of the answer is that in both *Ivan Ilych* and "Tell Me a Riddle" doctors are portrayed as scarcely necessary to the dying people. Olsen is not negative about them;[13] they simply do their jobs at the periphery of the central drama. Tolstoy goes farther. His physicians make themselves irrelevant by virtue of their self-importance. They deceive their patient and themselves. After putting on an inappropriately cheerful, "there now" face in the mornings, they cannot take it off. Ivan Ilych eventually consults several doctors, each of whom disagrees pompously with the others. If their characterizations were not set into the midst of an otherwise tragic tale, their essential natures—which are straight out of a Molière comedy—would be clearer.

The nurses are another matter altogether. The servant

Gerasim performs nursing functions for Ivan Ilych, and, in "Riddle" Eva's granddaughter Jeannie, who is in fact a professional nurse, does the nursing alongside Eva's husband. Neither Gerasim nor Jeannie accomplishes very much in terms of a conventional plot. Gerasim has very few sentences to himself, and Jeannie does nothing overtly dramatic. Oddly, that is good news for everyone who attends a dying person. It seems to demonstrate that in these two situations, at least, a great deal can be accomplished with the simple means available to most of us. On the plot level that I have been developing, the nurses are really midwives who assist in the paradox of the eleventh-hour birthing.[14]

Gerasim exemplifies Tolstoy's well-known view of the peasant as a kind and simple type. Innocent of the supercilious posturing of Ivan Ilych's family, friends, and doctors, Gerasim alone acknowledges directly that Ivan Ilych is going to die: "Only Gerasim recognized it and pitied him." The young servant finds caring for Ivan Ilych's body neither distasteful nor burdensome, but a natural, democratic act that he hopes will one day be done for him. He thereby helps Ivan Ilych in his central task of breaking down his rigid ideas about propriety. With Gerasim, Ivan Ilych is able to practice intimacy, never a valued part of his identity until now. Jeannie is more sophisticated than Gerasim, but her reactions to dying are, like his, direct, kind, and nonjudgmental. With perfect tact, she brings Eva a Mexican cookie, the "Bread of the Dead," made by a mother in the likeness of the little girl she has just lost. The cookie becomes the occasion for a conversation about grief in which Eva participates comfortably. She says that Jeannie is like the Russian Lisa, that mentor-midwife from long ago.

Eva is an atheist. I am not sure whether or not she is to be taken for a good person. But there is something deeply spiritual about how, in the face of physical agony, she yet makes a last-minute search for meaning among the shards of humankind's attempts to connect. Jeannie senses this. She is nearly incoherent in expressing it—but when has transcendent experience ever been easy to verbalize? To explain her "radiant" face of love to her grandfather, she replies "'my darling escape' . . . 'my darling Granny.'" Olsen expands the

207

thought: "(Shameful the joy, the pure overwhelming joy from being with her grandmother; the peace, the serenity that breathed.)" Thus is the midwife paid.[15]

As for Eva herself, has she reached her goal by the time she dies? We have only Jeannie's report: "On the last day, she said she would go back to when she first heard music, a little girl on the road of the village where she was born. She promised me. It is a wedding and they dance, while the flutes so joyous and vibrant tremble in the air." Vibrant flutes—this is not the way Eva remembered the scene earlier: "*a bare-footed sore-covered little girl . . . danced her ecstasy of grimace to flutes that scratched at a cross-roads village wedding.*" Therefore, if Jeannie has repeated her grandmother's words accurately, it may be that Eva has indeed seen through to the truth.

> And the end of all our exploring
> Will be to arrive where we started
> And know the place for the first time.

We can follow Eva no farther towards her wished-for reunion.

Tolstoy lets us experience the fulfillment. When Ivan Ilych realizes that his life has been false, his task is almost completed, though he does not yet know it. He has not only broken down the past, he appears to have emptied himself of any identity at all. He is like an empty vessel, waiting to be filled. And he is filled, with light and with joy. His rebirth occurs just as his pathetic little son comes into the room, takes up his hand, and, weeping, kisses it.

People have offered theological, psychological, and something like scientific interpretations of such a phenomenon. For Tolstoy, the theological, as understood in the Western world, is paramount. Ivan Ilych is rewarded with peace at that moment when he asks for forgiveness from God. Suddenly, "there was no fear because there was no death." This cannot mean that there is no dying, for Ivan Ilych goes on immediately to die, but that because of faith, death has no sting, the grave no victory.[16] His pain too is still real, but now just a given, and no longer a reminder of his absurdity: "'Let the pain be.'" Therefore, he is infused with light and joy. Psychologically, Ivan Ilych changes at the moment when he sees oth-

208

ers as real. He feels his son's pain, and later his wife's, and he is relieved of the burden of himself. The result is light and joy. Using the methods of the social sciences, the authors of two recent books have concluded that, whether for physiological reasons or others, many dying people do in fact report seeing light, feeling joy, and going gladly.[17]

Much mystery remains. Fortunately, I am obliged to pick up only one small part of it. I have tried to establish that Olsen's and Tolstoy's literary styles parallel the lifestyles of their main characters—loose, personal, and fragmented in the first case; tight, social, and linear in the second—and that, to die happily, the characters must at least partially revise the authors. If I am right, why does this revolt of character against creator happen? It is possible, though unlikely in these cases, that the authors intend it. So the unconscious gapes. I cannot believe that the revolt is due to the authors' unconscious self-hatred, wherein they are punished by their very own creatures. In fact, something healthy may be going on. Here is how my thinking runs: These authors are enormously successful. But success tends to reinforce past methods, and the method that succeeds sooner or later becomes the method that limits. Maybe the unconscious minds of these two deeply creative writers have allowed their characters to break down old forms, not in revolt but in exploration of new possibilities for Tolstoy and Olsen. If so, the pattern is recognizable. It is that type of death labor we call evolution.

☐ Notes ∎

1. I have used the Louise and Alymer Maude translation of Leo Tolstoy's 1886 novella *The Death of Ivan Ilych,* in *The Death of Ivan Ilych and Other Stories* (New York: New American Library/Signet, 1960), 95–156. Tillie Olsen's story "Tell Me a Riddle" was first collected in *Tell Me a Riddle* (New York: Dell, 1961), 63–116. All subsequent quotations are from these editions.

2. She is only sixty-nine, an age our society no longer considers old, but that is how Olsen conceives of her. In Tillie Olsen's *Silences* (New York: Dell, 1983), 58, she makes a reference to the character as "old mother, grandmother."

3. E.g., Harry Stack Sullivan and Kurt Lewin.

4. Like several others in the story, this phrase is italicized as if to underscore meaning seized on the run.

5. Olsen, *Silences*, 58.

6. "Outsider" is Virginia Woolf's term in *Three Guineas* (1938), a feminist volume that Olsen frequently cites in public lectures and private conversations.

7. D. H. Lawrence developed this concept throughout his work. See, e.g., his letter to Ernest Collings (17 January 1913) in *The Portable D. H. Lawrence* (New York: Viking, 1947), 563: "My great religion is a belief in the blood, the flesh, as being wiser than the intellect."

8. "Only connect the prose and the passion, and both will be exalted": a phrase from E. M. Forster's novel, *Howard's End* (1910), and used, in part, as its epigraph.

9. In the sense defined by Ralph Freedman in his influential study, *The Lyrical Novel: Studies in Hermann Hesse, André Gide, and Virginia Woolf* (Princeton, N.J.: Princeton University Press, 1963); that is, a fiction that emphasizes personal experience as revealed through poetic methods more than strictly narrative forms.

10. The clarity that derives from Tolstoy's fervent Christianity.

11. Olsen, *Silences*, 268.

12. Elisabeth Kübler-Ross, *On Death and Dying* (New York: Macmillan, 1970).

13. Eva's first physician misses the diagnosis, but this serves an aesthetic rather than moral goal in that it allows Olsen to observe what I have termed Eva's "Laurentian" behavior while the cancer is still unknown to her intellect.

14. It may be helpful to see their methods as Rogerian. Carl R. Rogers, who believed that the good therapeutic relationship was paradigmatic of any good interpersonal activity—and that the object of both was to help others become persons—outlined three conditions for the helper. He or she was to be "congruent" (i.e., genuine), to have "unconditional positive regard" for the client, and to evince "accurate empathy." See "The Necessary and Sufficient Conditions of Therapeutic Personality Change," *Journal of Consulting Psychology* 21 (1957): 95–103.

15. Cf. Mary de Santis, the private duty nurse in Patrick White's novel, *The Eye of the Storm* (New York: Viking, 1974), for

whom the care of an elderly, disintegrating woman is a religious experience.

16. I Corinthians 15:55 (KJV).

17. Karlis Osis and Erlendur Haraldsson, *At the Hour of Death,* rev. ed. (New York: Hastings House, 1986); and Raymond A. Moody, Jr., *Life After Life* (New York: Bantam Books, 1976). Cancer, or any lingering terminal illness, provides time for this kind of death labor, but Moody accumulates evidence that the same process, much condensed, also occurs in some traumatic near-death experiences.

Motherhood as Source and Silencer of Creativity

From one of her earliest pieces of writing—"I Want You Women Up North to Know" (1934)—to one of her most recent—*Mother to Daughter, Daughter to Mother* (1984)—Tillie Olsen has been passionately interested in mothers as writers and as subjects of literature. Motherhood as both source and silencer of creativity is one of Olsen's main themes, and she has spent her life rescuing mothers from silence, inarticulate awe, distortion, and sentimentality.

In her afterword to *Mother to Daughter, Daughter to Mother,* Olsen says that even in this book about mothers, "least present is work written by mothers themselves. . . . Whatever the differences now (including literacy, small families), for too many of the old, old reasons, few mothers while in the everyday welter of motherhood life, or after, are writing it. That everyday welter, the sense of its troublous context, the voice of the mother herself, are the largest absences in this book. And elsewhere" (275–76).[1]

It does not take much imagination to discover what the "old, old reasons" are. One reason mothers have not written their stories is that women have been told, blatantly or subtly, that they must choose between motherhood and other creative work, including writing. (Olsen lists in *Silences* the many women writers who were childless, some by choice, many because they were convinced they had no choice.) Another old

From *Protest and Possibility in the Writing of Tillie Olsen* (Charlottesville: University Press of Virginia, 1993), 35–63. Condensed with the permission of the author.

reason is the myth that motherhood is ineffable, that it is an experience so immured in nature that no one can find the words to write about it. According to this myth, mothering is something mothers intuitively know how to do but cannot explain to anyone else. This notion sets them apart from everyone—their childless sisters, the fathers of their children, and a sterile society. The underside of the myth of ineffability says that even should a woman have the confidence and time to write about motherhood, that experience is too ordinary, narrow, and dull to interest anyone except, perhaps, mothers themselves. A third reason why mothers have not told their stories is "the patriarchal injunction" Olsen describes in *Silences,* which tells women writers to avoid subjects belonging to the "woman's sphere," not because they are ineffable but simply because they are female. This injunction says to women, "If you are going to practice literature—a man's domain, profession—divest yourself of what might identify you as a woman" (250). Since mothering is an undeniably gendered mark of identification, women writers who want to succeed should avoid this subject at all costs.

Mothers have not fared much better as subjects. Their sons and daughters have often settled for grim or glowing stereotypes, and those stereotypes have passed for truth. As Adrienne Rich writes in *Of Woman Born,* it is "easier by far" for daughters to "hate and reject a mother outright than to see beyond her to the forces acting upon her."[2] Of course, some few writers in every generation have challenged the stereotypes. Daughters of immigrant mothers and daughters growing up in poverty have created portraits of mothers that are both loving and unstintingly honest, and are filled with grief, anger, and, sometimes, admiration. Edith Sumner Kelly's *Weeds* comes to mind, as do Agnes Smedley's *Daughter of Earth* and the novels of Anzia Yezierska. This is the tradition in which Olsen wrote her stories about mothers and mothering. But because most of these works went out of print soon after their publication and have only recently been reprinted, the tradition has been invisible to most readers.[3]

A more contemporary reason for the silence by and about mothers is that feminist writers and critics disagree about the value of this subject. While many contemporary feminists share Olsen's interest, there is by no means a consensus. In a review of May Sarton's 1985 novel, *The Magnificent Spinster,* Valerie Miner reveals this uneasy split: "For anyone dismayed by the current feminist infatuation for motherhood, it is refreshing to read a novel in which the women do stand on their own."[4] Olsen's interest in mothering can hardly be termed infatuation—it is neither fleeting nor romantic— yet she is determined to bring to light not only the oppression mothers have suffered but also "the yields possible in circumstanced motherhood," as she says in *Silences.* She is well aware that loving and admiring depictions of motherhood might be read as reproaches by women who have chosen to remain childless. Several years after her famous 1971 talk at the Modern Language Association Forum on Women Writers in the Twentieth Century, Olsen reflected that she barely touched the subject of the gifts mothers give, fearing that the many childless professional women in the audience would hear her remarks as one more version of the "traditional (mis)use" of the joys of motherhood "to rebuke and belittle the hard-won achievement of their lives; more of the societal coercion to conform; family as the only suitable way of life for a female" (*S* 202).

A stanza from "Cellar Door," a recent poem by Sue Standing which Olsen includes in *Mother to Daughter, Daughter to Mother,* expresses another familiar dilemma Olsen shares with other women writing about their mothers:

> Her hands stained and nicked
> from all the peeling, cutting, blanching—
> beautiful how she touched things,
> how quickly she could thread a needle.
> I'm not supposed to love her for this—
> smoothing our hair, sewing our clothes,
> or on her knees waxing the floor.

Showing mothers' domestic work as beautiful and admirable might seem to women readers like reinforcements of limiting roles or as calls to duplicate the patterns of their mothers' lives.

Olsen's life and the content of her work stand in direct opposition to these reasons, old and new, that have made motherhood "the least understood, the most tormentingly complex experience to wrest to truth" (*S* 254). Her life as a writer and working mother of four daughters contradicts the idea that mothering and writing are by their very nature mutually exclusive activities. Although she writes eloquently in *Silences* of the domestic and economic structures that limited her writing and almost prevented it altogether, she writes just as eloquently of the ways in which her life as mother gave her the substance of her work.

In almost everything she has written, Olsen delineates the distorted shape motherhood has taken in patriarchal society and critiques the cluster of beliefs about it that have been passed on as truth from generation to generation. It is part of her revolutionary work of helping to change "what will not let life be" for women. But Olsen's repudiation of patriarchal motherhood, that "last refuge of sexism," as she calls it,[5] is not in any sense a rejection of mothers or mothering. On the contrary, Olsen considers mothering one of the great untold stories of women's lives and one of the great unmined sources of literary marvels. (Unlike Rich, who uses the word *mothering* to mean the experience and *motherhood* to denote the institution, Olsen uses these words interchangeably. Only the context makes her meaning clear. I will follow Rich's usage throughout this chapter, however.) Olsen insists in *Silences* that the losses to literature and to many other fields of knowledge and endeavor have been incalculable "because comprehensions possible out of motherhood (*including,* among so much invaluable else, *the very nature, needs, illimitable potentiality of the human being—and the everyday means by which these are distorted, discouraged, limited, extinguished*) . . . have had . . . to remain inchoate, fragmentary, unformulated (and alas, unvalidated)" (202). The task she has set for herself is to bring those comprehensions to "powerful, undeniable, useful expression" (202). . . .

She writes in *Silences* that "conscience and world sensibility are as natural to women as to men; men have been freer to develop and exercise them, that is all" (42). This conviction seems to have come to her . . . from her own life experiences and from knowing committed socialist women like her mother and the Bundists Seevya and Genya Gorelick, the

216

women to whom she dedicates "Tell Me a Riddle." This is the story in which a mother's "world sensibility" is most evident, and it seems to be more than coincidence that Olsen began writing it in 1955–56, the year in which all three women died.[6] Olsen found in them and in her own life the combination of experiences that do lead mothers to political consciousness and a commitment to change that reaches far beyond their own families. That combination includes early political involvement, wide reading, and a knowledge of history. In several of her characters, most notably Eva in "Tell Me a Riddle," Olsen brings to "useful expression" a mother's world consciousness.

Finally, Olsen understands well the chasms that exist between mothers and their daughters, and between women who are mothers and those who are not. Yet her work reveals her belief that only full and honest remembering, neither distorted by bitterness nor softened by nostalgia, can bridge those chasms. One of the ways in which Olsen accomplishes this many-faceted task is by embodying in three complex sets of images a blight-fruit-possibility paradigm. Specifically, she uses three constellations of images, centering on hunger, stone, and flood, to describe the blighted circumstances of mothers' lives, to express wonder at the fruit of endurance and beauty their lives have borne, and to sketch the joyful possibilities that mothering could hold for women and for the world. But Olsen transforms these three sets of images into one another with the logic of poetry or dream, setting up echoes and oppositions both within and between works. In the discussion that follows, I will try to show what these image patterns mean and, at the same time, follow their intertwined, shifting course through Olsen's work.

The first of these image patterns revolves around hunger and food. In everything Olsen has written—her poetry, fiction, essays—she uses the language of eating, of feast and famine, of nurturing and starvation, of fat bellies and skeleton children to show a blighted world. In several works—most notably *Yonnondio*—hunger is a literal fact of life, the obvious result of chronic, institutionalized poverty; but in every work, spiritual, emotional, and intellectual hungers gnaw even at those characters who are well fed.

The images of food and eating also suggest that life is meant to be a banquet in a plentiful, generous world. In a world of possibility, feeding is an expression of gracious and generous nurturance in an interlocking human and natural ecology; and hungers for food, justice, knowledge, and beauty are all part of the healthy reaching out to life. Even the dead become nourishment for the living. But, at least on the surface, that is not the world of Olsen's stories. She shows us instead a world where to survive one must take food from others. Hunger, of necessity, becomes savagery; food snatched from others and hastily devoured is tasteless; and nourishment given binds people to each other through unending need.

Although Olsen is concerned with all hungry people, the hungers of mothers and children preoccupy her most. Even one of her earliest poems, "I Want You Women Up North to Know," is filled with the familiar images of starving mothers and their children. There is Catalina Rodriguez, age twenty-four, her "body shrivelled to a child's at twelve, / and her cough, gay, quick, staccato, / like a skeleton's bones clattering"; and Catalina Torres, who "to keep the starved body starving, embroiders from dawn to / night," spurred on by "the pinched faces of four huddled / children / the naked bodies of four bony children, / the chant of their chorale of hunger."[7]

Yonnondio picks up these images of physical deprivation, showing impoverished mothers and their families living in a world that feeds on them instead of providing nourishment. Through Olsen's multiple vision we see both men and women caught in poverty; this same vision, however, shows us the further devastation suffered by poor women, as the additional overlay of sexism leads husbands to feed off their wives and forces mothers and children to devour each other's substance. . . .

In "Tell Me a Riddle," Olsen shows even more clearly than in *Yonnondio* the grotesque shape of motherhood in the patriarchy and the immense cost of the institution to mother and children. Again, she totals up the cost by filling this story with the language of starvation, feeding, and eating. Eva, the central character, is a grandmother, with her years of pregnancy and child rearing far behind her. Yet in describing her, Olsen uses images that suggest both pregnancy and starvation. Eva is a little gnome, "all bones and swollen belly," with clawlike hands and a "yellow skull face"—the portrait of starvation that stares at us daily from posters and television screens. Those closest to her see her as something edible. David, her husband, and Nancy, her daughter-in-law, try to persuade her to move from her familiar home to the Haven, a "cooperative for the aged" run by David's lodge. When she refuses, they leave her to "stew a while," as Nancy puts it. But perhaps more important, the language of food both expresses and shapes Eva's perception of herself and of the people and events surrounding her. When David complains to the children about her harsh tongue, she thinks, "(Vinegar he poured on me all his life; I am well marinated; how can I be honey now?)" Her quarrel with David over selling the house becomes a "bellyful of bitterness," her sickness she feels as a "ravening inside," and her children are "morsels" with "lovely mouths" that "devour."

Linda Yoder describes well one purpose of this "overwhelming concentration of [food] imagery." It underlines, she says, Eva's overidentification with her role as mother "against which Eva will wisely, though painfully, struggle."[8] In other words, Eva's life has been so completely absorbed by nurturing others that these activities have taken over her ways of thinking and feeling and even her language. To borrow Olsen's imagery, they have eaten her up.

It was a brilliant stroke on Olsen's part to make Eva a grandmother living in the relatively affluent fifties rather than in the hungry twenties of *Yonnondio*. For Eva, the tasks of mothering that used up Anna's life are only memories, or have dwindled into unimportance. Instead of skimpy meals stretched to feed nine, now "a herring out of a jar is enough." While David worries about money, Eva shrugs, "In America, who starves?" The ironic answer to this question is that mothers starve even in America and even long after they have stopped being responsible for their children and no longer have to contend with physical hunger.

Against her family's urging, Eva refuses to nurture her grandchildren in the traditional mothers'/grandmothers' ways—holding, comforting, feeding—because she knows she dare not let herself be drawn again into the "long drunkenness" of needing and being needed, of devouring and being devoured by trusting children. Yet it is significant that she never abandons the language of food and hunger, and at the end of her life talks deliriously about "bread, day-old" and "one pound soup meat." Furthermore, Olsen's omniscient narrator continues to use this language to describe Eva, suggesting that motherhood as defined and structured in patriarchal society starves mothers by absorbing them body and spirit. Eva is hungry for all the nourishment that her life has refused her or that she has resolutely given away to be true to herself and her beliefs. She is hungry for both solitude and community, silence and language. (Eva even *tastes* and *chews* words and ideas.) Unaware that he is accurately describing her spirit as well as her body, David reminds Eva that she is "all bones and a swollen belly." All David sees are the symptoms of her illness; but here, as in *Yonnondio,* Olsen wants her readers to see mocking visual echoes of starvation and pregnancy which, mirroring each other and her illness, together form the shape of Eva's life.

In her fine essay "The Hungry Jewish Mother," Erika Duncan sets "Tell Me a Riddle" in the context of Jewish-American literature by women. In this literature, writes Duncan, "mothers are the 'bread givers' who try to make feeding into a replenishing, ecstatic act. But the mothers are themselves starved in every way, sucked dry and withered from being asked almost from birth to give a nurturance they never receive. They are starved not only for the actual food they are forced to turn over to others, but for the stuff of self and soul, for love and song."[9] That is the blighted life mothers lead in patriarchal society. As Olsen would say, that is the life of most women, past and present, as they carry the full weight of gender, class, and sometimes racial bias. We also see clearly the ways in which the mothers' hungers are visited upon their children, especially their daughters, who, like Anna's Mazie and Eva's Clara and Hannah, are reduced to "hands to help."

But to stop with grief and anger is to stop far short of Olsen's destination. The second element of her structuring paradigm, the fruit borne by the blighted tree, is nowhere more evident than in her portraits of mothers. For Olsen's fictional mothers possess intelligence, courage, and a gritty determination to survive, no matter how insurmountable the obstacles they face. What is more, in every story, mothers reach beyond survival to make their children's lives richer and wider than theirs have been. Sometimes they succeed; more often they fail. But even in failure, Olsen says, the most nourishing bread they give future generations is the coarse grain of their courageous effort. An important part of the task Olsen has set for herself is to acknowledge this nurturance. She does so by setting remembered moments of beauty and exaltation in mothers' lives in their context of pain and struggle.

This combination of beauty and struggle is evident in a remarkable passage from *Yonnondio,* in which the rhythms of Olsen's prose transform work that might be seen only as absolute drudgery into grace. It is no accident, of course, that the work Olsen describes is that of preserving food. The scene occurs on an unbearably hot day in a long line of such days, and Anna is in her kitchen canning fruit, making jelly, and tending her children all at the same time. Here is a portion of that scene. Read aloud, its rhythms work their way into the body:

> In the humid kitchen, Anna works on alone. . . . The last batch of jelly is on the stove. Between stirring and skimming, and changing the wet packs on Ben, Anna peels and cuts the canning peaches—two more lugs to go. If only all will sleep awhile. She begins to sing softly—*I saw a ship a-sailing, a-sailing on the sea*—it clears her head. The drone of fruit flies and Ben's rusty breathing are very loud in the unmoving, heavy air. Bess begins to fuss again. *There, there, Bessie, there, there,* stopping to sponge down the oozing sores on the tiny body. *There.* Skim, stir; sprinkle Bess; pit, peel, and cut; sponge; skim, stir. Any second the jelly will be right and must not wait. Shall she wake up Jimmie and ask him to blow a feather to keep Buss quiet? No, he'll wake cranky, he's just a baby hisself, let him sleep. Skim, stir; sprinkle; change the wet packs on Ben; pit, peel and cut; sponge. This time it does not soothe—Bess stiffens her body, flails her fists, begins to scream in misery, just as the jelly begins to boil. There is nothing for it but to take Bess up, jounce her on a hip (*there,*

there) and with her free hand frantically skim and ladle. *There, there*. The batch is poured and capped and sealed, all one-handed, jiggling-hipped. There, there, it is done. (148–49)

In a recent talk, Olsen said that only when she read this scene aloud to an audience did she realize that Anna's movements had the economy and disciplined grace of dance. "We gladly applaud for dancers on the stage," she said, "but do not recognize the similar grace and miracle of synchronization" of a mother, her baby on one hip, canning and tending her other children. Olsen added that she likes to imagine Anna's granddaughters as dancers, whose freer lives Anna had made possible with her hard work and loving determination. [10]

There is danger in this kind of writing. Turning relentless work into a dance could lead to the kind of sentimentality that perpetuates the work by casting the softening glow of nostalgia over it and that encourages daughters to repeat the surface patterns of their mothers' lives. That Olsen is alert to this danger is clear from the scenes following this domestic dance, in which the same event is seen as a mother's daily deadly toil; her skilled and useful labor to feed her family; and a moment of beauty that is as necessary and nourishing as canned peaches and amber jelly.

The multiple tasks push Anna to trembling, and her tenderness with the children is mixed "with a compulsion of exhaustion to have done, to put Bess outside in the yard where she can scream and scream outside of hearing and Anna can be free to splash herself with running water, forget the canning and the kids and sink into a chair, lay her forehead on the table and do nothing" (149–50). But Anna does not stop; she keeps working through the afternoon, surrounded by her heat-sickened children. Late in the day, as Anna still works, the sun—shining through a prism salvaged from the dump—sheds rainbows on the room. Mazie watches as the rainbow falls on Anna: "Not knowing an every-hued radiance floats on her hair, her mother stands at the sink; her knife seems flying. Fruit flies rise and settle and rise." Mazie, with her quick appreciation for beauty of any kind, says lovingly, "Momma" (152).

222

Light and shadow chase each other across these few pages, as Olsen's style turns drudgery into dance and back into drudgery, and then, for a fleeting moment casts "the stammering light" of beauty and promise over the whole scene. The cycles of poverty and sexism that rule *Yonnondio* will end this moment and perhaps steal it from Mazie's memory. (In "Tell Me a Riddle," Eva's delirious, deathbed singing reminds her oldest daughter, Clara, of a sound she has not heard or remembered since childhood. Clara cries in silent anguish, *"Where did we lose each other, first mother, singing mother?"* Even knowing well that moments like this one are often lost to daughters, Olsen has chosen to preserve it as precious and nourishing without in any way exalting the toil or urging future generations of daughters to repeat it.

To return to Duncan's phrase, Olsen's fictional mothers are "bread givers" dedicated to feeding their children's bodies, minds, and hearts. But Olsen shows another, equally important yield of "circumstanced motherhood." Because the experience of mothering, coupled with the other crucial experiences I described earlier, gives them what Olsen calls "a profound feeling about the preciousness of life on earth,"[11] the other fruit their lives sometimes bear is an awareness of justice and injustice that reaches beyond the walls of home and family. Olsen dramatizes this sense of justice most powerfully in Eva, who like the Seevya and Genya of Olsen's dedication, had been a revolutionary during her girlhood in Russia, has memorized her few books, and knows both past history and the United States of the 1950s. To understand what Olsen is saying about Eva's wide-ranging consciousness we need to return to the image of bread, this time superimposed on the recurring image of stone.

Bread and stone run parallel to each other through most of "Tell Me a Riddle." In the scene just before Eva's death, they leave their parallel tracks, meet, and undergo that transmutation of shape and meaning that Olsen uses so powerfully. In Eva's last delirious words, these two images reveal that her embattled love for her family and her desire to create a more just world for everyone are somehow the same passion, felt with the same intensity and fed by the same springs. David keeps watch by her deathbed and listens as she repeats bits from her memorized books, the facts of destruction in human history, snatches of songs, and speeches from their revolutionary past. They are litanies of courage, hope, and terror for the human race:

> *Slaveships   deathtrains   clubs   eeenough*
> *The bell   summon what enables*
> *78,000 in one minute* (whisper of a scream)
> *78,000 human beings   we'll destroy ourselves?*

and:

> *Lift high banner of reason* (tatter of an orator's voice)
> *justice   freedom   light*
> *Humankind   life worthy   capacities*
> *Seeks* (blur of shudder) *belong   human being*

As David listens, it seems to him that Eva is "maliciously . . . playing back only what said nothing of him, of the children, of their intimate life together." He says to her, knowing she cannot hear him, "A lifetime you tended and loved, and now not a word of us, for us." Finally Eva's words work their way into his consciousness, and he too remembers the idealism of their youth, the ways he has conspired with society to betray those ideals, "and the monstrous shapes of what had actually happened in the century." To ease himself, he thinks of their grandchildren, "whose childhoods were childish, who had never hungered, who lived unravaged by disease in warm houses of many rooms, had all the school for which they cared, could walk on any street, stood a head taller than their grandparents, towered above—beautiful skins, straight backs, clear straightforward eyes. . . . And was this not the dream then, come true in ways undreamed?"

The answer to David's question is *yes*, but only if one is thinking in individualistic terms. For Eva, *family* and *children* have meanings that extend far beyond tight biological definitions. Thoughts of the well-being of her own family have never allowed Eva to escape into complacency, and now, having fallen under her spell, David cannot escape either. He answers his own question "as if in her harsh voice":

> *And are there no other children in the world? . . .*
> *And the flame of freedom, the light of knowledge?*
> *And the drop, to spill no drop of blood?*

Eva's sense of responsibility for all the children of the world also deepens her sense of helplessness and grief. One of her hungers is surely the hunger and thirst for justice, and her starving body, that "swollen thinness," imitates as if by sympathetic magic the bodies of children not so well-fed as her own. Now, under Eva's influence, David begins to feel her lifelong starvation. He piles a tray with food, eats it, but "still was there thirst or hunger ravening in him."

As David realizes how much of his own idealism has been lost, he is filled with wonder that Eva has not lost or betrayed her dreams. But when David asks her to affirm their wide-ranging vision, Eva answers with memories of their private life together, and bitter memories at that:

> *Still she believed?* "Eva!" he whispered. "Still you believed? You lived by it? These Things Shall Be?"
>
> "One pound soup meat," she answered distinctly, "one soup bone."
>
> "My ears heard you. Ellen Mays was witness: 'Humankind . . . one has to believe.'" Imploringly: "Eva!"
>
> "Bread, day-old." She was mumbling. "Please, in a wooden box . . . for kindling. The thread, hah, the thread breaks. Cheap thread"—and a gurgling, enormously loud, began in her throat.
>
> "I ask for stone; she gives me bread—day-old." He pulled his hand away, shouted: "Who wanted questions? Everything you have to wake?" . . .
>
> Words jumbled, cleared. In a voice of crowded terror:
>
> "Paul, Sammy, don't fight.
>
> "Hannah, have I ten hands?
>
> "How can I give it, Clara, how can I give it if I don't have?"
>
> "You lie," he said sturdily, "there was joy too." Bitterly: "Ah how cheap you speak of us at the last."

This short scene is, among other things, a small masterpiece of ironic humor; even this close to death, David and Eva talk

225

in parallel monologues, their memories as unsynchronized as their lives in America have been.

What interests me most, though, is David's remark, "I ask for stone; she gives me bread—day-old." This is a witty reversal of the New Testament passage in which Jesus describes the mercy of God with this homely comparison: "Is there a man among you who would hand his son a stone when he asked for bread?" (Matt. 7:9).[12] The reversals move in every direction. David asks not God or his father for sustenance, but rather his dying wife. He also reverses the usual connotations of bread and stone. The nourishment David asks for to feed his ravenous hunger is the stone of unshakeable faith in life rather than bread, which at best is perishable; day-old, it is a mark of poverty and defeat. Of course, David attributes Eva's refusal to give him the nourishment he needs to her contrariness. The fact is that she is not answering his questions at all, but following the associative drift of her own memories. What Olsen gives us is a picture of Eva's thoughts and a hint of her influence, finally, on David. Although Eva can articulate the link only in fragments, in her mind, the personal and the political are knitted together. In the early part of this scene, Eva will not let David rejoice in his own family's health and lose sight of the world's hungry children; here she will not let him take refuge in dreams of political change that do not encompass the often dreary realities of family life, where mothers must struggle alone to make ends meet.

That familiar split between the personal and political has no place in Olsen's writing. As Catharine Stimpson writes: "Given her sense of American politics, Olsen cannot show the achievement of the good dream, only its transformation into terror or its dissolution. When the dream is dissipated, as it is for the American-born children of Russian revolutionaries in 'Tell Me a Riddle,' its political contents, its sense of 'the flame of freedom, the light of knowledge,' are lost. Only its personal contents are gratified. Without the political, the personal is merely materialistic."[13] I would add, however, that in Olsen's feminist vision, the reverse is also true: in patriarchal America, without the personal, and especially without a consideration of the lives of women and children, the political is empty theory, espousing equality on street corners or in labor halls while ignoring the deep ills of family life.

Just as the personal and the political, reality and idealism are fused in this scene, so are the images of bread and stone. If we read the rest of the story with this fusion in mind, earlier references to stone take on unexpected meanings. Two such references give insights into the marvels Eva's life can yield to the alert reader and the ways in which her life breaks out of the isolation of motherhood.

Early in the story, as part of his campaign to get Eva to move to the Haven, David shouts at her, "You sit, you sit—there too you could sit like a stone." Critic Mary DeShazer says that this description, along with David's epithet, Mrs. Word Miser, turns Eva into a "silent, Sphinx-like hoarder of words" who, in struggling with the Sphinx's question, "What is Man?" finds both the question and the answer inadequate to human experience, and more specifically, to women's experience. As DeShazer writes, "Man has been too long the seeker of and answer to the riddle . . . ; woman too must identify the quest. Traditionally woman has been unable to riddle, for she has lacked the power to name her own experience."[14] While David glibly matches his grandchildren riddle for riddle, the silent, searching Eva says she knows no riddles. It would be more accurate to say that she knows no answers to the riddles that torment her and certainly none that she could tell a child.

While this image of Eva as Sphinx is provocative, I think Olsen expects or, more realistically, hopes that her readers will also see in this woman sitting "like a stone" Rebecca Harding Davis's korl woman from *Life in the Iron Mills*, the book Olsen rescued from oblivion. The korl woman is rock hard, "crouching on the ground, her arms flung out in some wild gesture of warning." She is hungry, her maker Hugh Wolfe says, not for meat but for "summat to make her live." Far from being inscrutable like the Sphinx, she has a "wild, eager face like that of a starving wolf's." She is the product not of an ancient civilization, but of American industrial society, carved from the waste material from the iron mill. Her maker is an illiterate miller who, with no hope of ever becoming anything better, is cursed or blessed with an artist's eye and hands and heart. The korl woman's form is "muscular, grown coarse with labor"; one of the visitors to the mill, looking at the "bony wrist" and "the strained sinews of the instep," describes her as a "working woman,—the very type of her class." The visitors see in her gesturing arms both "the peculiar action of a man dying of thirst" and "the mad, half-despairing gesture of drowning." Finally, the sympathetic narrator of the story, who keeps the carving after Hugh Wolfe's suicide, says that the korl woman has "a wan, woeful face, through which the spirit of the dead korl-cutter looks out, with its thwarted life, its mighty hunger, its unfinished work. Its pale, vague lips seem to tremble with a terrible question. 'Is this the End?' they say,—'nothing beyond?—no more?'"[15]

These are Eva's questions. She asks them not only about her own life and the life of her son, Davy, who was killed in World War II, but also about all those lives wasted by war and by many kinds of starvation. In her delirium, she says: "Tell Sammy's boy, he who flies, tell him to go to Stuttgart and see where Davy has no grave. And what? . . . And what? where millions have no graves—save air." Her most tormenting questions are "when will it end?" and "Man . . . we'll destroy ourselves?"

Whether as Sphinx or korl woman or both, after a lifetime of being bread, Eva has conspired with the circumstances of her life to change herself into stone. This becomes clear if we look at another important passage, shortly after she has refused to hold her newest grandson. She spends the afternoons shut in the closet in her daughter's home, trying to protect herself from her family and their needs. As her mind travels impressionistically from subject to subject, she repeats to herself her grandson Richard's lesson on rocks: "Of stones . . . there are three kinds: earth's fire jetting; rock of layered centuries; crucibled new out of old (igneous, sedimentary, metamorphic). But there was that other—frozen to black glass, never to transform or hold the fossil memory . . . (let not my seed fall on stone). . . . (stone will perish, but the word remain). And you, David, who with a stone slew, screaming: Lord, take my heart of stone and give me flesh." Shortly before this, Richard had given her two specimens to start her own rock collection, the first a trilobite fossil, the second a piece of obsidian, shiny and impervious as glass. It is as if Eva is pondering which kind she is, seeing the risks of being stone rather than bread. In her pondering, the meanings of stone shift, reach back into myth and history, and take on a dizzying ambiguity. Eva wants to become, and somehow leave for the world, something that will last, outliving her body and keeping her beliefs alive, green and burning in its heart. She knows that bread spoils or is devoured, leaving children always hungry for more. She wants instead to be the kind of rock that is shaped by history or the kind that holds "the fossil memory," to be cherished by a future generation of children collecting the wisdom of the past.

The line, "And you, David, who with a stone slew, screaming: Lord, take my heart of stone and give me flesh," is puzzling at first. David is of course the biblical David who killed Goliath with a stone from his slingshot, but from there on, the scriptural reference will lead us astray if we follow it too closely. (The David story is from the first Book of Samuel [17:36–58], while the second half of the quotation comes from the Book of Ezekiel, where it is reported as the word of God spoken to the people of Israel through the prophet [36:26–27].) By this time Olsen has made it clear that Eva is not an observant Jew, having rejected her religion as a young girl. What she knows of Scripture is probably meant to be a mixture of early memories and gleanings that are simply a part of Judaeo-Christian culture. Olsen frequently shifts the meanings of biblical passages, sometimes slightly, sometimes radically, often with ironical results. Here David is not the heroic savior of his people but a slayer in a world where death breeds death. He might represent David her husband, whose imperviousness to her needs has been in some way deadly to both of them; he might be her son Davy, who killed and was killed in World War II; he might be her gentle friend Lisa, who killed an informer with her teeth; he might be humankind, all of us implicated in death even as we pray for the ability to love. David might be Eva herself, hardening her heart, and in so doing betraying herself and others. For Eva faces the danger that she will simply be "frozen to black glass," closed to love or pity, a stone on which no seed can grow. (In another kaleidoscopic shifting of images, seed comes to mean life itself, the grain made into bread, children, and the word.) Eva continues her pondering, "(stone will perish, but the word remain.)" She is no doubt thinking of her beloved authors and orators and, with despair, of all her own unspoken words, which, if she could only say them, would outlive her.

In creating a character like Eva, a woman and a mother who has somehow kept all these supposed opposites alive within her, Olsen shows that even in the patriarchy mothering bears fruit. In the scene from the end of the story that I described earlier, day-old bread and inedible stone are transformed into a feast, as Eva and her granddaughter Jeannie teach each other the intricate relationships between life and death and together teach David. Jeannie gives Eva the easeful knowledge that at last someone has heard and understood the lessons her life taught her.

I have said that in describing Eva's swollen body, Olsen superimposes the images of fatal illness, starvation, and pregnancy in order to show the terrible cost exacted by poverty and patriarchal motherhood. For Olsen, even this nightmare image suggests possibilities that for me were completely unexpected. In this scene David finally comes to understand the breadth and fidelity of Eva's life. For the first time in years, perhaps for the first time in their marriage, he sees her in her full humanity, "dear, personal, fleshed," and instead of coining one more ironic epithet, he calls her by name. He sees Jeannie's sketch of himself and Eva, their hands clasped, "feeding each other"; obeying the images, he lies down, "holding the sketch (as if it could shield against the monstrous shapes of loss, of betrayal, of death) and with his free hand [takes] hers back into his." In this scene, David and Eva feed each others' starvation (the "ravening" each feels) and in some way give birth to each other, their hands umbilical cords, and Jeannie the midwife. The tragedy here is that it is her life as mother, as bread and bread giver, that made Eva's perceptions possible and at the same time commanded her silence. For Eva the birth and the saving nourishment come too late. But Olsen gives the wisdom of Eva's life to her readers through the words of this story, this imperishable stone.

Although Olsen is convinced that even "circumstanced

motherhood" is the source of marvels in life and in literature, her writing always urges her readers to look beyond the circumstances, beyond marvels that can be enjoyed by future generations but never by mothers themselves and rarely by their own children. Her radical subtext—the possibility beneath her prose—insists that mothering in its literal meaning and in all the extended meanings she gives it in her fiction and nonfiction is meant to be tender, ecstatic, explosively creative, and revolutionary, not in some yet-to-be-created utopia, but in this world. This may seem at first like a rash misreading, since Olsen continues to argue as she has throughout her writing career that the circumstances in which mothers and children live make full human development impossible. Almost fifteen years ago, she wrote in *Silences:*

> Except for a privileged few who escape, who benefit from its effects, it remains a maiming sex-class-race world for ourselves, for those we love. The changes that will enable us to live together without harm . . . are as yet only in the making (and we are not only beings seeking to change; changing; we are also that which our past has made us). In such circumstances, taking for one's best achievement means almost inevitably at the cost of others' needs.
>
> (And where there are children. . . . And where there are children. . . .) (258)

One might expect her view to have changed to match the changes that have occurred in women's lives in the intervening years. But while Olsen acknowledges gratefully that at least in some places technology and the women's movement have combined to broaden mothers' horizons and lessen the drudgery of their lives, she insists rightly that mothers still bear "the major responsibility for the maintenance of life, for seeing the food gets there, the clothing, the shelter, the order, the cleanliness, the *quality* of life, the binding up of wounds, the attention to what is happening, roof after roof." She also asserts that societal structures in the United States still make it impossible for mothers to raise their children except "at the cost of [their] . . . best, other work." [16] Finally, she continues to point out to anyone who will listen that for many mothers, in the United States and throughout the world, even the meager gains of the past few decades are out of reach.

On the other hand, since the beginning of Olsen's writing career, she has implied that things do not need to be the way they are for mothers. *Silences,* for example, is filled with statements like these: "No one's development would any longer be at the cost of another" (222n); the silencing of mother-writers is "(unnecessarily happening, for it need not, must not continue to be)" (39); and of the mother-artist Käthe Kollwitz, she marvels at what might be "if—needed time *and* strength were available simultaneously with 'the blessing,' the 'living as a human being must live' . . . (as, with changes, now could be)" (212). "Could be," "not yet," "so far"—these persistently hopeful phrases, scattered like seed in *Silences* and in her talks and interviews, are the explicit counterparts of the hopeful subtext of her fiction.

I do not believe that Olsen's sketching of the creative possibilities of mothering falls into the "current infatuation with motherhood" Valerie Miner deplores. In her fiction, Olsen never suggests that mothering should take the place that romantic love, or more recently, sexual experience, has held in literature as the one and only route to maturity and selfhood available to women. On the contrary, in suggesting the possible, Olsen deflates many overblown features of the motherhood mystique. That deflation is an important strategy in making the possible real. Once again, the imagery of hunger, eating, and feeding shows us how she accomplishes this multilayered task.

In Olsen's fiction, the language of hunger almost always holds two elements of her basic paradigm folded within one image: starvation, greed, and something close to cannibalism on the one hand, and a passionate give-and-take that replenishes the body and spirit on the other. This imagery suggests that when hunger of any kind is not distorted by inequality and injustice, it is healthy, generous, curious, and eager for connections. It leads to equality rather than domination. Even on the most literal level, hunger expresses a desire to stay alive; and giving food both sustains life and expresses a faith that life is worth sustaining. On the figurative level, her imagery acknowledges that, consciously or unconsciously, each generation feeds on the wisdom and work of ancestors and contemporaries as well as on the promise of children. In the face of no matter what betrayal or hypocrisy, meals in Olsen's work are communal, the flat-out denial of individualism.

A few examples will serve to show that, for Olsen, being healthily hungry is almost synonymous with being healthily human, not just for mothers and children but for everyone. In a fine passage from *Silences*, she quotes Whitman's belief that "American bards . . . shall be Kosmos, without monopoly or secrecy, glad to pass anything to anyone—hungry for equals by night and by day." Olsen adds her impassioned interpretation of what this hunger for equality means:

> O yes.
>
> The truth under the spume and corrosion. Literature is a place for generosity and affection and hunger for equals—not a prizefight ring. We are increased, confirmed in our medium, roused to do our best, by every good writer, every fine achievement. Would we want one good writer or fine book less? . . .
>
> Hungry for equals. The sustenance some writers are to each other personally, besides the help of doing their best work.
>
> Hungry for equals. The spirit of those writers who have worked longer years, solved more, are more established; reaching out to the newer, the ones who must carry on the loved medium. (174)

Given favorable conditions, creation and relation feed each other. Again from *Silences*, "So long they fed each other—my life, the writing—; —the writing or hope of it, my life" (20). Even the conscious and subconscious levels of the human person feed each other: "Subterranean forces can make you wait, but they are very finicky about the kind of waiting it has to be. Before they will feed the creator back, they must be fed, passionately fed, what needs to be worked on" (13). In Olsen's fiction, everything is meant to be tasted and chewed. David urges Eva to taste the beauty of the California seacoast, and in "Hey Sailor, What Ship?" Lennie and Whitey share the pleasure of "chewing over . . . the happenings of the time or the queerness of people." For Olsen, literal and figurative images of hunger express the healthy, essential needs of every part of the human psyche and of the human community, becoming a wedding of body and spirit and a powerful force drawing people out of isolation toward each other.

The logic of Olsen's imagistic connections between hunger and mothering raises a further question: What would mothering look like if it were not maimed by the "sex-class-race world" in which it now exists? I believe Olsen's answer is exactly the same as the answer to the same question about hunger: mothering could be, *can* be healthy, generous, curious, eager for connections, even rapturous. Olsen's language again suggests possibilities of both starvation and plenty. Eva calls her children *morsels*. Suggesting something small, fragile, and tasty, this word holds both potential menace and tenderness. David says to Eva, "You are the one who always used to say: better mankind born without mouths and stomachs than always to worry for money to buy, to shop, to fix, to cook, to wash, to clean." Eva's answer—"How cleverly you hid that you heard. I said it then because eighteen hours a day I ran. And you never scraped a carrot or knew a dish towel sops"—reveals that she was not renouncing hungry people or the task of feeding them but rather the unspoken rules of the patriarchal family.

David calls Eva "a woman of honey," meaning, of course, the opposite; Eva concurs with his opinion of her, thinking during an argument, "(Vinegar he poured on me all his life; I am well marinated; how can I be honey now?)." This exchange would seem to reinforce the image of Eva as food, and bitter food at that, but Olsen gives neither David nor Eva the last word. As she often does, here she uses David's ironical epithet to tell some deeper truth about Eva, . . . whose wisdom she wants her readers to taste, and find nourishing and even delicious.

Another important passage linking mothering and hunger goes even further in suggesting possible yields. It is the famous one in which Eva tries to explain to herself why she cannot hold her grandson: "Immediacy to embrace, and the breath of *that* past: warm flesh like this that had claims and nuzzled away all else and with lovely mouths devoured; hot-

234

living like an animal—intensely and now; the turning maze; the long drunkenness; the drowning into needing and being needed." Eva uses similar words to describe her daughter Vivi, caught in "the maze of the long, the lovely drunkenness" of mothering. With some justification, critics have described this passage on mother love as "violent" and the language that of addiction or even cannibalism.[17] I propose a parallel—or perhaps subterranean—interpretation, suggested by words like *intensely, maze, lovely drunkenness,* and *drowning,* all of which say that mothering can be an ecstatic experience having much in common with intense creative and communal activity. Olsen creates here something far more interesting than a new version of the cliché that turns mothering into a metaphor for the creative process. Instead, she suggests that mothering is one of many analogous human experiences that involve one wholly, dissolving tight boundaries and sweeping one into "the seas of humankind." Because of their power, such experiences are both dangerous challenges and exhilarating adventures; they threaten annihilation and at the same time promise fullness of life.

The images Olsen uses for all these experiences—the flood, the high tide, the powerful underground river—seem to have come to her early from the 1934 San Francisco longshoremen's strike. At any rate, they appear for the first time in "The Strike," her account of that event. The longshoremen are a river "streaming ceaselessly up and down, a river that sometimes raged into a flood, surging over the wavering shoreline of police, battering into the piers and sucking under the scabs in its angry tides. HELL CAN'T STOP US. . . . That was the meaning of the seamen and the oilers and the wipers and the mastermates and the pilots and the scalers torrenting into the river, widening into the sea."[18] Flood images almost disappear in the landlocked heat of *Yonnondio;* we hear them only briefly in Anna's songs—"Oh Shenandoah I love your daughter / I'll bring her safe through stormy water," and "I saw a ship a sailing / And on that ship was me." They reappear more than twenty years later in the stories collected in *Tell Me a Riddle* and later still in *Silences.* I suspect that the expanded meaning of this imagery in later works reflects what twenty years as mother and writer taught Olsen about the hidden

235

emotional similarities among seemingly disparate experiences. Several passages that use flood images to characterize such experiences will show what those lessons were.

In "O Yes," innumerable images of drowning and baptism mingle with each other to describe Carol's experience of being drawn into black religious experience and into caring for lives other than her own. The church choir sings:

> *Wade,*
> *Sea of trouble all mingled with fire*
> *Come on my brethren it's time to go higher*
> *Wade wade*
> (*R* 57)

Carol tries to separate herself from the explosive pain and joy of the black congregation by focusing on "a little Jesus walk[ing] on wondrously blue waters to where bearded disciples spread nets out of a fishing boat." But the voices sweep over her "in great humming waves" and she feels herself drowning into "the deep cool green": "And now the rhinestones in Parry's hair glitter wicked; the white hands of the ushers, fanning, foam in the air; the blue-painted waters of Jordan swell and thunder; Christ spirals on his cross in the window—and she is drowned under the sluice of the slow singing and the sway" (57–58).

A passage from "Tell Me a Riddle" picks up similar images of flood and drowning to describe Eva's experience of mothering: "It was not that she had not loved her babies, her children. The love—the passion of tending—had risen with the need like a torrent; and like a torrent drowned and immolated all else" (92). Olsen then describes Eva's early revolutionary spirit and the new tasks she believes old age holds for her; the flood imagery declares the commonalities between these three phases of Eva's life: "On that torrent she had borne [her children] on their own lives, and the riverbed was desert long years now. Not there would she dwell, a memoried wraith. Surely that was not all, surely there was more. Still the springs, the springs were in her seeking. Somewhere an older power that beat for life. Somewhere coherence, transport, meaning" (92–93).

Finally, Olsen echoes both "O Yes" and "Tell Me a Riddle" when she describes in *Silences* the experience of writing and how it feels when writing has to be deferred. For her and for the writers she quotes (James, Woolf, Gide, Kafka), writing is "*rapture;* the saving comfort; the joyous energies, pride, love, audacity, reverence wrestling with the angel, Art—" (173). She describes the many times in her life when she had to "leave work at the flood to return to the Time-Master, to business-ese and legalese" (21).

In using this flood imagery to forge links between mothering and other absorbing, creative work, Olsen obviously is not repeating the "moldy theory" that all women must be biological mothers in order to claim their womanhood (*S* 16); nor does she mean that mothering can or should absorb a woman's whole life. Finally, she is not bitterly or ironically setting mothering alongside political action, religious experience, or writing only to reveal by contrast its dull passivity. On the contrary, her imagery suggests that, far from being dull and repetitive, mothering could and should be high adventure, calling forth compassion, courage, and wonder. It could and should be like art, Olsen says in *Silences,* in "the toil and patience," but also in the "calling upon total capacities; the reliving and new using of the past; the comprehensions; the fascination, absorption, intensity" (18). In addition, viewing mothering as art and as a source of art can help dismantle the walls between women who are mothers and women engaged in other creative work and, at the same time, help bring together the often fragmented selves within individual women.

By demonstrating that her life as mother was one of the main sources of her writing, and in taking the further step of making mothers' lives the center of much of her fiction, Olsen counters one of the old notions about mothers I described at the beginning of this chapter. This notion claims that mothering is an experience so immured in nature there are no words to express it. Olsen's imagery tells a homelier truth: that mothering is neither more nor less expressible, neither more nor less sunk in silence than any other experience that involves one's whole being. Just as it is difficult but possible to write about making love, creating a poem, teaching well,

237

marching on a picket line, or nursing a dying grandmother, it is difficult but possible to write about mothering.

Annie Gottlieb's 1976 book review entitled "Feminists Look at Motherhood" helps me to understand the weight of Olsen's influence in bringing mothering out of the hazy, romantic half-light that has obscured it for so long. Gottlieb writes about an honest and joyous dialogue between her, a writer with no children, and her youngest sister, who had just given birth to her first child. It is a dialogue, says Gottlieb, that would have been impossible only a few years earlier:

> The birth of my sister's baby would have divided us irrevocably from each other—and from ourselves. She would have passed, for me, into a closed, dim world, inarticulate, seductive and threatening, made up of equal parts of archetypal power and TV-commercial insipidity. And for her, it would have been hopelessly beyond the reach of words she could not begin to formulate and would in any case not have dared to utter, because they would have violated all the accepted canons of motherhood.
>
> She might have feared my educated contempt, for motherhood, while cloyingly idealized, was in no way honored as either a source or an accomplishment of human intelligence.[19]

Gottlieb attributes the newfound possibility of communication between herself and her sister to the women whose books about motherhood she is reviewing (Alta, Jane Lazarre, and Adrienne Rich). Their work was made possible, she says, by the Women's Movement, "which in turn has drawn inspiration from the work of a few pioneers—foremost among them Tillie Olsen." For Gottlieb, Olsen "*feels* like the first, both to extend 'universal' human experience to females and to dignify uniquely female experience as a source of human knowledge."[20] Although Olsen would hasten to name many predecessors to whom she herself is indebted, I agree with Gottlieb that Olsen is certainly the first whose works have been widely read, studied, and discussed.

In the fifteen years since Gottlieb wrote that tribute, dozens of books about mothers, mothering, and motherhood have appeared, and it is true that what Valerie Miner terms "this current infatuation with motherhood" might be traced to Olsen. But Olsen never sets mothers against women like May Sarton's magnificent spinster who "stand on their own." In fact, she does the opposite. As Gottlieb says, Olsen's writing has directly and indirectly helped to create connections "between body and mind, between female experience and the realm of thought, between a woman who at this moment is predominantly a mother and one who at this moment is a writer."[21] While Olsen continues to show clearly the differences among women, including those between women who are mothers and those who are not, she steadfastly affirms that those differences are not inherently divisive, ought not to be used as weapons of reproach or sources of guilt, and do not lend themselves to ranking except when one is obeying the dictates of patriarchal thought.

Gottlieb writes that "between the 'experience' of motherhood and the patriarchal 'institution,' a system of man-made myths and 'false-namings' exists that twists the experience itself into something far more anguished and confining than it would naturally be. What it could be under vastly different circumstances we cannot fully know."[22] Olsen's stories express more powerfully than those of any other writer I know the needless anguish and confinement, asking that her readers, sons and daughters all, "enter the pain" of their mothers' lives.[23] But Olsen never gives up on the possibility that pregnancy, birth, and the essential arts of mothering could be one way for a woman to give birth to herself; they could be replenishing acts for mothers, their children, and a hungry society. In the imagery of Olsen's fiction, they could be hearty bread, stone that preserves the valuable lessons of the past, and a flood filled with life.

☐ Notes ■

1. Citations of Olsen's major works appear in the text. I have used the following editions and abbreviations: *Mother to Daughter, Daughter to Mother* (Old Westbury, N.Y.: Feminist Press, 1984); *Silences* (New York: Dell, 1980), designated as *S*; *Tell Me a Riddle*

(New York: Laurel-Dell, 1981); and *Yonnondio: From the Thirties* (New York: Laurel-Dell, 1981), designated as *Y.*

2. Adrienne Rich, *Of Woman Born: Motherhood as Experience and Institution* (New York: Bantam, 1976), 237.

3. For example, Edith Sumner Kelly's *Weeds* was published in 1923 and was not reprinted until 1972, in the appropriately named Lost American Fiction series of the Southern Illinois University Press. Agnes Smedley's *Daughter of Earth,* published in 1929 and reprinted in a shortened version in 1935, did not reappear until 1973, when The Feminist Press reprinted it.

4. Valerie Miner, "The Light of the Muse," review of May Sarton, *The Magnificent Spinster, Women's Review of Books* 3, No. 3 (December 1985), 7.

5. Lisa See, "PW Interviews: Tillie Olsen," *Publisher's Weekly* (23 November 1984), 79.

6. Olsen's Personal Statement, in *First Drafts, Last Drafts: Forty Years of the Creative Writing Program at Stanford University,* prepared by William McPheron with the assistance of Amor Towles (Stanford: Stanford University Libraries, 1989), 63.

7. Tillie Lerner, "I Want You Women Up North to Know," reprinted in Selma Burkom and Margaret Williams, eds., "De-Riddling Tillie Olsen's Writings," *San Jose Studies* 2, No. 1 (February 1976), 67–69.

8. Linda Kathryn Yoder, "Memory as Art: The Life Review in Contemporary American Fiction," Ph.D. diss., West Virginia University, 1983.

9. Erica Duncan, "The Hungry Jewish Mother," in Cathy Davidson and E. M. Broner, eds., *The Lost Tradition: Mothers and Daughters in Literature* (New York: Frederick Ungar, 1980), 232.

10. Olsen, lecture/reading and correspondence, 8 March 1992.

11. Olsen, quoted in See, "PW Interviews," 79.

12. The Jerusalem Bible, 1966.

13. "Tillie Olsen: Witness as Servant," *Polit: A Journal for Literature and Politics* 1 (Fall 1977), 5.

14. Mary K. DeShazer, "'In the Wind of the Singing': The Language of Tillie Olsen's 'Tell Me a Riddle'," paper presented at the symposium, "Tillie Olsen Week, The Writer and Society," 21–26 March 1983. Sponsored by Augustana College, Rock Island, Illinois, *et al.*

15. Rebecca Harding Davis, *Life in the Iron Mills; or The Korl Woman* (Old Westbury, N.Y.: The Feminist Press, 1972), 31–33, 64.

16. Olsen, quoted in Linda Matchan, "The Staggering Burden of Motherhood," *Boston Sunday Globe* (11 May 1986), 98.

17. See Yoder, "Memory as Art," 100; and Judith Arcana, *Our Mothers' Daughters* (Berkeley: Shameless Hussy Press, 1979), 188.

18. Tillie Lerner, "The Strike" reprinted in Jack Salzman, ed., *Years of Protest: A Collection of American Writings of the 1930's* (New York: Pegasus, 1967), 139.

19. Annie Gottlieb, "Feminists Look at Motherhood," *Mother Jones* (November 1976), 51.

20. Ibid., 51, 52.

21. Ibid., 53.

22. Ibid., 52.

23. Duncan, "The Hungry Jewish Mother," 232.

RACHEL BLAU DuPLESSIS ■

To "Bear My Mother's Name": *Künstlerromane* by Women Writers

> No song or poem will bear my mother's name. . . .
> Perhaps she was herself a poet—though only her
> daughter's name is signed to the poems that we know.
> ALICE WALKER,
> "In Search of Our Mothers' Gardens" (1974)

The love plot and *Bildungs* plot are fused in a particular fictional strategy, a figure emerging in a range of narratives from Elizabeth Barrett Browning's *Aurora Leigh* to Margaret Atwood's *Surfacing.** And the central struggle between designated role and meaningful vocation is negotiated by different narrative tactics in nineteenth- and twentieth-century texts.[1] The figure of a female artist encodes the conflict between any empowered woman and the barriers to her achievement.[2] Using the female artist as a literary motif dramatizes and heightens the already-present contradiction in bourgeois ideology between the ideals of striving, improvement, and visible public

---

From *Writing beyond the Ending: Narrative Strategies of Twentieth-Century Women Writers* (Bloomington: Indiana University Press, 1985), 35–63. Condensed with the permission of the author.

* Ed. note. In an introductory chapter, DuPlessis argues that prior to the twentieth century, gender ideologies are inscribed in two primary, sometimes overlapping, plots: the romance, or love plot, and the quest, or *Bildung,* involving the character's growth and development. Twentieth-century women's fiction writes multiple, complex plots displacing the conventional endings for women protagonists in either marriage or death. "Künstlerromane" means, literally, "artist-novels." These are novels in which the artist's development is central.

243

works, and the feminine version of that formula: passivity, "accomplishments," and invisible private acts.

For bourgeois women, torn between their class values and the subset of values historically affirmed for their gender caste, the figure of the female artist expressed the doubled experience of a dominant ideology that was supposed to be muted in them and that therefore became oppositional for their gender. Making a female character be a "woman of genius" sets in motion not only conventional notions of womanhood but also conventional romantic notions of the genius, the person apart, who, because unique and gifted, could be released from social ties and expectations.[3] Genius theory is a particular exaggeration of bourgeois individualism, and its evocation increases the tension between middle-class women as a special group and the dominant assumptions of their class. Because it is precisely expression and the desire to refuse silence that are at issue in artistic creation, the contradiction between dominant and muted areas can also be played out in the motif of the imbedded artwork, another narrative marker of these *Künstlerromane*.

Aurora Leigh (1856) by Elizabeth Barrett Browning is the mid-century text of an emergent ideological formation, as *Ruth Hall* (1855), a sweet American book, is that of dominant sentiments. *Aurora Leigh* is a booklength narrative poem about the fusing of artist and woman, and the testing of values surrounding class and spiritual vision.[4] In the final moments of this work, the artist Aurora accepts her suitor in marriage, having discovered that all her notable successes are compromised without affection.[5]

> Passioned to exalt
> The artist's instinct in me at the cost
> Of putting down the woman's, I forgot
> No perfect artist is developed here
> From any imperfect woman.
> (380)

Aurora's expostulation of Love's primacy at the end of the work ("Art is much, but Love is more. / O Art, my Art, thou'rt much, but Love is more!" 381) is well separated from

244

the even more powerful statements of her allegiance to art and her meditations on craft, in Books II and V, which describe the upsurge of her passionate inspiration as the "lava-lymph" (195).

> Never flinch,
> But still, unscrupulously epic, catch
> Upon the burning lava of a song
> The full-veined, heaving, double-breasted Age:
> That, when the next shall come, the men of that
> May touch the impress with reverent hand, and say
> "Behold,—behold the paps we all have sucked!"
>
> (201–202)

Aurora Leigh is irrepressibly rich in imagery of volcanoes and breasts, of maternal power to nourish; and by evoking the physical female, the poem claims both biological and cultural authority to speak.[6]

Heterosexual love may have moral and ideological primacy in *Aurora Leigh*, as articulated at the end, but vocation, itself bound with maternal bliss and the power of love/hate relations among women, has textual primacy.[7] Vocation, asserted early and often, is, moreover, stated in the critical context of a beady-eyed analysis of female education for domesticity, acquiescence, and superficiality. Aurora's choice of vocation is made against the will of her closest relatives, including Romney. She asserts female right to a profession not because of financial exigency or family crisis, but out of sheer desire and for the sake of sheer power. Her ecstatic commitment to the vocation of poet and her achievement tend to make valid the ideology of striving and success that she embodies, joining that set of values to female possibility.[8]

Between the beginning and the end, Romney and Aurora have exchanged roles, in a chiastic move that tends to make their marriage somewhat credible, despite the plot mechanism that has him involved with three women, representing three social classes and three female types. Aurora has seen the centrality of love, he the vitality of her art. While he had, in Book II, been the fountainhead of smugly discouraging statements about women as artists ("We get no Christ from

245

you,—and verily / We shall not get a poet, in my mind," 81), at the end he comes to recognize that her achievement was more vital than his in inducing the conversion experiences that are the real root of any social change. This readjustment takes shape in a distinct and punitive shock to his views. For Romney, like an escapee from *Jane Eyre,* is first rejected, like St. John Rivers, and then, like Rochester, blinded. This wounding of male heroes is, according to Elaine Showalter, a symbolic way of making them experience the passivity, dependency, and powerlessness associated with women's experiences of gender.[9] And, as in Brontë's *Shirley,* the rebellious lower orders express, in unacceptable form, the rancor and hostility of all the powerless, women included. For Romney's blindness is direct punishment for his political theories. A mean-spirited, animalistic rebellion causes the accident that blinds him. The poor have been so brutalized that their souls are nasty, unawakened, unspiritual; their true awakening will be brought about only by poetry and God, not by politics.

Because he can no longer continue these handicapped reformist activities, the private sphere of love and the cosmic sphere of religion become the world in which all his needs can—must—be satisfied. So the man is made to live in the "separate sphere," in the feminine culture of love and God. The creation of Romney's short-fall, his "castration" by the malicious verve of the unwashed masses, creates a power vacuum where the upper-class or upper-middle-class hero used to be. Aurora is then available to claim both masculine and feminine rewards—the hero's reward of success and the heroine's reward of marriage—in a rescripting of nineteenth-century motifs that joins romantic love to the public sphere of vocation.

> Shine out for two, Aurora, and fulfil
> My falling-short that must be! work for two,
> As I, though thus restrained, for two, shall love!
>
> (389)

Since Aurora had offered to sacrifice and to be used (381), what more aggrandizing way to fulfill her desire for abasement than to demand that she do twice as often and twice as intensely what she has already proven she can do very well. Being an artist is, at the end, reinterpreted as self-sacrifice for the woman, and thus is aligned with feminine ideology. This work, then, created a powerful reference point, but it did not change the nineteenth-century convention of representation that saw the price of artistic ambition as the loss of femininity.

Most of the nineteenth-century works with female artists as heroes observe the pieties, putting their final emphasis on the woman, not the genius; the narratives are lacerated with conflicts between femininity and ambition. There are works in which the only reason for an artistic vocation is the utterly desperate and melodramatic destitution of the main character—say a widow with young children, cast out from sanctimonious, petty family. Such is the case with Fanny Fern's *Ruth Hall: A Domestic Tale of the Present Time,* published (in America) a year before *Aurora Leigh.* In this work, when a child asks, "When I get to be a woman shall I write books, Momma?" the proper answer is clearly Ruth's "God forbid . . . no happy woman ever writes. From Harry's grave sprang Floy [her pen name]."[10] This statement may be taken as the mid-century base line of attitudes, in which a woman's entry into public discourse elicits a shudder of self-disgust and is allowable only if it is undertaken in mourning and domesticity.

Self-realization and ambition as a female crime, and the absolute separation of love and vocation are also grimly coded into a moral tale by Rebecca Harding Davis.[11] An older woman, Hetty, vividly discontented with the dullness and ordinary struggles of her life, is alienated from her new baby and from her husband. The focus of her discontent is her ambition to succeed in the public world with "fame and an accomplished deed in life" (10). The climax of this conflict comes in a sequence that we later learn is a hallucinatory dream of an artist's life. She is hissed on stage, sexually exposed, homeless, mistaken for a prostitute, and responsible for her husband's death from grief: surely an intense catalogue of punishments for the crime of ambition. This transposition of desire for vocation to shame and disgust is achieved by Davis's manipulation of the dual connotations of the artist as soul and body. At first her ambition is boldly justified as "the highest soul-utterance," a "mission," "a true action of the creative power," but the sordid intervention of a "greasy" impresario refracts these spiritual claims and collapses them. There is no third or mediating way out of the paradox that the apparently romantic aspirations have a sordid reality, while humdrum domestic life is, instead, the real sphere of divine mission. Here, as in *Aurora Leigh,* class questions subtly shift the ground: the preindustrial farm in which all participate, the family work in unity and interdependence, is clearly better than the protocapitalist exploitation of artist/woman by impresario/man, a relationship all too suggestive of prostitute to pimp. Reunited with family, baby, and husband, Hetty thanks God that she was purged of selfishness, willful dreams, and her delusive claims to talent. "A woman has no better work in life than the one she has taken up: to make herself a visible Providence to her husband and child" (19). God is usefully recruited to bolster the solution. The public sphere is tempting but shallow; the transcendent "Self" without ties is desolate; the private sphere, rather than stultifying and "mawkish," is a cozy and ennobling realm of human love (15, 8). The either/or ending of love versus vocation is created with a newly honed edge in this tale. Although it does offer a pointed vocabulary of critique, the narrative just as pointedly discredits it.

Kate Chopin's *The Awakening* (1899) summarizes these nineteenth-century motifs, working them allusively, testing their limits, considering how they might be broken.[12] The way the life of the artist can be mistaken for the life of the demimondaine, the way "the children" come in and are narratively presented, and an allusion to the sacredness of home ties by a woman suffering in childbed are motifs shared with Rebecca Harding Davis. The death of Edna Pontellier as an artist figure is a plain statement that the character rejects the binary, either/or convention of love versus vocation. However, the fact that her rejection of complicity takes the form of suicide attacks the binary division between selves only by the monism of obliteration. Chopin hints that there might be some socially plausible, if marginalized, third way open to Edna, who is too attached to her privileges of class (the dovecote, the smart set) and gender (her beauty) to pursue it. In this narrative the binary choice still has force, but not finality; the main character cannot experiment further and punishes herself for her mixture of ambition to transcend feminine norms and complicity with them by an act (swimming) that both celebrates and destroys that awakening. . . .

The Story of Avis (1877) by the prolific American writer Elizabeth Stuart Phelps takes up the challenge of *Aurora Leigh* to examine the relation of a woman to artistic vocation after the declaration of love and the marriage that conclude Browning's poem. This deft book is formed like a quilt of neatly fitted and boldly colored discourses—sentimental, realistic, and, of course, allegorical (the death of a bird [Latin: avis] given to her future husband for safekeeping).

Avis is another of the large-spirited and gifted artist heroes torn between human energy and feminine ideology. Phelps's version of a tragicomic wedlock plot will show that marriage and vocation should not be combined for women.

> Success—for a woman—means absolute surrender, in whatever direction. Whether she paints a picture, or loves a man, there is no division of labor possible in her economy. To the attainment of any end worth living for, a symmetrical sacrifice of her nature is compulsory upon her. I do not say that this was meant to be so. I do not think we know what was meant for women. It is enough that it is so.[13]

Women are trained to a personality, formed by social constraints that compel an undivided commitment to one path; allusions to the psychological economy of romance makes change seem impossible. Avis argues that even a woman of genius cannot break the imposed pattern of sacrifice, of an either/or choice. Her future husband claims that a talented and dynamic woman painter, once married, would be able to create and housekeep in fair and equal balance. He is, not incidentally, feckless, although persuasive. The book is built to test their opposing propositions; Avis "wins" the argument by losing her art, a plot mechanism that recapitulates the double bind of femininity and vocation.

Shrewdly observed details of daily life in a household that does not compromise its bourgeois solidity make the novel a study in frustration.[14] Not only the arrival of children but, in sharply executed scenes, their behavior—seductive tantrums outside the studio door—dramatizes the conflicts that daily impede the practice of her talent. Her paints grow dusty; domesticity encroaches constantly. Then the home itself falters: one child dies, the husband is invalided by tuberculosis, the marriage is an alienating stalemate. The author's attention shifts to the prevention of the spiritual and emotional divorce she has so cunningly suggested, as if Avis would be dishonored as a character if she could not recapture love or respect for her husband. With this shift of attention, the burden of the novel falls on the wedlock plot, and the *Bildung* of the female artist is put aside. But even her husband's death does not set Avis free. In a conservative scene of surrender, the character discovers that being married had "eaten into and eaten out the core of her life, left her a riddled, withered thing, spent and rent" (447). She can no longer create, for her genius has been used up in love; she is reduced to teaching art school. This mercantilist view of the psychic economy of women suggests that a fixed amount of energy exists in her life; what is spent is never replenished or recreated. Hence the either/or choice persists and controls the character.

The book ends by the generational displacement of the mother's ambition onto her daughter.[15] The mother reads her child the story of the Quest for the Holy Grail, and we understand that while the first generation (Sir Lancelot) failed, the second, purer generation of seekers will achieve the quest. The thwarted mother bequeathes her ambition to the child, and that emergent daughter becomes, as we shall see, the main character of the twentieth-century *Künstlerroman*.[16]

Avis's two major art works embody the conflict between vocation and love. One is the catalyst for her marriage, a portrait of her future husband. The other is the sphinx, a work of a thwarted artist, encoding both the powers and failures of her genius.[17] In the sphinx is depicted the muted, riddling, and inarticulate drive of woman artists in particular and of women in general, suggesting vocation and its erosion, potential speech and actual silencing, the whole "mutilated actuality" of her career (150).

In a number of works that center on female artists, characters from the conventional heterosexual love plot . . .

make strong demands for conformity to exactingly interpreted feminine roles. Both lover and maternal figures compel the processes of silencing and thwart the preternatural articulateness of the female artists. In the nineteenth-century works, the husband or suitor is the major problem for the artistic career. The husband/suitor's concerted disapproval of the artist's vocation (*Aurora Leigh,* until the end), his lack of sustained understanding of the nature of her needs (*The Story of Avis*), his view of wife as bourgeois possession (*The Awakening*) and his controlling of her artistic and intellectual activity (as we shall see in "The Yellow Wallpaper") are some of the motifs.

The major modulation from the nineteenth- to the twentieth-century *Künstlerroman* involves the position of heterosexual love and the couple within the narrative. The romance plot, which often turns into a stalemate, is displaced in twentieth-century narratives and replaced by a triangular plot of nurturance offered to an emergent daughter by a parental couple. Whenever the heterosexual bond remains central to the main character, she is usually a "thwarted mother" type of artist. Charlotte Perkins Gilman's "The Yellow Wallpaper" may be taken as a transitional work; the nurturing that the potential artist receives is a form of social and emotional control, repressive tolerance at its shrewdest. But Gilman's text is transitional because, instead of submitting to the complicity or battered resignation we see in works like *The Story of Avis,* Gilman's hero performs the act signaling a shift in female narrative politics, the critique of narrative and ideology by writing beyond the ending.

"The Yellow Wallpaper" is an obdurate account of the conflict between an artist's calling and external constraints, telling of the literal entrapment of a potential writer in the room in which she is suffering from a breakdown.[18] Her journal of self-analysis (the work is constructed as a diary) is written furtively, under her husband's ban. The external controls on the woman's activity are very persistent, so her creative energy is baffled except for one completed document—the text we hold.

The room of her imprisonment epitomizes the doubled public and private power characteristic of the social pressures brought to bear on women. As the marital bedroom, it recalls love and trust; with its bars and fixed furniture, it mimics such impersonal corrective institutions as jails and asylums. In the double character of the husband/doctor, Gilman has expressed this nexus of patriarchal love, power, and force; he combines the professional authority of the physician with the legal and emotional authority of the husband.[19] The cause of the character's worsening depression is written—and with the proper eyes can be read—in the yellow wallpaper of the sickroom and in the diary secretly kept by the woman.

The symptoms have a double impact, involving her fixation on the wallpaper and her decoding of it. In the inability of the trained professional to read her symptoms (but in his power to enforce his interpretation), in the ability of the untrained patient to understand the semiology of her illness (but her powerlessness to have her reading credited), Gilman has constructed a dramatic statement illustrating the difficulty of the muted group* to "deny or reverse a universal assumption."[20] When the ill woman makes the climactic separation of the wallpaper's front pattern and its hidden female figure, she makes the crucial analytic distinction between a muted ("creeping") woman and the "central, effective and dominant system of meanings" in her society.[21] By making the wallpaper pattern represent the patterns of androcentric society, Gilman underscores the dailiness and omnipresence of the universal assumption of male dominance, its apparent banality and harmlessness—just one modest feature of home decor. But like any system of social and ideological dominance, it is pervasive, extensive, and saturating.[22] All who live within this fixed pattern of institutions and values are affected by it, no matter what their social benefits or sufferings or how "careful" they are; Gilman reports that "the paper stained everything it touched" (27).

At the ending, depending on one's interpretive paradigm, two contradictory opinions about the main character can be held. The conflicting judgments are simultaneously present, as the narrator, tearing the wallpaper, tries to release

---

* Ed. note. In anthropological thought, as brought into feminist literary criticism by Elaine Showalter, a "muted group" is a group silenced by its lack of access to social power.

her double, the muted subtext with its unsaid meanings. "Much Madness is divinest Sense" here. But from the standpoint of "Much Sense—the starkest Madness—" that is, from the perspective of normalcy, her statement demanding freedom for the muted meanings looks like irrationality and delusion.[23] By an ending that calls attention to interpretive paradigms and powers, Gilman highlights the politics of narrative.

The autobiographical sources of this short story have been well-documented, from the breakdown itself to the infantalizing rest cure, prescribed by an eminent Philadelphia doctor.[24] As Gilman was massaged and fattened, she could "Have but two hours' intellectual life a day. And never touch pen, brush or pencil as long as you live." "The Yellow Wallpaper," dramatizing the mental cruelty of that dependent inactivity, was written with an explicitly didactic purpose—"to reach Dr. S. Weir Mitchell, and convince him of the error of his ways."[25] It is less noted that the inspiration for this story parallels the provocation of *The Story of Avis:* a compensatory defense of a thwarted mother and a highly critical eye cast at the institution of heterosexual romance and marriage—in Gilman's case both the marriage of her parents and her own first marriage.[26]

The motif in which the maternal parent becomes the muse for the daughter has more than fictional status; we can trace it through the biographies of women authors from Virginia Woolf and H. D. to Alice Walker. In a Woolfean essay, Walker "thinks back," tracing the sources of her art to the parent whose artistry is vital.

> Whatever she planted grew as if by magic, and her fame as a grower of flowers spread over three counties. . . . And I remember people coming to my mother's yard to be given cuttings from her flowers; I hear again the praise showered on her because whatever rocky soil she landed on, she turned into a garden. A garden so brilliant with colors, so original in its design, so magnificent with life and creativity, that to this day people drive by our house in Georgia—perfect strangers and imperfect strangers—and ask to stand or walk among my mother's art.[27]

253

Judging from the evidence in Gilman, Phelps Ward, Woolf, and Walker, there seems to be a specific biographical drama that has entered and shaped *Künstlerromane* by women. Such a narrative is engaged with a maternal figure and, on a biographical level, is often compensatory for her losses (which may themselves be imaginatively heightened by being remembered by her child). The daughter becomes an artist to extend, reveal, and elaborate her mother's often thwarted talents. "No song or poem will bear my mother's name" (240). Still, "perhaps she was herself a poet," summarizes Walker, "though only her daughter's name is signed to the poems that we know" (243).

The younger artist's future project as a creator lies in completing the fragmentary and potential work of the mother; the mother is the daughter's muse, but in more than a passive sense. For the mother is also an artist. She has written, sung, made, or created, but her work, because in unconventional media, is muted and unrecognized. The media in which she works are often the materials of "everyday use" (to borrow a phrase from Alice Walker), and her works are artisanal.[28] The traditional notion of a muse is a figure who gives access to feeling or knowledge that she herself cannot formulate. In contrast, this maternal muse struggles with her condition to forge a work, usually one unique, unrepeatable work—an event, a gesture, an atmosphere—a work of synthesis and artistry that is consumed or used.

By entering and expressing herself in some more dominant art form (poem, not garden, painting, not cuisine, novel, not parlor piano playing) the daughter can make prominent the work both have achieved. Mother and daughter are thus collaborators, coauthors separated by a generation. Because only the daughter's work is perceived as art within conventional definitions, it will challenge these formulations of decorum, so the mother or muted parent too can be seen as the artist s/he was.[29] This intellectual, aesthetic, and ethical defense of the mother becomes involved with the evocation of the preoedipal dyad, matrisexuality, or a bisexual oscillation deep in the gendering process. In these works, the female artist is given a way of looping back and reenacting childhood ties, to achieve not the culturally approved ending in heterosexual romance, but rather the reparenting necessary to her second birth as an artist.

In the nineteenth-century texts sampled here, heterosexual ties and the marriage relation come under considerable critical scrutiny, but no change in narrative modes occurs. In twentieth-century texts, the proportion of successful artist figures increases, by virtue of a keen change in the terms of the conflict between role and vocation. Instead of meaning marriage, motherhood, and housewifery, "role" comes to mean the filial completion of a thwarted parent's task. The daughter artist and the blocked, usually maternal, parent are, then, the central characters of twentieth-century women's *Künstlerromane*. The maternal or parental muse and the reparenting motifs are strategies that erode, transpose, and reject narratives of heterosexual love and romantic thralldom.

Precisely this is at stake in Virginia Woolf's *To the Lighthouse*, which concerns Lily Briscoe's long development, revealed through the interrupted process of completing her painting over the ten years in which the novel is set. The painting, a vivid formulation of the novel's themes in an imaginary plastic structure, is "about" a mother and child, Mrs. Ramsay and James, or even Lily herself, poised between strong opposing forces representing male and female—Mr. and Mrs. Ramsay. The creation of that dynamic poise has been the central aesthetic struggle for Lily.[30]

Because of her double and contradictory status, Mrs. Ramsay exists twice in Lily's painting, first as one of the two conventional sides that must be balanced, but then as the inspiration for the revelatory stroke in the middle. For Mrs. Ramsay is central to the two systems: she is the stereotypical feminine side of that dichotomy between male and female which will be superseded, yet at the same time she is the final line at the center of the painting: the dome of the mother-child dyad, the lighthouse of quest-love, the wedge-shaped mark of life infused with the void of oceanic death. . . .

By the midpoint of the novel, both of the traditional endings—marriage and death—have occurred, a sharp critical statement on Woolf's part that clears the ground of any rival solutions to Lily's plot. The third part of *To the Lighthouse* surpasses these classic resolutions, moving beyond the endings they propose, to brother-sister links, to male-female friendship, and, even more, to a vision that overwhelms all the binary systems on which the novel has been built. The final stroke, the placement of Lily's last line, an abstraction of the mother-child dyad wedged into the divided picture, makes her work emotionally complete and aesthetically unified. The either/or division between masculine and feminine reaches a both/and resolution in the art work of the female artist, who joins oedipal to preoedipal materials and expresses the hive, dome, and secret hieroglyphs of matrisexual passion.[31] This synthesis of polarities is even recorded in Woolf's response to her text: on one hand she can characterize it as a "hard muscular book," yet she can also see it as "soft and pliable, and I think deep. . . ."[32]

In the first part of the novel, Lily opts for the pure quest plot of artistic ambition. . . . Yet Lily cannot finish her painting, not because "women can't paint, women can't write"—Tansley's taunt and an external goad—but because she has split her formalist vision from her emotional life (238). Woolf further insists that Lily's painting can be completed only if she immerses herself in vulnerability, need, exposure, and grief, only through empathy—a set of feelings usually called womanly—and not through exclusive attention to aesthetics in a vacuum. The point is illustrated in the later scene with Mr. Ramsay, when "The sympathy she had not given him weighed her down. It made it difficult for her to paint" (254). In short, the painting can be achieved only through the fusion of love with quest.

The love here is not of the classic novelistic kind: Lily's helpful and genuine admiration for Mr. Ramsay's boots, saving him from yet another depressive attack, is hardly a prelude to their courtship. But love it is, alluding to familial love, friendly love, comradely ties, some "of those unclassified affections of which there are so many" (157). She helps him without dissolving into romantic thralldom or powerful self-abnegation, an important distinction from Mrs. Ramsay's way. Not only in offering affection to him but in admitting vulnerability to love and loss in herself, Lily is able to complete her painting. Thus love enables quest; quest is given meaning because of love. The two arcing and interconnected actions that complete the novel—Mr. Ramsay's sail across the bay with his children and Lily's completion of the painting—are both journeys that had been becalmed until love, grief, and need were admitted. . . .[33]

On the last page of *Surfacing* (1972) by Margaret Atwood, the narrator hovers between past and future, between her dead parents and her unborn child, between meretricious commercial art and the art she promises to make. *Surfacing* also shows an emergent daughter who focuses the heritage of both parents in order to bring herself to maturity. The man in the book, a woodsy impregnator, is set aside when his task is done. The art work is a ritual performance piece that the protagonist constructs in order to gain access to her parental, Canadian, mythic (especially matriarchal) roots. Through this performance ritual, she sloughs off the victimization and deadness of nationality and gender. Alone in the wilderness, the protagonist choreographs visions of her parents, dreams, and symbolic acts, like eating or not, into a unity both aesthetic and transformative. The ritual functions in this character's life much as Lily's painting did, closing the past and readying the self for the future. The liminal ending in which the narrator crosses over into love (for her unborn child) and achievement (her unborn art) mingles quest and love; the acceptance of female role—the pregnancy was deliberately sought—is, like the scenes of empathy in *To the Lighthouse*, the enabling act.[34]

Despite any use of the words "mother" and "daughter'" to characterize the preoedipal implications of this reparenting, some of these figures are either displaced by some generations or are not the biological daughters of the mothers they seek. The generational displacement in the twentieth-century works covertly announces that the mother might be less than inspiring. Hence the mother may die in the story, as she does in Woolf and Tillie Olsen. In Christina Stead's novel *The Man Who Loved Children* (1940), the daughter artist Louie has even murdered Henny, her mother, with Henny's complicit understanding. Louie then emerges from her family, having broken the grip of the two embattled parents, escaping beyond the frame of the book in a liminal ending: "I have gone for a walk round the world."[35] The death or generational displacement of the mother in plots involving a daughter artist may be the writer's way of solving one form of the conflict between role and vocation, between the mutual costs, in Jane Flax's terms, of maternal nurturance and filial autonomy. The narrative death is a cold-blooded if necessary enabling act, which distinguishes the useful from the damaging in the maternal heritage. The useful part—empathy and symbiosis—is placed in the daughter's art work; the damaging part—envelopment and paralysis—lies buried in the grave.[36]

The doubled story in Tillie Olsen's "Tell Me a Riddle" is based on the complementary characters of artists who are thwarted and emergent, mother and daughter, dying and living. One major riddle—"How was it that soft reaching tendrils also became blows that knocked?"—refers in general to the ceaseless dialogue between possibility and betrayal that is carried on over a woman's lifetime, and in specific to the conflict between motherhood and Eva's political and artistic vocations.[37] The lifelong impoverishment of Eva's complex spirit, a narrowing carried out in the private realm of family life as well as in the public, historical realm, with its failure of revolutionary hopes, has made her a rancorous old lady. Eva is deaf, deliberately, bitterly silent, and filled with hostility and resentment: a paradigmatically muted figure.

During the story, she and her husband leave their house, site of many contentions and thematic issues about the meaning of home and family, and visit three "daughters." The first returns to the past, with her ghettoized emphasis on Jewish particularism; the second lives a life like her mother's, with its ever-present claims and pressures of children "intensely and now." The third figure, the grandchild Jeannie, completes the pattern, offering future promise. Resembling the revolutionary woman who taught Eva to read more than fifty years before, Jeannie expresses a continuity between the battered ideals of the century's struggles and the unknown future in which these revolutionary possibilities might be realized.

At the last stage of her journey, with her death from cancer imminent, Eva becomes the point upon which past, present, and future converge. She recovers her long-repressed identity as "First mother, singing mother," beginning her "incessant words," which resemble the *Sprechstimme* of modernist musical style.[38] Her suffering and her memories crack her

258

open; her voicing makes a broken, poetic song-speech with a pedal-point of unanswerable riddles: "So strong for what? To rot not grow": "Man . . . we'll destroy ourselves?" Like the pageant music in Woolf's *Between the Acts*, Eva's song is a communal one, and her individual person is like a conduit through which a collectivity chants: "night and day, asleep or awake . . . the songs and the phrases leaping." In Eva's cantata of voices, memories, stories, bits of speeches and books, Olsen makes a manifesto of long-muted voices, a political and aesthetic statement of power from the apparently powerless, who sometimes can hear the music of human struggle and destiny.

The granddaughter Jeannie, a Visiting Nurse, only gradually emerges as an artist in the course of the story. For if Jeannie is a muse for Eva, the reverse is also true: the grandmother's vision will reorient the younger woman. In the sketch of her grandmother "coiled . . . like an ear," Jeannie shows she has understood Eva's essence: sensitivity to the music of struggling humanity. Another of Jeannie's sketches, of her grandparents lying, hands "clasped, feeding each other," makes the grandfather forgive Eva for her bitterness. Jeannie "remarries" them at their last moments together. So, like Eva's, her art is a moral and didactic act.

Human creativity in its boldest and broadest senses inspires Eva's cantata. The collective strength and "zest" of voices at a community chorale break through her defenses. The stories of Chekhov and Balzac are high cultural sources; a Pan del Muerto—folk-art cookie for a dead child—comes from popular culture. "Like art," this decorated cookie recalls the songs of Anon in *Between the Acts,* the moment "almost like a work of art" in *To the Lighthouse,* and "my mother's art" of the garden for Alice Walker. Like Woolf and Walker, Olsen obliterates the distinction between high culture and folk art in the array of Eva's sources.[39] Yet while immersion in the human condition compels artistic expression, such an immersion also prevents it. Olsen's own career is a negotiation with this contradiction. She chooses to look for the unsaid, absent, or missing elements, constructing a literary and political stance "dark with silences" of the unspoken.[40] Olsen has testified to the thematic and moral center provided by her recognition, like Woolf's in *A Room of One's Own*, of the social,

259

material, and emotional circumstances that prevent, or give a certain twisted cast to, fruition and achievement.

If, in these women writers, the function of the artist with the tools of dominant culture is to embody muted experiences, then the figure of the female artist counters the modernist tradition of exile, alienation, and refusal of social roles—the *non serviam* of the classic artist hero, Stephen Dedalus. The woman writer creates the ethical role of the artist by making her imaginatively depict and try to change the life in which she is also immersed. This differentiates the figure in the female *Künstlerromane* from the fantasies of social untouchability or superiority that are prevalent in modernist depictions. These issues of change and stasis emerge in Doris Lessing's *The Golden Notebook* (1962).[41] A published writer of a book that she now regards with contempt, Anna Wulf can no longer "write," but keeps four notebooks, separated explanations for the political and sexual strains that caused her professional stalemate. The major formal project of Lessing's book is to explore and surpass meretricious, abandoned, or incomplete stories, sometimes love plots, but also a whole novel called *Free Women*, in order to arrive at some precious dialectical "golden" amalgam, through which a more dynamic statement about history, politics, and personal relations can be articulated. . . .

Anna had argued endlessly that it is impossible to create art, since the only wholeness people exhibit occurs by virtue of pastiche and ersatz imitations of order. She learns that it is not art that should be rejected but a limiting conception of artistic order. Thus another kind of narrative must be invented—the multivocal, palimpsestic, personal, autobiographical, documentary, analytic, essayistic diary-novel. This is not the encyclopedic form of the authoritative *summa* but something that has switched the poles of authority—an encyclopedia with its categories unformed, its indices unmade, its alphabets unorganized, without fixed grids of judgment, exclusion, concision, or categorization. Anna has found that to write fiction as it was once written would constitute a premature resolution of conflict, confining contradictions rather than releasing them the length and breadth of the work. Narrative based on nostalgia, on manipulative transpositions, on small-minded, riskless reaches into the expressive are obsessively set forth and rejected. Thus the novel is an encyclopedia of the critique of narrative and hegemonic orders. . . .

The fictional art work, distinctively described in these works, has a poetics of domestic values—nurturance, community building, inclusiveness, empathetic care.[42] The poetics of the fictional art work begins with its ethics, not its aesthetics; it has its source in human ties and its end in human change. The work is described as having a clear ethical function and is not severed from the personal or social needs that are its source—for example, the mourning or rage expressed by the characters. This art work can only be made with an immersion in personal vulnerability, a breakdown, or a breakthrough, as in Gilman, Lessing, and Atwood, or as an articulation of long-repressed grief or love, usually the experiences of a daughter in relation to parents, as in Woolf and Olsen.[43] This saturation in buried, even taboo emotions, first resisted, then sought, and finally claimed, is the preferred process by which the fictional artist comes into her own. Since this art work annuls aesthetic distance and is based on vulnerability and need, it is very like "life."[44]

But the work is not exclusively expressive in its poetics. While often begun in situations of psychic desperation, these works are not satisfied simply to confess this fact, or to transform the fictional artist through her knowledge. In contradistinction to purely expressive theories of art, here sincerity is valued because it clarifies the ethical and social bases of the experience. Expression, in the fictional art works, is informed with critical purpose. Anna Wulf's breakdown, the subject of her most dramatic and fructifying notebook, is a decisive rupture with the paradigms of intellectual and emotional order in which she once believed. Eva's cantata begins in hostile anger and ends with a vision of social and revolutionary hope. The hero of "The Yellow Wallpaper" resists the definitional grids that imprison her double in the wallpaper.

The depicted art work is charged with the conditions of its own creation. Maintaining self-reflexive emphasis on the process of creation, this art work is not presented as an artifact free from the stresses and limits of the time in which it was formed. Instead, it is both fabricated from and immersed in the temporal, social, and psychic conditions of muted female life that we are compelled to understand in reading the work: interruptions, blockage, long censorship, derision, self-hatred, internalized repression. Nor does the art work seek the status of a masterpiece or great work, which will be severed from its everyday connections, stored in a museum or gallery, published or sold. The imaginary art work takes its cue from the artisanal experience, in which the object is made for use and has its existence in the realm of necessity, as an expression of ties or needs. Art defined in this fashion is not a property dependent upon its market price and the level of rarity or specialness that it has attained. The fictional art work, drawing on the artisanal, not only expresses its connection with the parental or maternal handicrafter but also registers a protest against art as a salable commodity. The thing precious only because it is hoarded, saved, unconsumed is rejected. Instead, craft (gardening, cooking, storytelling, singing, quilting) and art (painting, sculpting, writing) are viewed as varient parts of one spectrum of human production. This pointed fusion of craft and high art makes a critical assessment of the value placed on activities elevated above the material and conflictual realm.[45]

The division between high and decorative arts is a historical construct, not a universal, and it can be linked to the view of the artist as a separated, isolated genius. By inserting the artist in a social group, the family—but a family reconceptualized so that parental and especially maternal ties are a nurturing source, not an impediment—and by structuring an ethics of emotional service, the idea of the artist as social outcast is contested.

So the fictional art works are carefully built to end what Theodor Adorno calls "the pure autonomy of mind" in the relation of art to culture. Culture—high bourgeois culture—"originates in the radical separation of mental and physical work. It is from this separation, the original sin, as it were, that culture draws its strength."[46] William Morris also points to the historical specificity of the moment when "the great and lesser arts" separate, the one to become "ingenious toys" for the rich, the other to become trivial and unintelligent.[47] It is clear that the fusion of the artisanal and high art has been

262

an analytic dream for radical thinkers. The ideological importance of this fusion for solving the narrative dilemma of role and vocation is apparent when one remembers the completely binary alternatives of the nineteenth-century texts—either domestic life or artistic life. The twentieth-century female *Künstlerromane* solve that binary opposition between work and domesticity by having the fictional art work function as a labor of love, a continuation of the artisanal impulse of a thwarted parent, an emotional gift for family, child, self, or others. This may or may not be realistic, but it is a compelling narrative solution to a prime contradiction. In their artist novels, women writers present a radical oppositional aesthetics criticizing dominance.

☐ *Notes* ∎

1. There are two parallel discussions of the *Künstlerroman*. Grace Stewart discusses mother-daughter ties as "often central to the novel of the artist as heroine," but focuses on their negative character. *A New Mythos: The Novel of the Artist as Heroine, 1877–1977* (St. Alban's, Vt.: Eden Press Women's Publications, Inc., 1979), p. 41. In another consideration of this topic, Susan Gubar argues that two scripts felt to have been absolute alternatives—artistic production and biological reproduction—are joined in twentieth-century women's *Künstlerromane,* allowing female images of creativity to dominate the works. "The Birth of the Artist as Heroine: (Re)production, the *Künstlerroman* Tradition, and the Fiction of Katherine Mansfield," in *The Representation of Women in Fiction,* ed. Carolyn G. Heilbrun and Margaret R. Higonnet (Baltimore: The John Hopkins University Press, 1983): pp. 19–59.

2. A note on terminology. "Female artist" will refer only to the fictional figure; the person who invented the narrative is a woman writer. "Art work" will mean the imaginary text, painting, or performance described, the production of the female artist.

3. Janet Wolff, *The Social Production of Art* (London: Macmillan Press, Ltd., 1981), p. 27.

4. Elizabeth Barrett Browning, *Aurora Leigh and Other Poems,* introduced by Cora Kaplan (London: The Woman's Press, Ltd., 1978).

5. Although, by its focus on closure, my interpretation emphasizes the relations of romance, this work, like *Jane Eyre,* has a powerful subtext of female love-hate relations among the women of all three social classes. Especially the tie between Marian Earle ("a monumental Madonna") and Aurora is discussed by Nina Auerbach, *Woman and the Demon: The Life of a Victorian Myth* (Cambridge: Harvard University Press, 1982), p. 151.

6. Cora Kaplan is admirable on this point, as on many others in her introduction.

7. In another reading, it is heterosexual romance that becomes a metaphor for creative identity. For Barbara Charlesworth Gelpi, Romney is first the interior, self-hating critic and then a "dramatic projection of . . . blind faith" in oneself." "*Aurora Leigh:* The Vocation of the Woman Poet," *Victorian Poetry* 19, 1 (Spring 1981): 48.

8. But this was also a shocking affirmation, for it violated "the social and public silence of women after puberty which was central to the construction of femininity in the nineteenth century." The Marxist Feminist Literature Collective, "Women's Writing: Jane Eyre, Shirley, Villette, Aurora Leigh," in *1848: The Sociology of Literature,* ed. Francis Barker (Colchester: University of Essex, 1978), p. 202.

9. Elaine Showalter, *A Literature of Their Own: British Women Novelists from Brontë to Lessing* (Princeton, N.J.: Princeton University Press, 1977), p. 152.

10. Fanny Fern [Mrs. Sarah Payson (Willis) Parton], *Ruth Hall: A Domestic Tale of the Present Time* (New York: Mason Brothers, 1855), p. 333.

11. Rebecca Harding Davis, "The Wife's Story," *The Atlantic Monthly* XIV, 81 (July 1864): 1–19.

12. Kate Chopin, *The Awakening* (New York: Capricorn Books, 1964).

13. Elizabeth Stuart Phelps, *The Story of Avis* (Boston: James R. Osgood & Co., 1877), p. 126.

14. Indeed, in a notable conduct book, a sister writer deplores Phelps's sympathetic depiction of Avis's dilemma, insisting that even an "emancipated schoolgirl" still needs practical knowledge of womanly, domestic tasks. With sharply selective citation, she makes Avis's complaints seem self-indulgent. Marion Harland, *Eve's Daughters, or*

Common Sense for Maid, Wife and Mother (New York: J. R. Anderson and H. S. Allen, 1982), p. 326.

15. The same kind of ending is visible in Rebecca Harding Davis, *Earthen Pitchers* (1873–74), which offers similar motifs: the ruining of female talent, the insensitive but ill husband (here he is blind), the heritage in the child.

16. Phelps was presenting a compensatory analysis of her own family. Her exacting and punctilious father had, in her view, stifled the ambitions and spirit of her talented mother, a writer, whose name the eight-year-old Elizabeth took in tribute after her mother's untimely death. The bond between Avis and her daughter takes on an extra dimension in the biographical context, in which the author, a daughter, did feel she was completing her mother's thwarted work. For the biographical information, see Christine Stansell, "Elizabeth Stuart Phelps: A Study in Female Rebellion," in *Women: an Issue,* ed. Lee Edwards, Mary Heath and Lisa Baskin (Boston: Little, Brown and Co., 1972): pp. 239–56. About this, Phelps wrote, "Her last book and her last baby came together, and killed her. She lived one of those rich and piteous lives such as only gifted women know; torn by the civil war of the dual nature which can be given to women only." Cited from Phelps [Ward], *Chapters from a Life,* 1897, in the Afterword by Mari Jo Buhle and Florence Howe to *The Silent Partner* (1871) (Old Westbury: The Feminist Press, 1983), p. 362.

17. Because Avis cites *Aurora Leigh,* it is likely that the subject of her painting was inspired by these lines in Barrett Browning: "Or perhaps again, / In order to discover the Muse—the Sphinx, / the melancholy desert must sweep round, / Behind you as before" (*AL,* 70).

18. Charlotte Perkins Gilman, *The Yellow Wallpaper* (1899) (New York: The Feminist Press, 1973).

19. That powerful and loving doctor/lawgiver is a recurrent figure in women's writing, as in their lives, for he sums up the fascinated ambivalence of male culture toward the ambitious female as speaking subject: Freud and "Dora"; S. Weir Mitchell and Gilman; Otto Rank and Anaïs Nin; Freud and H. D. He recurs, transposed, in the Sir William Bradshaw—Septimus Smith tie in Woolf's *Mrs. Dalloway.*

20. "That one sex should have monopolized all human activi-

ties, called them 'man's work,' and managed them as such, is what is meant by the phrase 'Androcentric Culture.'" Referring to the difficulty of even naming "our androcentric culture" in a convincing way, Gilman remarks, "It is no easy matter to deny or reverse a universal assumption." *The Man-Made World, or, Our Androcentric Culture* (New York: Charlton Company, 1911), pp. 25, 21.

21. Raymond Williams, "Base and Superstructure in Marxist Cultural Theory," *New Left Review* 82 (November–December 1973): 9.

22. A veiled citation from ibid.

23. The gloss is Emily Dickinson, 435. "Much Madness is divinest Sense—To a discerning Eye— / Much Sense—the starkest Madness— / 'Tis the Majority / In this, as All, prevail— / Assent— and you are same— / Demur—you're straightway dangerous— / And handled with a Chain—" *The Complete Poems of Emily Dickinson,* ed. Thomas H. Johnson (Boston: Little, Brown and Company, 1960), p. 209.

24. As early motherhood and the strains of domesticity, added to a well-meaning but awkward marriage, overtaxed the ambitious Gilman and contributed to her breakdown, it was not more injunctions to domesticity and femininity that she needed. But this is what S. Weir Mitchell offered his female clients. Mitchell's treatment reflected nineteenth-century attitudes, inducing conformity with the duties of womanhood rather than exploring the conflict and anger within the individual. This point is made by Mary A. Hill, *Charlotte Perkins Gilman: The Making of a Radical Feminist, 1860–1896* (Philadelphia: Temple University Press, 1980), p. 149. In S. Weir Mitchell's home city there is, near 16th on Walnut Street, a plaque commemorating his accomplishments as "physician, physiologist, poet, man of letters" adding, "He taught us the use of rest for the nervous."

25. Gilman, *The Living of Charlotte Perkins Gilman: An Autobiography* (1935) (New York: Harper and Row, 1975), pp. 96, 121.

26. After her own first marriage, she sank into a profound depression, which lifted almost the instant she separated from that husband, but whose effects lasted in what she perceived as a compromise of her abilities. Earlier, Gilman has seen her parents' marriage as "a long-drawn, triple tragedy," and said "mother's life was one of the most painfully thwarted I have ever known" (*Living*, p. 8). Her mother was a pianist who sold the instrument to pay her bills; again

the thwarted mother as artist motivates the achievements of the daughter. Gilman felt that it was possible to combine marriage, motherhood, and vocation, but in her specific case, "it was not right." This may stem from the self-denial and deprivation to which she subjected herself.

27. Alice Walker, "In Search of Our Mothers' Gardens," in *In Search of Our Mothers' Gardens* (San Diego: Harcourt Brace Jovanovich, 1983), p. 241.

28. In Alice Walker's story "Everyday Use," the maternal heritage of quilts belongs to the down-home daughter, who will use them and who has the skills to replenish the stock, not to the urban chic daughter, who, discovering her rural roots, wants to hang the quilts on the wall and alienate them into quaintness. The story is a revisionary telling of the Jacob-Esau story, in which the matriarch works to equalize the "portion" of both sisters, when the more favored quick child has schemed to take part of that heritage although she does not honor it.

29. Where the writer is also concerned to show the artist completing the work of the thwarted father, the father will come from a historically marginalized, nondominant group. For example, in Doris Lessing's *The Golden Notebook,* the parental couple is transposed to Mother Sugar, Anna's analyst, and Charlie Themba, a (correctly) paranoid African leader. This use of parental figures often involves a distinct rewriting or an idealization, for example, using characters who are surrogate parents or grandparents, generationally displaced, or otherwise reassembled.

30. Virginia Woolf, *To the Lighthouse* (1927) (New York: Harcourt, Brace and World, Inc., 1955).

31. It is striking how, in *Moments of Being,* the maternal and the visionary moments are both expressed in the image of a translucent dome of light: the "globular, semi-transparent" early ecstatic sensations, the "arch of glass" that domed Paddington Station, burning and glowing with light. *Moments of Being,* ed. Jeanne Schulkind (New York: Harcourt Brace Jovanovich, 1976), pp. 66, 93. So Mrs. Ramsey at that preoedipal moment of yearning (associated with both hieroglyphs and bees) ends as "the shape of a dome" (80).

32. Virginia Woolf, *A Writer's Diary,* ed. Leonard Woolf (New York: Harcourt, Brace and Company, 1954), pp. 102, 105.

33. How to achieve this ending was the subject of Woolf's entry on 5 September 1926, which interestingly reveals that in the

original conception, Lily and her picture were secondary, and "summing up [Mr.] R's character" seemed to be primary. The shift from a patrifocal narrative to one focused on balance between the generations and on the daughter's vision of the mother serves as further evidence of the thesis of this chapter (*Writer's Diary*, p. 98).

34. Margaret Atwood, *Surfacing* (Ontario: Paperjacks, 1973).

35. Christina Stead, *The Man Who Loved Children* (New York: Avon Books, 1966), p. 491. The book contains an imbedded art work—Louie's play, in an invented language, which depicts to her father a distinct, bitter message about the tie between Snake Man and his daughter: "You are killing me" (378).

36. See Jane Flax, "The Conflict Between Nurturance and Autonomy in Mother-Daughter Relationships and Within Feminism," and Judith Kegan Gardiner, "A Wake for Mother: The Maternal Deathbed in Women's Fiction," which discusses how "mothers in death embody the negative aspects of female personality and role," both in *Feminist Studies* 4, 2 (June 1978): 171–89; 146–65.

37. Tillie Olsen, "Tell Me a Riddle," in *Tell Me a Riddle* (New York: Dell Publishing Company, 1960), p. 86.

38. The term *Sprechstimme* (literally "speech voice") is a distinctive form of writing for the voice in twentieth-century music. Grove's *Dictionary of Music and Musicians* defines it as a "kind of vocal declamation which partakes of the characteristics of both song and speech."

39. The same multiple populist inspiration, double artist figures, mother-daughter and father-daughter ties, and proliferating works of art occur in Margaret Laurence's *The Diviners* (New York: Alfred Knopf, 1974). By stories, ballads, and novels, the politically outcast Canadian strains—Celtic, French, and Indian—are synthesized and become oppositional to the powerful British minority.

40. Tillie Olsen, *Silences* (New York: Delta, 1979).

41. Doris Lessing, *The Golden Notebook* (New York: Ballantine Books, 1968).

42. In her analysis of artist novels, Gubar calls this "revisionary domestic mythology" (*The Representation of Women in Fiction*, p. 39).

43. The particularly privileged mother-daughter connection for creative women was verified in Bell Gale Chevigny's "Daughters Writing: Toward a Theory of Women's Biography," *Feminist Studies* 9, 1 (Spring 1983): 79–102.

44. Judith Kegan Gardiner corroborates this connection between art and life, tracing it to fluid ego boundaries in women's psychological identity. "On Female Identity and Writing by Women," *Critical Inquiry* 8, 2 (Winter 1981): 347–61. In considering stances plausible for a feminist poetics, Lawrence Lipking discusses several issues that this study has also put forth: the pressure on women of an injunction to silence, the personal, rather than objective, stake women have in analyses made of them, and therefore the lack of aesthetic distance and the attempt to build a poetics and a criticism based on affiliation, not authority. "Aristotle's Sister: A Poetics of Abandonment," *Critical Inquiry* 10, 1 (September 1983): 61–81.

45. Herbert Marcuse, "The Affirmative Character of Culture," *Negations: Essays in Critical Theory* (Boston: Beacon Press, 1968), pp. 95–96. One might fruitfully compare the black aesthetic, as enunciated by Gwendolyn Brooks in her introduction to *Jump Bad,* an anthology of black poetry from Chicago. "These black writers do not care if you call their product Art or Peanuts. Artistic survival, appointment to Glory, appointment to Glory among the anointed elders, is neither their crevice [*sic*] nor creed. They give to the ghetto gut. Ghetto gut receives. Ghetto giver's gone." *Report from Part One* (Detroit: Broadside Press, 1972), p. 195.

46. Theodor W. Adorno, "Cultural Criticism and Society," *Prisms* (London: Neville Spearman, 1967), p. 26.

47. William Morris, "The Lesser Arts" (also given under the title "The Decorative Arts," 1877), in *The Political Writings of William Morris,* ed. A. L. Morton (London: Lawrence and Wishart, 1973), p. 32.

"No One's Private Ground": A Bakhtinian Reading of Tillie Olsen's *Tell Me a Riddle*

> "Commitment" is more than just a matter of presenting correct political opinions in one's art; it reveals itself in how far the artist reconstructs the artistic forms at his [/her] disposal, turning authors, readers and spectators into collaborators.
>
> TERRY EAGLETON,
> referring in his *Marxism and Literary Criticism*
> to Walter Benjamin's "The Author as Producer"

In the stories collected in *Tell Me a Riddle* Tillie Olsen examines the marginalization and potential empowering of various groups of oppressed people, particularly women, by experimenting with potentially democratizing modes of discourse. Deborah Rosenfelt has rightly placed Olsen in

> . . . a line of women writers, associated with the American Left, who unite a class consciousness and a feminist consciousness in their lives and creative work, who are concerned with the material circumstances of people's lives, who articulate the experiences and grievances of women and of other oppressed groups—workers, national minorities, the colonized and the exploited—and who speak out of a defining commitment to social change. ("Thirties" 374)

Reprinted (with revisions) from *Feminist Studies* 18, no. 2 (Summer 1992): 257–81.

Although *Tell Me a Riddle* shows a range of marginalized lives, Olsen is far from content with merely portraying this multiplicity in American society. As Rosenfelt observes, Olsen writes out of a "commitment to social change," and I will discuss some of Olsen's narrative/political strategies that exemplify that commitment.

The modes of discourse with which Olsen experiments in developing her narrative strategies are those she has derived and recreated from long and careful listening to the voices of marginalized people. The cacophany of their voices, Olsen recognizes, comprises a potentially democratizing force. Noting some of Olsen's uses of empowering discursive forms in *Silences*, Elizabeth A. Meese writes that "by means of a polyvocal chorus she [Olsen] questions silence and allows others to participate in the same process. . . . She then calls upon the reader to write the text—no longer her text, but occasioned by it and by the voices speaking through it" (110). The experiments noted by Meese as well as several other experiments pervade *Tell Me a Riddle*.

Some of Olsen's specific uses of discursive modes and the political/social changes they work to bring about are prefigured in Mikhail Bakhtin's general concept of "heteroglossia." For Bakhtin there are two competing forces in language use: "Every concrete utterance of a speaking subject serves as a point where centrifugal as well as centripetal forces are brought to bear" (*Dialogic* 272). The "centripetal" or "monologic" force presses toward unity, singularity of meaning; it attempts to assert its dominance by silencing uses of language that deviate from it. On the other hand, the "centrifugal" or "heteroglossic" force resists the dominance of monologism by fragmenting and disrupting it. The myriad heteroglossic voices of the marginalized comprise a social and political force against the tyranny of dominant discursive modes in any language community. Those such as Olsen who observe, record, and honor the multiple heteroglossic voices engage in the democratizing enterprise of amplifying dominated and marginalized voices.

Bakhtin's metaphor of "carnival" displays the nexus of heteroglossia and political/social power. Carnival, with its various simultaneous activities, is a site in which many of the

272

usual societal impositions of class and order are suspended while the populace participates in multiple ways of parodying or mimicking the dominant culture's behavior. Terry Eagleton has described Bakhtin's notion of carnival in these terms: "The 'gay relativity' of popular carnival, 'opposed to all that [is] ready-made and completed, to all pretence at immutability,' is the political materialization of Bakhtin's poetics, as the blasphemous, 'familiarizing' language of plebeian laughter destroys monologic authoritarianism with its satirical estrangements" (*Against* 117). In *Tell Me a Riddle,* in several instances of carnival-like atmosphere, heteroglossia is unleashed to engage in a powerful, playful satirizing of the dominant culture.

The nurturing and recording of heteroglossia has democratizing potential, but heteroglossia itself and the recording of it also contain hazards both for the multiplicity of speakers and for those who listen to their voices. The collection of stories in *Tell Me a Riddle* presents a wide range of individual, marginalized voices competing for our attention. Unless readers/listeners make connections among a variety of voices, many of which are foreign to their own, the potential for genuine democracy latent within the cacophony of heteroglossia is lost. If they remain unconnected from each other, the competing voices lapse into a white-noise excess of sound that becomes unintelligible. Rejecting many traditional modes of authorial control, Olsen refuses opportunities to make connections for us and presses us to make connections among those voices ourselves. The social/political act of connecting otherwise isolated and marginalized voices realizes the democratizing potential of heteroglossia, and Olsen demands that we participate in such action.

To participate properly, we must be permeable to multiple voices, and in some characters in *Tell Me a Riddle,* Olsen shows us both the benefits and risks of receptivity to heteroglossia. Multiple voices often compete within a single character, displaying that character's complex web of ties to others and to the past. Heteroglossia on this level often operates in *Tell Me a Riddle* and other works by Olsen to undermine and offer alternatives to bourgeois individualism. But Olsen does not idealize the individual permeable to heteroglossia; she shows us hazards that exist in individual manifestations of heteroglossia (e.g., Whitey's isolation in "Hey Sailor, What Ship?" and the multiple voices that threaten to overwhelm the narrator of "I Stand Here Ironing"). *Tell Me a Riddle* asks us to be cognizant of the dangers we face as we assume the role Olsen insists we assume—that of active readers alert to the connections among a multiplicity of marginalized voices.

Throughout the stories in *Tell Me a Riddle* Olsen pits heteroglossic modes of discourse she associates with the oppressed against oppressors' monolingual/monological modes of discourse. In the title story, Jeannie's sketch of Eva "coiled, convoluted like an ear" suggests Olsen's narrative/political strategies. Olsen's writing, like an ear "intense in listening," is permeable to the heteroglossic differences constitutive of a complex social field. The stories collected in *Tell Me a Riddle* strain away from the prevailing narrative and social order by "hearing" and incorporating the suppressed voices of mothers, those of the working class, and the dialects of immigrants and African-Americans; by deconstructing the opposition between personal and political; and, in the title story, by honoring the communal polyphony of a dying visionary.

A second and related narrative/political strategy is a reworking of traditional relationships among writer, text, and reader. The stories collected in *Tell Me a Riddle* subvert the concept of textual ownership, affirming the reader not as an object but, reciprocally, as another subject. Many dominant discursive practices still take for granted that the act of reading will be a subjection to a fixed meaning, a passive receiving of what Bakhtin terms "monologue." In Bakhtin's view of monological discourse, the writer directly addresses the readers, attempting to anticipate their responses and deflect their objections; meanings are seen as delivered, unchanged, from source to recipient. In Bakhtin's terms, monologue is "deaf to the other's response; it does not await it and does not grant it any *decisive* force" (cited in Todorov 107).

Heteroglossic discourse, on the other hand, acknowledges "that there exists outside of it another consciousness, with the same rights, and capable of responding on an equal footing, another and equal *I* " (107). *Tell Me a Riddle*'s heteroglossia acknowledges the other consciousnesses that exist outside the text. As Meese indicates about similar strategies in *Silences, Tell Me a Riddle* activates its reader-subjects while subverting authorial domination; in the tradition of Bertolt Brecht's theater and Jean-Luc Godard's cinematic montage, it turns writer and readers into collaborators.

The two categories of Olsen's narrative/political strategy I have identified—her recording of heteroglossia and her reworking of relationships among writer, text, and reader—constitute this essay's two major divisions.

In *Tell Me a Riddle's* first story, "I Stand Here Ironing," Olsen begins her recording of heteroglossia by exploring problems that fragment lives and discourse and by experimenting with narrative forms that display that fragmentation. Emily, the daughter of the unnamed narrator, had been born into "the pre-relief, pre-WPA world of the depression," and her father, no longer able to "endure . . . sharing want" with the 19-year-old mother and child, had left them when Emily was eight months old (10). The infant "was a miracle to me," the narrator recalls, but when she had to work, she had no choice but to leave Emily with "the woman downstairs to whom she was no miracle at all" (10). This arrangement grieved both mother and child: "I would start running as soon as I got off the streetcar, running up the stairs," the narrator remembers, and "when she saw me she would break into a clogged weeping that could not be comforted, a weeping I can hear yet" (10–11). Then came months of complete separation, while the child lived with relatives. The price for reunion was Emily's spending days at "the kinds of nurseries that [were] only parking places for children. . . . It was the only place there was. It was the only way we could be together, the only way I could hold a job" (11). Their situation improved with the presence of "a new daddy" (12). Although the narrator still worked at wage-earning jobs, she was more relaxed with her younger children than she had been with Emily: "it was the face of joy, and not of care or tightness or worry I turned to them." But, the narrator adds, by then it was "too late for Emily" (12).

The narrative is laced with references to the pressure of circumstance, the limits on choice: "when is there time?";

"what cannot be helped" (9); "it was the only way" (11); "We were poor and could not afford for her the soil of easy growth" (20); "She is the child of her age, of depression, of war, of fear" (20). Both mother and daughter have been damaged: While Emily expresses fear and despair casually ("we'll all be atom-dead"), her mother suffers because "all that is in her [Emily] will not bloom" (20). All the narrator asks for Emily is "enough left to live by" and the consciousness that "she is more than this dress on the ironing board, helpless before the iron" (21).

The story includes two major discursive forms. The form that appears through most of the story is indirect, circling, uncertain; it is heteroglossic. The other form, which Olsen points out and discards in one paragraph near the story's end, is direct, clipped, and assertive.[1] It is a version of the reductive dominant discourse contributing to the pressure of the circumstances in which Emily and her mother struggle to survive. With these two forms of discourse Olsen introduces issues that concern her in all the stories in *Tell Me a Riddle:* language as power; dominant versus subversive modes of discourse; heteroglossia.

The second major discursive form, the direct, is introduced by the narrator of "I Stand Here Ironing" in this way: "I will never total it all. I will never come in to say: She was a child seldom smiled at. Her father left me before she was a year old. I had to work her first six years when there was work, or I sent her home and to his relatives. There were years she had care she hated" (20). What the narrator offers here is what she will not say and what she will not do. She will not "total"—sum up—Emily's life in a direct, linear, cause-and-effect way.

The other major discursive form—with its many modes of indirectness, false starts, and uncertainties—is signalled in the form of address at the beginning of the story. The narrator says, "I stand here ironing, and what you asked me moves tormented back and forth with the iron" (9). This "you" (never clearly identified, but likely one of Emily's high school teachers, a guidance counselor, or a social worker) is the ostensible audience to whom the narrator's discourse is directed. However, in this most indirect form of address, the entire story takes place in the mind of the narrator, who is speaking to herself as though rehearsing her discourse for the "you." We do not know whether this discourse ever passes from the silence of the mother's mind to the hearing of the audience (the teacher or counselor) for whom it is being rehearsed.

The narrator's discourse is persistently marked by indirectness, false starts, and uncertainties—the forms on which the narrator must rely as she looks back over her life with Emily: "Why do I put that first? I do not even know if it matters, or if it explains anything" (10); "In this and other ways she leaves her seal, I say aloud. And startle at my saying it. What do I mean? What did I start to gather together, to try and make coherent?" (18). These fitful "digressions" typify the movement of the story's first major discursive form. The user of that form, far from reducing her subjects to linear, cause-and-effect patterns, displays in multifaceted discourse her own complicated and ultimately irreducible forms of interdependence with her subjects. The form is heteroglossic; it is a "voice" made of many voices: Caught in the memory of conflicts between Emily and her sister, Susan, "each one human, needing, demanding, hurting, taking," the mother says, "Susan telling jokes and riddles to company for applause while Emily sat silent (to say to me later; that was *my* riddle, Mother, I told it to Susan)" (16–17). As employed in this and other stories in the collection, heteroglossia is not solely a matter of multiple voices within or among cultures or subcultures; it is often the multiple and conflicting voices that make up one person. Olsen's displays of individual heteroglossia, the fragmenting of voices constituting a self and that self's interdependence with others, become one means by which her work offers alternatives to bourgeois individualism.

At the beginning of the story, the words of the unidentified teacher or counselor and the mother's reaction to those words create a complex intermingling of voices. The mother has been asked to assist in helping Emily: "'I wish you would manage the time to come in and talk with me about your daughter. I'm sure you can help me understand her. She's a youngster who needs help and whom I'm deeply interested in helping.'" The next line of the story is "'Who needs help.'. . . ." (9; ellipsis Olsen's). Who indeed? This entangling of the helpers and the helped, including the suggestion that the mother is being asked for the very aid she herself may need in order to assist Emily, is indicative of the ways in which the narrator's thinking and discourse proceed. She cannot, in language, fully demarcate herself from Emily or from those whose lives became entangled with Emily's in the past, such as an unsympathetic nursery school teacher: "And even without knowing, I knew. I knew the teacher that was evil because all these years it has curdled into my memory, the little boy hunched in the corner, her rasp, 'why aren't you outside, because Alvin hits you? that's no reason, go out, scaredy'" (11). Facing the incessant pressure of time and circumstances—"And when is there time to remember, to sift, to weigh, to estimate, to total?"—the narrator recognizes that multiple voices and memories constantly threaten to engulf her (9).

The nonlinear mode of discourse is so often replete with complexity of meaning that it risks falling into meaninglessness and the equivalent of silence. In this story that risk is most acute at moments when the mother cannot find the language to respond to Emily. While looking back over her life with Emily, the mother returns to times when she could respond to her daughter with nothing more than silence.

> There was a boy she loved painfully through two school semesters. Months later she told me how she had taken pennies from my purse to buy him candy. "Licorice was his favorite and I bought him some every day, but he still liked Jennifer better'n me. Why, Mommy?" The kind of question for which there is no answer. (15–16)

On the night in which this story takes place the mother is remembering such details of Emily's life and instances of failed communication between mother and daughter. The cumulative details from the various stages of Emily's life and the crowding of voices force the narrator to say near the story's end: "because I have been dredging the past, and all that compounds a human being is so heavy and meaningful in me, I cannot bear it tonight" (20). A richness of meaning approximating meaninglessness and the equivalent of silence weighs on the mother when she says of Emily, "This is one of her communicative nights and she tells me everything and nothing as she fixes herself a plate of food" (19). Yet for the narrator a reliance on nonlinear discourse with its attendant hazards is not only a matter of what her circumstances have forced upon her. It is also a matter of choice.

The narrator must use nonlinear heteroglossic modes if her goal in telling Emily's story is, as she says it is, to "Let her [Emily] be." The complicated, conflicting stuff of which human beings are made can be discussed only nonreductively in nonlinear discourse, in a manner that has some chance of "letting them be." To adopt the dominant, linear, reductive mode of discourse is to usurp and control Emily, and it is to abandon the hope with which the story ends: the narrator's hope that Emily will know "that she is more than this dress on the ironing board, helpless before the iron" (20).

The two major discursive forms in "I Stand Here Ironing"—the indirect, uncertain, circling form, and the direct, clipped, assertive form—appear again in "Tell Me a Riddle," and, again, Olsen uses them to explore language as power; dominant versus subversive modes of discourse; and heteroglossia. The story begins with a battle between Eva and David, who have been married for forty-seven years, most of them spent in poverty. In the dialect of Russian-Jewish immigrants, they bitterly dispute whether to sell their home and move to a retirement cooperative operated by David's union. He craves company while Eva, after raising seven children, will not "exchange her solitude for anything. *Never again to be forced to move to the rhythms of others.*" David and Eva use a not-always-direct, but relentlessly assertive, and minimal form of discourse in their perpetual quarreling. We find that mode of discourse in their opening fray:

> "What do we need all this for?" he would ask loudly, for her hearing aid was turned down and the vacuum was shrilling. "Five rooms" (pushing the sofa so she could get into the corner) "furniture" (smoothing down the rug) "floors and surfaces to make work. Tell me why do we need it?" And he was glad he could ask in a scream.
>
> "Because I'm use't."
>
> "Because you're use't. This is a reason, Mrs. Word Miser? Used to can get unused!"

They poke at each other with as few words as possible, using words not as instruments of communication but as weapons of combat and control. Further, each uses any available means to suppress the other's minimal discourse. She turns down her hearing aid and turns on the vacuum cleaner. He turns on the television "loud so he need not hear."

The text only gradually reveals Eva's long-ago status as a revolutionary orator; only through fragments of dialogue and interior monologue do we learn that this obdurate, rancorous woman, who now wields power only by turning down her hearing aid, was once an orator in the 1905 Russian revolution. Models for Eva's revolutionary commitment included that of Olsen's own mother, Ida Lerner. Another was Seevya Dinkin, who shares "Riddle"'s dedication with Genya Gorelick.[2]

"Tell Me a Riddle" illuminates, as no polemic could, the terrible cost of a sexual division of labor. David, who has worked outside the home, has sustained a vitality and sociability. But he has lost the "holiest dreams" he and Eva shared in their radical youth, seems to accept American "progress," and would rather consume TV's version of "This Is Your Life" than reflect on his own. Insulated at home, Eva has felt less pressure to assimilate, to compromise her values, and has preserved those dreams. But the many years of 18-hour days, of performing domestic tasks "with the desperate ingenuity of poverty" (years in which David "never scraped a carrot") have transformed her youthful capacity for engagement into a terrible need for solitude (Rosenfelt, "Divided" 19).

As Eva is dying she slips into the indirect discursive mode. After years of bitter silence, she begins to speak, sing, and recite incessantly. Fragments of memories and voices, suppressed during her years of marriage and motherhood, emerge as the old woman nears death. Eva, like the mother in "I Stand Here Ironing," becomes an individual embodiment of heteroglossia. Eva had announced her desire for solitude, but ironically she returns in her reverie to the time when she was engaged with others in a revolutionary movement. She sings revolutionary songs from her youth and in a "gossamer" voice whispers fragments of speeches she had delivered in "a girl's

280

voice of eloquence" half a century before. Her babble is a communal one; she becomes a vehicle for many voices.

Eva's experiences while dying may have been partly modelled on those of Ida Lerner. "In the winter of 1955," Olsen reports in *Mother to Daughter, Daughter to Mother,* "in her last weeks of life, my mother—so much of whose waking life had been a nightmare, that common everyday nightmare of hardship, limitation, longing; of baffling struggle to raise six children in a world hostile to human unfolding—my mother, dying of cancer, had beautiful dream-visions—in color." She dreamed/envisioned three wise men, "magnificent in jewelled robes" of crimson, gold, and royal blue. The wise men ask to talk to her "of whys, of wisdom," but as they began to talk, *"she saw that they were not men, but women: That they were not dressed in jewelled robes, but in the coarse everyday shifts and shawls of the old country women of her childhood, their feet wrapped round and round with rags for lack of boots. . . . And now it was many women, a babble"* (261, 262). Together, the women sing a lullaby.

Like Ida Lerner, on her deathbed Eva becomes the human equivalent of a heteroglossic carnival site.

> *One by one they* [the thousand various faces of age] *streamed by and imprinted on her—and though the savage zest of their singing came voicelessly soft and distant, the faces still roared—the faces densened the air—chorded into*
>
> children-chants, mother-croons, singing of the chained love serenades, Beethoven storms, mad Lucia's scream, drunken joy-songs, keens for the dead, working-singing. . . .

Olsen blurs the distinction between high and popular culture in the diversity of cultural forms that sustain Eva; her beloved Chekhov, Balzac, Victor Hugo; Russian love songs; revolutionary songs; a "community sing" for elderly immigrants; and *Pan del Muerto,* a folk-art cookie for a dead child.

The barrage of voices and references that constitute Eva at her death return us to the danger I referred to in discussing "I Stand Here Ironing"—that multivocal, heteroglossic discourse may result in the equivalent of silence. Despite the danger, heteroglossia's cacophony is preferable to the dominant discourse's reductive forms. As for Emily in "I Stand Here Ironing," what will "let Eva be" is heteroglossia. After years of living in silence and near silence, Eva emerges in heteroglossia. Yet in both stories the richness of meaning released in Emily's and Eva's heteroglossic utterances threaten to result in the equivalent of silence.

In *Tell Me a Riddle* mimicry provides examples of subversive, indirect modes of discourse jousting with dominant monolithic modes; however, in mimicry Olsen finds the occasion to examine hazards in marginalized discourse's competing with the dominant discourse. Like other forms of parody, mimicry comprises a powerful form of heteroglossia. Aimed against an official or monologic language, mimicry divides that system against itself. However, mimicry's ability to oppress the oppressor may be a snare for the mimic. To make her mother laugh, or out of the despair she felt about her isolation in the world, Emily, in "I Stand Here Ironing," imitates people and incidents from her school day. Eventually her gift for mimicry, pantomime, and comedy lead to first prize in her high school amateur show and requests to perform at other schools, colleges, and city- and state-wide competitions. However, her talent and achievement do not remedy her isolation: "Now suddenly she was Somebody, and as imprisoned in her difference as she had been in anonymity" (19). By exercising her parodic talent, Emily unwittingly exchanges one form of marginalization for another.

Like Emily, Whitey in "Hey Sailor, What Ship?" has a knack for mimicry, which he exhibits, for example, when telling Lennie about the union official who fined him: "(His [Whitey's] old fine talent for mimicry jutting through the blurred-together words.)" (44). Whitey, a seaman being destroyed by alcoholism, is no less isolated than Emily in "I Stand Here Ironing." Lennie and Helen, who have been Whitey's friends and political comrades for years (Whitey saved Lennie's life during the 1934 Maritime Strike), and their three daughters are his only friends—indeed, the only people he can "be around . . . without having to pay" (43).[3]

Mimicry deals Whitey a fate similar to Emily's. However, an irony of "Hey Sailor, What Ship?" is that it is mimicry of the mimic, Whitey, that contributes to Whitey's fate. The family engages in an affectionate mimicking of the salty language that sets Whitey apart from their other acquaintances:

> Watch the language, Whitey, there's a gentleman present, says Helen. Finish your plate, Allie.
>
> [Whitey:] Thass right. Know who the gen'lmum is? I'm the gen'lmum. The world, says Marx, is divided into two classes. . . . [ellipsis Olsen's]
>
> Seafaring gen'lmum and shoreside bastards, choruses Lennie with him.
>
> Why, Daddy! says Jeannie.
>
> You're a mean ole bassard father, says Allie.
>
> Thass right, tell him off, urges Whitey. Hell with waitin' for glasses. Down the ol' hatch.
>
> *My* class is divided by marks, says Carol, giggling helplessly at her own joke, and anyway what about ladies? Where's *my* drink? Down the hatch. (35)

Thus mimicry functions in "Hey Sailor, What Ship?" as one form that entices Whitey out of isolation and into the family, while simultaneously diminishing the importance of Whitey as "other." The behavior of the family in relation to Whitey, despite what seems to be their shared political beliefs and practice, becomes a microcosm for the dominant culture's behavior in relation to much marginalized discourse. Charmed by difference (the history of music in U.S. popular culture exemplifies the point), the mainstream culture co-opts the marginalized discourse, stripping it of its power as "difference," and diminishes its force in a process of homogenization. Olsen's references to mimicry in these stories comprise part of her running commentary on the power of dominant and subversive modes of discourse and the complications of identity that marginalized people and their discourses face.

In addition to mimicry, "Hey Sailor, What Ship?", like other stories collected in *Tell Me a Riddle,* manifests heteroglossia by incorporating genres that "further intensify its speech diversity in fresh ways" (Bakhtin, *Dialogic* 321). Although this strategy is not uncommon among fiction writers, Olsen employs it more than many. In "Hey Sailor, What Ship?" Olsen has inserted a valediction (because the story is a farewell to Whitey, this insertion becomes a valediction within a valediction). Whitey learned it as a boy from his first shipmate, and one of the children asks him to recite it. Originally delivered in 1896 by the Phillipine hero Jose Rizal before he was executed, it concludes:

> Little will matter, my country,
> That thou shouldst forget me.
> I shall be speech in thy ears, fragrance and color,
> Light and shout and loved song. . . .
>
> Where I go are no tyrants. . . .
>   (42)

Jose Rizal would have been an insurgent against both Spanish and American domination of the Philippines, and the recitation implicitly condemns American imperialism and the Cold War, at its height when Olsen wrote "Hey Sailor, What Ship?"

Whitey's recitation also eulogizes his (and Olsen's) youthful hopes for a socialist America, which have been snuffed out by Cold War strategists:

> Land I adore, farewell. . . .
> Our forfeited garden of Eden. . . .
>
> Vision I followed from afar,
> Desire that spurred on and consumed me,
> Beautiful it is to fall,
> That the vision may rise to fulfillment.
>   (41)

Moreover, the valediction associates Whitey, who has been destroyed as much by "*the death of the brotherhood*" as by alcoholism, with political martyrdom. Whitey, who has attempted to keep thirties militancy alive in a period of political reaction, feels estranged from the complacent younger seamen. "These kids," he complains to Lennie, "don't realize how we got what we got. Beginnin' to lose it, too." One "kid," who had overtime coming to him, "didn't even wanta beef about it" (44). As the

284

ship's delegate, Whitey nevertheless took the grievance to the union, which had become a conservative, alien bureaucracy, and was fined for "not taking it [the grievance] up through proper channels" (44). The younger seamen also lack the sense of solidarity Whitey and Lennie experienced during the thirties: "'Think anybody backed me up, Len?' . . . *Once, once an injury to one is an injury to all. Once, once they had to live for each other. And whoever came off the ship fat shared, because that was the only way of survival for all of them. . . . Now it was a dwindling few . . .*" (45). And, finally, because Whitey's efforts to stay sober have consistently failed and his health is rapidly deteriorating, Jose Rizal's valediction also functions as his own farewell address.

Yet there is a dimension to Whitey that cannot be explained in political or economic terms. Even in his youth, when both he and the Left were robust, Whitey was tormented by an emotional disorder that manifested itself in an inability to have sexual relations except when "*high with drink.*" Many years later, at "the drunken end of his eight-months-sober try," Lennie and Helen hear a "torn-out-of-him confession" that the psychosexual problem persists, and likely, it will remain a riddle (44, 46). The story ends with its plaintive refrain—"Hey Sailor, what ship?"—which mourns the tragic waste of Whitey's life as well as suggests the disorientation, diminished options, and uncertainty of radicals in a period of right-wing ascendancy.

Both Whitey and Emily exemplify dangers in heteroglossic, subversive modes of discourse. Emily's and Whitey's individual talent allows each of them to joust with the dominant discourse. However, those individual talents, unlinked to other heteroglossic voices also intent upon jabbing at the dominant discourse, leave both Emily and Whitey without the supporting network of similar subversive voices. Without that support, they experience the dominant discourse's subsuming power and are returned to marginalized positions and forms of silence.

Mimicry and the two major forms of discourse—the direct and the indirect, and the risk that the cacophony of multivocal discourse may result in the equivalent of silence—play major roles in "O Yes." Helen, Lennie, and their daughters appear again in this story about the difficulty of sustaining a friendship across racial lines. Lennie and Helen's 12-year-old, Carol, is white; Parialee, her neighbor and closest friend from their earliest years, is African-American. "O Yes," which begins with Helen and Carol's attending Parialee's baptismal service, is permeable to the speech of "others"—songs by three church choirs; parishioners' shouts; Parialee's newly-learned jivetalk; and Alva's African-American dialect. Carol, who has never before experienced the intense emotionalism that erupts during the service (chanting, shrieking, fainting), is a stranger in the world of an all-African-American congregation. Trapped in heteroglossia's cacophony, Carol falls into the silence of a near faint, and once again, an abundance of meaning approaches silence.

Yet, in the first of the story's two parts, a far more reductive and controlling mode of discourse—an assertion/affirmation form of "dialogue"—presents itself as a counter to heteroglossia. In the dialogue's highly structured environment, the preacher takes the lead by making assertions that the congregation affirms. The dialogue includes the preacher's words, such as "And God is Powerful," and the congregation's response, "*O Yes*" and "I am so glad" (52, 54). The reductive and controlling mode of discourse in which the assertions are assigned to the figure of power, the preacher, and the affirmations to his followers, the congregation, replicates the structure of society outside the church. Exercising their role in the dialogue, the parishioners seem to be playing out the subservient parts African-Americans have so often been assigned within the society. Yet, within the church, heteroglossia persistently strains against the constraining mode of discourse. In "O Yes," as throughout *Tell Me a Riddle,* two major discursive forms—heteroglossia and, in this case, the countering assertion/affirmation dialogue—vie for power.

A complicated version of mimicry is prominent in "O Yes." What I identified earlier as a conventional assertion/affirmation structure placed in the midst of a swirling heteroglossia contains complex elements of a form of mimicry in which the preacher and congregation wittingly or unwittingly dramatize the roles of dominant and marginalized people, oppressor and oppressed. As the drama of the dialogue in-

286

tensifies, it threatens to overpower heteroglossia by reducing it to the near monological assertion/affirmation exchanges between a leader and followers. Much of that drama takes place in the sermon delivered at Parialee's baptismal service. The narrator tells us that the subject of the sermon is "the Nature of God. How God is long-suffering. Oh, how long he has suffered" (51). The narrator has shown us a version of the classic Christian mystery of incarnation: God as the maker of human beings who suffer and God as the human victim of suffering. This dual role of perpetrator and victim becomes central to the sermon-response's dialogic structure. Early in the sermon the preacher chants, "And God is Powerful," to which the congregation responds "*O Yes*" (52). Here, again, we find an assertion/affirmation structure in which the preacher assumes the lead in the dialogue by making assertions that the congregation, in its role as follower, responds to by affirming.

Other dimensions of the dialogue quickly emerge. The preacher, working the theme of the great judgment day, blows an imaginary trumpet and announces: "And the horn wakes up Adam, and Adam runs to wake up Eve, and Eve moans; Just one more minute, let me sleep, and Adam yells, Great Day, woman, don't you know it's the Great Day?" (53). The basic assertion/affirmation structure is still operating, but within that structure the preacher in godlike fashion now creates characters who in turn engage in their own dialogues. The scene becomes increasingly heteroglossic. Immediately after the created Adam's rousing call to a sleeping Eve ("Great Day, woman, don't you know it's the Great Day?"), one of the choirs responds, "*Great Day, Great Day*" (53). Is the choir responding to the voice of the created Adam or to the preacher? The answer is of little consequence. What is important here is that the structure of the assertion/affirmation dialogue has dictated conditions that the congregation follows. Whichever "leader," real or imaginary, they respond to in the course of the sermon, they persistently replicate their role as affirmers of the leader's assertion. Thus what emerges from this heteroglossic scene is a powerful counter to heteroglossia, a discursive structure that imposes unity and control by locking participants into predetermined traditional roles.

The force for unity within heteroglossia intensifies

as the imaginary dimension of the dialogue escalates. The preacher moves from assertions about God and the creation of characters such as Adam and Eve to assuming the role of God, and with that move the form of his discourse shifts from assertion/affirmation to promise/affirmation. Having just asserted the multiple roles of God in relation to human beings (friend, father, way maker, door opener), the preacher proclaims: "I will put my Word in you and it is power. I will put my Truth in you and it is power." The response is "*O Yes*" (55). Soon after, the narrator says, "Powerful throbbing voices. Calling and answering to each other" (56). The narrator captures the vibrant force of the unity within the heteroglossia when she says, "A single exultant lunge of shriek" (56).

What are we to make of this univocalizing of heteroglossia? The sexual implications that have been accumulating in this scene and that culminate in the orgasmic "single exultant lunge of shriek" invite an instructive digression into Mae Gwendolyn Henderson's discussion of an orgasmic "howl" in Toni Morrison's *Sula*. Henderson, who skillfully employs Bakhtinian analysis, observes of Sula's orgasmic cry: "The howl, signifying a prediscursive mode, thus becomes an act of self-reconstitution as well as an act of subversion or resistance to the 'network of signification' represented by the symbolic order. The 'high silence of orgasm' and the howl allow temporary retreats from or breaks in the dominant discourse" (33). The "single exultant lunge of shriek" has very similar functions in the church scene in "O Yes." The parishioners have repeatedly experienced the intense repetition of the constraining assertion/affirmation and promise/affirmation structures that mimic the dominant discourse of power to which the congregation members are subjected outside the church. The shriek becomes an act of "self-reconstitution" and, at the same time, a "subversion or resistance to the 'network of signification'" that constrains the parishioners.

Henderson argues persuasively that Sula's orgasmic howl occurs at the moment at which she is located "outside of the dominant discursive order" but also when she is poised to re-enter and disrupt the discursive order. For Henderson, Sula's howl becomes a primary metaphor for African-American women writers whose objective is not "to move from margin to center, but to remain on the borders of discourse, speaking from the vantage point of the insider/outsider" (33, 36). This point of difficult balance is, I suggest, where Olsen places the African-American congregation at the moment of the "single exultant lunge of shriek."

But what more is there in the story to justify such a reading of this univocalizing of heteroglossia? Alva, Parialee's mother, will give us some indications. After Carol's near-faint, Alva blames herself for not having been more attentive to Carol's being brought into a situation she had no basis for understanding. Attempting to explain the situation to Carol after the fact, Alva says, "You not used to people letting go that way. . . . You not used to hearing what people keeps inside, Carol. You know how music can make you feel things? Glad or sad or like you can't sit still? That was religion music, Carol." Speaking of the congregation Alva says, "'And they're home Carol, church is home. Maybe the only place they can feel how they feel and maybe let it come out. So they can go on. And it's all right'" (59–60). So we seem to have our answer. The univocalizing of heteroglossia is a shared singular escape of people who are trapped in multiple ways. They seem to choose to surrender the heteroglossia of their suffering to the univocal escape of the church/home. But is it "all right"?

The story's first section ends with an italicized rendering of what Alva did not say to Carol. This reverie—which remains silent, unspoken to Carol—stands as a response (like the earlier italicized responses of the congregation and the choirs) to an earlier series of the preacher's assertions. Earlier in the sermon the preacher proclaims: "He was your mother's rock. Your father's mighty tower. And he gave us a little baby. A little baby to love." The congregation responds: "*I am so glad*" (54). Alva's silent reverie begins:

> *When I was carrying Parry and her father left me, and I fifteen years old, one thousand miles away from home, sin-sick and never really believing, as still I don't believe all, scorning, for what have it done to help, waiting there in the clinic and maybe sleeping, a voice called: Alva, Alva. So mournful and so sweet: Alva. Fear not, I have loved you from the foundation of the universe.* (61)

Alva follows the voice *"into a world of light, multitudes sing-ing,"* and the reverie ends: *"Free, free, I am so glad"* (61). The reverie's mixture of dream and reality parallels the mixture of the imaginary and the real in the sermon situation and seems to stand as Alva's singular response (not an affirmation) to the preacher's assertions in the sermon. But this is not a com-pletely singular response, and it is not totally devoid of affir-mation. When Alva acknowledges, "still I don't believe all," she locates herself, like Henderson's African-American female writer, both within and outside the church, inside yet resist-ing the univocality, outside yet resisting the conflation of the imaginary and the real. But we must remember that this is what Alva does *not* say to Carol, or to Helen, or as far as we know to anyone other than us. What is the force that creates this silence? Is it the circumstances of Alva's daily life? Is it the church?

We cannot begin to answer these questions without looking at the structure of the second part of the story. Just as Alva's reverie functions as a response to the sermon, the second part of the story stands as a response to the first part. In the second part, which takes place in the world of Helen and Len (or Lennie) and their daughters, Carol and Jeannie, a univocalizing force parallels that of the church in part one. In the second part the force against heteroglossia is the junior high school, which officially and unofficially at-tempts to separate Carol and Parialee, univocalizing Carol and other white students while shutting out Parialee and other African-American students. Because she is African-American, Parialee will not be tracked into Carol's accelerated classes; and even if she were initially admitted to them, the necessity to care for younger siblings while her mother works the four-to-twelve-thirty night shift would quickly put her behind in her studies. Carol is "college prep," whereas Parialee will likely not finish junior high, predicts Jeannie, a 17-year-old veteran of the public school system. According to Jeannie, "you have to watch everything, what you wear and how you wear it and who you eat lunch with and how much homework you do and how you act to the teacher and what you laugh at. . . . [ellipsis Olsen's] And run with your crowd" (63). Peer pressure is tremendous, and Carol and Parialee would be ostracized for

290

attempting to be friends. Jeannie contrasts their "for real" working-class school with one in a nearby affluent neighborhood where it is fashionable for whites and African-Americans to be "buddies": ". . . three coloured kids and their father's a doctor or judge or something big wheel and one always gets elected President or head song girl or something to prove oh how we're democratic" (65).

The junior high school has its parallel to the preacher—the teacher, Miss Campbell (nicknamed "Rockface")—and in this parallel Olsen further suggests dangers in the monologic impulses within the church's heteroglossia. Godlike in the junior high school kingdom, the bigoted teacher has the power to decide whether Parialee can be trusted to take Carol's homework assignments to her when Carol has the mumps: "Does your mother work for Carol's mother?" Rockface asks Parialee. "Oh, you're neighbors! Very well, I'll send along a monitor to open Carol's locker but you're only to take these things I'm writing down, nothing else" (67). Like the preacher, Rockface has the power to make Parialee respond. In drill master fashion, Rockface insists: "Now say after me: Miss Campbell is trusting me to be a good responsible girl. And go right to Carol's house. . . . Not stop anywhere on the way. Not lose anything. And only take. What's written on the list" (67). However, we know of this not because Parialee told Carol. The account of Rockface appears in a passage that parallels Alva's reverie—what she did not say to Carol. The passage in which Parialee accounts for Rockface appears in a section in which she has been talking to Carol, but the Rockface passage begins: "*But did not tell.*" The knowledge we have of Rockface from Parialee is, like the knowledge we have of Alva's inner world, one more silence in Carol's world.

What are we to make of this chilling structural parallel between the worlds of the dominant and the marginalized, the oppressor and the oppressed? Certainly we must hear Olsen's warning that the marginalized imperil their identities by replicating, even through mimicry, structures of the dominant discourse. The African-American congregation risks imposing on itself the dominant culture's reductive and oppressive structures. But has the congregation yet succumbed? Perhaps not. Perhaps they as a collective, unlike the individuals Emily and Whitey, keep their identities apart from what they mimic (or in Whitey's case, what mimics him). Perhaps insofar as the assertion/affirmation structure (so dangerously reminiscent of the dominant discourse's reductive structures) remains embedded in a cacophonous atmosphere of heteroglossia, it remains a viable form of mimicry and the African-American church maintains a delicate ecology of inside/outside with alternative structures and voices constantly checking and offsetting the structures of an oppressive discourse. Certainly the scene within the church approximates what Bakhtin identifies as heteroglossia in its fullest play—carnival—in which people's multiple voices play in, around, and against the dominant culture's hierarchical structures. Perhaps insofar as the African-American church remains a world about which Alva can say, "still I don't believe all," a world where she can be simultaneously inside and outside, it remains a dynamic social unit capable of resisting its own oppressive impulses.

Those readers who are strangers to the powerful culture of the African-American church cannot be sure how to assess that world and, like Carol, experience an abundance of meaning that approaches silence. In fact, Carol is a very useful point of reference for Olsen's readers. The story is a tangled web of explanations Carol never hears about historical circumstances that have enmeshed her. Carol hears neither Alva's reverie, which partly explains the phenomenon in the church, nor Parialee's account of Rockface. Further, as the story nears its end, Carol in desperation asks Helen a basic question, openly pleading for a response: "Mother, why did they sing and scream like that? At Parry's church?" But in place of a response we find:

> *Emotion,* Helen thought of explaining, *a characteristic of the religion of all oppressed peoples, yes your very own great-grandparents*—thought of saying. And discarded.
>
> *Aren't you now, haven't you had feelings in yourself so strong they had to come out some way?* ("what howls restrained by decorum")—thought of saying. And discarded.
>
> Repeat Alva: *hope . . . every word out of their own life. A place to let go. And church is home.* And discarded.
>
> *The special history of the Negro people—history?—just*

> *you try living what must be lived every day*—thought of say-
> ing. And discarded.
>
> And said nothing. (70)

Once more, Carol is met with silence.

We as readers may, like Carol, expect answers to our many questions about the disjunctures and potential connections among the lives and worlds of the story's characters. But Olsen, no more than Helen, supplies definitive answers. We are privileged to hear more than Carol hears, but Olsen does not answer our questions about how the lives and worlds might be connected. Is Helen's silence at the end of "O Yes" a failure in relation to her daughter? Is Olsen's silence in relation to us a failure of authorial responsibility?

To address these questions I turn to my discussion's second major division, Olsen's reworking of relationships among writer, text, and reader. Helen's silence provides insight into Olsen's designs on us as readers and our relationships to issues of dominant and marginalized people and their discourses. To return to Meese's previously-cited observation, Olsen repeatedly "calls upon the reader to write the text—no longer her text, but occasioned by it and by the voices speaking through it" (110). Helen thinks but does not say: "*Better immersion than to live untouched*" (71). Structured immersion is what Olsen plans for us. Olsen demands that we not be passive receptors, but that we, in Bakhtinian terms, join in the heteroglossia. Olsen has skillfully structured textual gaps and developed strategies for readers' identifying with characters— structures and strategies that require readers to contribute to the emergence of heteroglossic meaning. In those gaps and moments of identification we are not given free rein as readers, but we are asked to act responsibly as members of a complex human community.

To observe Olsen's craft in teasing out our active participation, I return first to "Tell Me a Riddle." Eva craves solitude: "*Never again to be forced to move to the rhythms of others*." And she is tired of the talk: "All my life around babblers. Enough!" Eva exercises her greatest control and feels triumphant when she manages to gain and maintain periods of silence. Olsen has given us a difficult kind of central character, one whose fierce desire for the silences she believes she has earned resists the telling of her story. We as audience are caught in the uncomfortable position of hearing the story of someone who wants her story left in silence. We are interlopers. We, like David, violate Eva's solitude and silence, and the narrator, seemingly torn between telling the story and honoring Eva's longing for silence, contributes to our discomfort.

The story's title and the presence of the phrase "tell me a riddle" in the story itself indicate sources of our uneasiness. In the story, the phrase "tell me a riddle" appears in the context of the "command performance." On the visit to daughter Vivi's, a visit Eva felt forced to make when she really wanted to go home, the narrator tells us very nearly from Eva's own perspective: "Attentive with the older children; sat through their performances (command performance; we command you to be the audience). . . ." Here the traditional notion of "command performance" is reversed. It is not the performer who enacts her role by command; it is the audience who performs its role by command. Eva is trapped. She is once again at the mercy of others' needs and desires.

In her role as command audience, Eva "watched the children whoop after their grandfather who knew how to tickle, chuck, lift, toss, do tricks, tell secrets, make jokes, match riddle for riddle." She watched David interact with the grandchildren in the expected ways, in all the ways in which she would not: "(Tell me a riddle, Grammy. I know no riddles, child)." Eva, the command audience, plays her attentive role up to a point, but she does not fully meet expectations. To the command "Tell me a riddle" she responds with a form of her prized silence, thwarting conventional expectations about grandparent-grandchild interactions.

Conventional expectations about interactions between us as audience and Eva and her story are also thwarted. We cannot be merely passive listeners to Eva's story. Whereas monologic discourse is, again, as Bakhtin asserts, "deaf to the other's response," even the title "Tell Me a Riddle" signals the necessity of our response. From the moment we read the title, we are told to act: "Tell Me a Riddle." We expect to hear a story, but we are told to tell a riddle. We, like Eva, are a command audience, and we, like Eva, find ourselves responding with our own versions of silence. We, the command audience, have been identified with Eva, the command audience, and with her desire for silence. Again, we are put in the uncomfortable situation of wanting to be silent listeners to the story of someone who wants her story left in silence.

Why should we be submitted to this discomfort? On one level we are put in this position because of the narrator's sympathy with Eva's desires. Eva's is a story that needs to be told, yet the narrator sympathizes with Eva's hunger for silence. The compromise for the narrator is to disrupt our complacency as audience. We will hear the story, but not on our terms: We will hear the story as a command audience. What better way to force us to realize the complexity of Eva's situation than to force us into a position resembling Eva's experience as command audience? But there is another reason for our discomfort. As in *Yonnondio* and *Silences*, Olsen disrupts our passivity, demanding that we as readers share responsibility for completing Eva's story.

But how do we exercise our responsibility? We have some clues in David's response to Eva. To David it seemed that for seventy years she had hidden an "infinitely microscopic" tape recorder within her, "trapping every song, every melody, every word read, heard, and spoken." She had caught and was now releasing all the discourse around her: "you who called others babbler and cunningly saved your words." But the harsh realization for David was that "she was playing back only what said nothing of him, of the children, of their intimate life together." For David, the air is now filled with sound; yet that sound is the equivalent of silence. To him the danger referred to in my discussion of "I Stand Here Ironing"—that multivocal, heteroglossic discourse may result in the equivalent of silence—has become reality.

However, here we have a new perspective on the danger. The danger lies not in the discourse but in the audience. Because David hears nothing of Eva's life with him, the sounds become meaningless. His is an individualistic, self-centered response. But, crucially, what are these sounds to us as command audience? We have experienced the discomfort of being listeners to the story of one who does not want her story told, but now, at the end of her life, she speaks. If we identify with David's individualistic perspective, we will not understand Eva; her sounds will be the equivalent of silence. However, if we value Eva's identification with all humankind, we are an audience for whom Eva's last words have meaning.

Olsen aids us in valuing Eva's links to all humankind. One of those aids is a resuscitated David with whom we are invited to identify once he has remembered what he had long forgotten. Finally, David comes to a partial understanding of Eva's last words. When she brokenly repeats part of a favorite quotation from Victor Hugo, David remembers it, too, reciting scornfully: "'in the twentieth century ignorance will be dead, dogma will be dead, war will be dead, and for all humankind one country—of fulfillment'? Hah!" (120). But Eva's feverish cantata finally awakens in the old man memories of his own youthful visions:

> Without warning, the bereavement and betrayal he had sheltered—compounded through the years—hidden even from himself—revealed itself,
>> uncoiled,
>> released,
>> *sprung*
> and with it the monstrous shapes of what had actually happened in the century. (120)

David realizes with sudden clarity the full price of his assimilation into America's "apolitical" mainstream: "'Lost, how much I lost.'" (121). He and Eva "had believed so beautifully, so . . . falsely?" (ellipsis Olsen's):

> "Aaah, children," he said out loud, "how we believed, how we belonged." And he yearned to package for each of the children, the grandchildren, for everyone, *that joyous certainty, that sense of mattering, of moving and being moved, of being one and indivisible with the great of the past, with all that freed, ennobled.* Package it, stand on corners, in front of stadiums and on crowded beaches, knock on doors, give it as a fabled gift.

296

David also realizes that Eva's revolutionary faith did not die with his: "*Still she believed?* 'Eva!' he whispered. 'Still you believed? You lived by it? These Things Shall Be?'" (123). This story's epigraph, "These Things Shall Be," is the title of an old socialist hymn expressing hope for a future just society. Another riddle, then, is the puzzle of revolutionary consciousness: Under what circumstances does it develop, dissipate? How does it sustain itself when confronted by "monstrous shapes"—the rise of fascism, two world wars, the extermination of nine million Jews, the threat of global extinction?

The second aid Olsen provides us in valuing Eva's ties to all humankind is Eva's granddaughter, Jeannie (the same Jeannie of "Hey Sailor, What Ship?" and "O Yes," now in her twenties) to whom the legacy of resistance is passed on. Jeannie, who works as a visiting nurse and has a special political and artistic sensibility, cares for Eva in the last weeks of her life. "Like Lisa she is, your Jeannie," Eva whispers to Lennie and Helen, referring to the revolutionary who taught Eva to read more than 50 years before. It is at the end of the passage in which Eva compares Jeannie to Lisa that Eva says, "All that happens, one must try to understand'" (112, 113).

These words comprise Eva's hope for Jeannie and Olsen's most basic demand on us as active readers. Recognizing the persistent threat of being so flooded with meaning that we may be faced with meaninglessness and the equivalent of silence, we must persist in the attempt to understand. In that attempt we must recognize the dangers of the bourgeois individualism into which we, like David, are constantly tempted to retreat. Olsen provides structures, such as the command audience structure I have discussed, to force us out of our passive individualistic roles as readers and to invite us into a web of interconnected, heteroglossic roles.[4] If we accept the invitation, we must do more than value Eva's identification with all humankind: We must remember if we have forgotten (the model of David) or learn if we have never known (the model of Jeannie) the complicated histories of worlds like those in which Eva lived and struggled. At the least, we are required to do our part in keeping alive the historical circumstances of oppressive czarist Russia and the connections among all oppressed groups. Eva and Olsen require us to learn the very histories to which America's "apolitical" mainstream would have us remain oblivious. With Jeannie, we are challenged to carry on Eva's legacy of resistance.

Olsen provides one further aid in valuing Eva's links to all humankind, an aid not limited to the collection's final story. The subject of motherhood so prominent in "I Stand Here Ironing," "O Yes," and "Tell Me a Riddle" provides a crucial reference point for our accepting a heteroglossia linking all humankind. Olsen has rightly referred to motherhood "as an almost taboo area; the last refuge of sexism . . . the least understood" and "last explored, tormentingly complex *core* of women's oppression." At the same time, Olsen believes that motherhood is, potentially, a source of "transport" for women, moving them beyond some of the constraints of individualism.[5] Responsible for what Olsen terms "the maintenance of life," mothers are often exposed to forms of heteroglossia, with their attendant benefits and hazards (*Silences* 34). In exploring the complexity of motherhood, Olsen renders versions of it that are "coiled, convoluted like an ear"—versions that may serve as models for the necessary hearing of heteroglossia.

I return to Helen's silence at the end of "O Yes." We can read Helen's silence as one of several textual comments on the limits of authority; indeed, it may have been through the experience of parenting that Olsen learned the limits of authorial control, which her texts so willingly concede. As an involved parent, one is forced to live intensely "in relation to," as the boundary between self and other is constantly negotiated. Such negotiating provides a model in which the ability to listen to constantly changing, heteroglossic voices is prized. When Carol asks, "why do I have to care?", the narrator tells us the following about Helen:

> Caressing, quieting.
> Thinking: *caring asks doing. It is a long baptism into the seas of humankind, my daughter. Better immersion than to live untouched. . . .* [ellipsis Olsen's] *Yet how will you sustain?*
> *Why is it like it is?*
> Sheltering her daughter close, mourning the illusion of the embrace.
> *And why do I have to care?*

298

> While in her, her own need leapt and plunged for the
> place of strength that was not—where one could scream or
> sorrow while all knew and accepted, and gloved and loving
> hands waited to support and understand. (71)

Although we risk being flooded by a multiplicity of meaning
that approaches meaninglessness and the equivalent of silence, we as readers must submit to the "immersion," the
"long baptism" that allows us to be the proper "ear" for the
complexity of heteroglossia.

We have similar models at the end of "I Stand Here
Ironing" and "Tell Me a Riddle." The mother listens to Emily
on "one of her communicative nights . . . [when] she tells me
everything and nothing" (19). The mother does not respond to
Emily, but says to herself, to the teacher or counselor, and
to us, "Let her be. So all that is in her will not bloom—but
in how many does it? There is still enough left to live by"
(20–21). In "Tell Me a Riddle" Jeannie, who has listened carefully to Eva's dying heteroglossia, is not actually a mother; but,
like a mother, she is a caretaker, a nurturer, a listener.

However, Olsen asks more of us than listening. As
Helen says to herself, *"caring asks doing."* In none of these
models in *Tell Me a Riddle* is the mother figure a passive listener; rather, she is a listener responsive to heteroglossia.
Even when multiple voices so overwhelm her that she is
caught in silence (Emily's mother, Helen, Eva), she can sometimes caress or embrace, knowing the communicative power
of such actions. As active readers, then, we are provided models of careful listening, leading to action. Olsen does not pro-
scribe the field of political/social action that we as active
readers might enter. However, she does demand that we work
to understand the many voices of the oppressed. In "I Stand
Here Ironing," the mother says of Emily, "Only help her to
know," a command the dying Eva echoes: "All that happens,
one must try to understand." These words comprise impera-
tives for us. And these mother figures, who live compassionately and interdependently in a multicultural and heteroglossic dynamic, become models for us readers.

Olsen demands another, related form of action from her
readers. In the collection, *Tell Me a Riddle,* we have been ex-

posed to many moments in which characters sensitive to heteroglossia have been so inundated with complexity of meaning
they have lapsed into silence. We have heard what the unnamed mother in "I Stand Here Ironing," Alva, Helen, and
Eva have *not* been able to say to those most immediately
connected to them. If the silence is perpetuated, these characters risk, as do Emily and Whitey, being subsumed by the
dominant discourse. Olsen requires us, as readers of the complete collection, to hear the various oppressed voices and to
make and articulate connections among them, connections
the separate characters may not be able to see, or may only
partially see. With such actions we become collaborators with
Olsen in the democratizing enterprise of amplifying dominated and marginalized voices. We join her in a commitment
to social change.

The "riddle" which Olsen's work challenges us to engage requires that we consider political activity not as something confined to a single class, party, gender, ethnic group,
or cause but as something undertaken within a kaleidoscopic
social field and, simultaneously, within "the fibres of the self
and in the hard practical substance of effective and continuing
relationships" (Williams 212). Olsen's genuinely democratic
content articulates itself in multivocal texts that prefigure post-
individual cultural forms. In a sense, Olsen's sociopolitical vision has enabled her to write what cannot be written. *Tell Me
a Riddle*'s form represents a "*pre-emergence*, active and press-
ing but not yet fully articulated, rather than the evident emergence which could be more confidently named" (Williams
126). With Virginia Woolf in "The Leaning Tower," Olsen's
texts proclaim: "Literature is no one's private ground; literature is common ground" (125).

☐ *Notes* ■

1. For discussions of history of reading strategies and earlier
defenses of indirect and figurational structures against schemes for
linguistic reductionism, see Bartine.

2. In the edition of *Tell Me a Riddle* I have used for this essay,
the title story is "for two of that generation, Seevya and Genya." In

the 1989 edition, Olsen also dedicates the story to her parents. Genya Gorelick had been a factory organizer in Mozyr, a famous orator, and the leading woman of the Jewish Workers' Alliance, the Bund of pre-revolutionary Russia. Her son, Al Richmond, has written about the role Gorelick played in the 1905 revolution, when she was just nineteen:

> The 1905 revolution burst forth like the splendid realization of a dream, shaking the Czarist regime enough to loosen its most repressive restrictions, so that revolutionaries at last could address the public, not any more through the whispered word and the surreptitious leaflet but openly and directly in large assemblies. She discovered her gifts as a public orator. She was good, and in her best moments she was truly great. (8; cited in Rosenfelt, "Divided" 19)

3. Olsen told me in an interview (11 July 1986, San Francisco) that she modelled Whitey partly on Filipino men she knew "in the movement" who hungered for contact with families at a time when U.S. immigration law kept Filipino women and children from entering the U.S.

4. Patrocinio P. Schweickart outlines a promising model for reading based on a joining of reader-response theory and feminist theory. Her model contains some of the characteristics Olsen's writing demands of readers. Schweickart finds that feminist theory can move "beyond the individualistic models of [Wolfgang] Iser and of most reader-response critics" toward a "collective" model of reading. Describing the goal of that model, Schweickart observes that "the feminist reader hopes that other women will recognize themselves in her story, and join her in her struggle to transform the culture" (50, 51). It must be added that Olsen, like Schweickart, would have women and men "join her in her struggle to transform the culture."

5. *Silences* 202. For an enlightening discussion of *Tell Me a Riddle* in relation to other works dealing with motherhood, see Gardiner. Gardiner also suggests Jeannie's function as a model for readers when she notes that "at the end of the story, Jeannie has absorbed her grandmother's consciousness," allowing Eva to be "the agent of a revolutionary and transcendent ideal that can be passed from woman to woman, of a commitment to fully human values" (163).

☐ Works Cited ■

Bakhtin, M. M. *The Dialogic Imagination.* Ed. Michael Holquist. Trans. Caryl Emerson and Michael Holquist. Austin: University of Texas Press, 1981.

Bartine, David. *Early English Reading Theory: Origins of Current Debates.* Columbia: University of South Carolina Press, 1989.

———. *Reading, Culture, and Criticism: 1820–1950.* Columbia: University of South Carolina Press, 1992.

Eagleton, Terry. *Against the Grain, Essays 1975–1985.* London: Verso, 1986.

———. *Marxism and Literary Criticism.* Berkeley and Los Angeles: University of California Press, 1976.

Gardiner, Judith Kegan. "A Wake for Mother: The Maternal Deathbed in Women's Fiction." *Feminist Studies* 4 (June 1978): 146–165.

Henderson, Mae Gwendolyn. "Speaking in Tongues: Dialogics, Dialectics, and the Black Woman Writer's Literary Tradition." *Changing Our Own Words: Essays on Criticism, Theory, and Writing by Black Women.* Ed. Cheryl A. Wall. New Brunswick: Rutgers University Press, 1989.

Meese, Elizabeth A. *Crossing the Double-Cross: The Practice of Feminist Criticism.* Chapel Hill: University of North Carolina Press, 1986.

Olsen, Tillie. *Mother to Daughter, Daughter to Mother.* Old Westbury: Feminist Press, 1984.

———. *Silences.* New York: Dell, 1978.

———. *Tell Me a Riddle.* 1961. New York: Dell, 1979.

Richmond, Al. *A Long View from the Left: Memoirs of an American Revolutionary.* New York: Dell, 1972.

Rosenfelt, Deborah. "Divided against Herself." *Moving On,* April/ May 1980: 15–23.

———. "From the Thirties: Tillie Olsen and the Radical Tradition." *Feminist Studies* 7 (Fall 1981): 371–406. Reprinted here and in Judith Newton and Deborah Rosenfelt, eds., *Feminist Criticism and Social Change: Sex, Class, and Race in Literature and Culture* (New York: Methuen, 1985), 216–48.

Schweickart, Patrocinio P. "Reading Ourselves: Toward a Feminist Theory of Reading." *Gender and Reading: Essays on Readers, Texts, and Contexts,* eds. Elizabeth A. Flynn and Patrocinio

P. Schweickart. Baltimore: Johns Hopkins University Press, 1986.

Todorov, Tzvetan. *Mikhail Bakhtin: The Dialogical Principle*. Translated by Wlad Godzich. Minneapolis: University of Minnesota Press, 1984.

Williams, Raymond. *Marxism and Literature*. Oxford: Oxford University Press, 1977.

Woolf, Virginia. "The Leaning Tower." *The Moment and Other Essays*. London: Hogarth, 1952.

☐ Selected Bibliography ■

Works by Tillie Lerner Olsen

FICTION

"The Iron Throat." (Tillie Lerner). *Partisan Review* 1,2 (April–May 1934): 3–9. Became first chapter of *Yonnondio*.

"Not You I Weep For." Ca. 1931. In *First Words: Earliest Writings from Favorite Contemporary Authors,* edited by Paul Mandelbaum. Chapel Hill, N.C.: Algonquin Books of Chapel Hill, 1993.

"Requa." *Iowa Review* 1 (Summer 1970): 54–74. Reprinted as "Requa I" in *Best American Short Stories,* edited by Martha Foley and David Burnett. Boston: Houghton Mifflin, 1971. Reprinted as "Requa–I" in *Granta: New American Writing* (September 1979): 111–32.

Tell Me a Riddle. Philadelphia: Lippincott, 1961. Reprinted New York: Delacorte, 1979; reprinted New York: Delta, 1989. Includes "I Stand Here Ironing," first published as "Help Her to Believe," *Pacific Spectator* 10 (Winter 1956): 55–63; "Hey Sailor, What Ship?", *New Campus Writing* 2 (New York: Putnam, 1957); "O Yes," first published as "Baptism," *Prairie Schooner* 31 (Spring 1957): 70–80; and "Tell Me a Riddle," *New World Writing* 16 (Philadelphia: Lippincott, 1960), 11–57.

Yonnondio: From the Thirties. New York: Delacorte Press/Seymour Lawrence, 1974; reprinted New York: Dell, 1975; New York: Delta, 1981.

POEMS

"At Fourteen Years." In *First Words: Earliest Writings from Favorite Contemporary Authors,* edited by Paul Mandelbaum. Chapel Hill, N.C.: Algonquin Books of Chapel Hill, 1993.

"I Want You Women Up North to Know." (Tillie Lerner). *The Partisan* 1 (March 1934): 4. Reprinted in *Writing Red: An Anthology of American Women Writers, 1930–1940,* edited by Charlotte Nekola and Paula Rabinowitz. New York: The Feminist Press, 1987.

"There Is a Lesson." (Tillie Lerner). *The Partisan* 1 (April 1934): 4. Reprinted in Burkom and Williams (below).

NONFICTION PROSE

"Dream-Vision." In *Mother to Daughter, Daughter to Mother: Mothers on Mothering,* selected and shaped by Tillie Olsen. Old Westbury: The Feminist Press, 1984.

Foreword to *Black Women Writers at Work,* edited by Claudia Tate. New York: Continuum, 1986.

305

Introduction to *Allegra Maud Goldman,* by Edith Konecky. New York: The Feminist Press, 1987.

"Mothers and Daughters." With Julie Olsen Edwards. In *Mothers and Daughters: That Special Quality: An Exploration in Photography,* edited by Tillie Olsen, Julie Olsen Edwards, and Estelle Jussim, 14–17. New York: Aperture, 1987.

"Personal Statement." In *First Drafts, Last Drafts: Forty Years of the Creative Writing Program at Stanford University,* prepared by William McPheron with the assistance of Amor Towles. Stanford: Stanford University Libraries, 1989.

Silences. New York: Delacorte, 1978. Includes previous essays: "Silences in Literature," first published in *Harper's* 231 (October 1965): 153–61; "One Out of Twelve: Women Who Are Writers in Our Century," first published in *College English* 34 (October 1972): 6–17; and "Rebecca Harding Davis: Her Life and Times," first published as "A Biographical Interpretation," afterword for Rebecca Harding Davis, *Life in the Iron Mills* (Old Westbury: The Feminist Press, 1972; 1985).

"The Strike." (Tillie Lerner). *Partisan Review* 1, 4 (September–October 1934): 3–9. In *Years of Protest: A Collection of American Writings of the 1930's,* edited by Jack Salzman. New York: Pegasus, 1967. Reprinted in Nekola and Rabinowitz, above.

"The Thirties: A Vision of Fear and Hope." *Newsweek* (January 3, 1994): 26–27.

"Thousand-Dollar Vagrant." (Tillie Lerner). *New Republic* 80 (August 29, 1934): 67–69.

"The Word Made Flesh." In *Critical Thinking/Critical Writing.* Educational Service Publication. Cedar Falls, Iowa: University of Northern Iowa, 1984.

SELECTED FURTHER READING

Burkom, Selma, and Margaret Williams. "De-riddling Tillie Olsen's Writings." *San Jose Studies* 2 (February 1976): 64–83. Reprinted in Nelson and Huse.

Coiner, Constance. "Literature of Resistance: The Intersection of Feminism and the Communist Left in Meridel Le Sueur and Tillie Olsen." In *Left Politics and the Literary Profession,* edited by Lennard J. Davis and M. Bella Mirabella. New York: Columbia University Press, 1990. 162–85.

———. *Better Red: The Writing and Resistance of Tillie Olsen and Meridel Le Sueur.* New York: Oxford University Press, 1995.

Coles, Robert. "Reconsideration." Review of *Tell Me a Riddle. New Republic* 6 (December 1975): 29–39. Reprinted as "Tillie Olsen: The Iron and the Riddle." *That Red Wheelbarrow: Selected Literary Essays by Robert Coles.* Iowa City: University of Iowa Press, 1988. 122–127.

Duncan, Erica. "Coming of Age in the Thirties: A Portrait of Tillie Olsen."

Book Forum 6, 2 (1982): 207–22. Reprinted as "Tillie Olsen" in *Unless Soul Clap Its Hands: Portraits and Passages*. New York: Schocken, 1984. 31–57.

Faulkner, Mara. *Protest and Possibility in the Writing of Tillie Olsen*. Charlottesville: University Press of Virginia, 1993.

Frye, Joanne S. "Tillie Olsen: Probing the Boundaries between Text and Context." *Journal of Narrative and Life History* 3, No's 2 and 3 (1993): 255–268.

Gardiner, Judith Kegan. "A Wake for Mother: The Maternal Deathbed in Women's Fiction." *Feminist Studies* 4 (June 1978): 145–65.

Hedges, Elaine and Shelley Fisher Fishkin, eds. *Listening to 'Silences': New Feminist Essays*. New York: Oxford University Press, 1994.

Jacobs, Naomi. "Earth, Air, Fire and Water in 'Tell Me a Riddle.'" *Studies in Short Fiction* 23, 4 (Fall 1986): 401–06.

Kamel, Rose. "Riddles and Silences: Tillie Olsen's Autobiographical Fiction." *Aggravating the Conscience: Jewish-American Literary Mothers in the Promised Land*. New York: Peter Lang, 1988. 81–114.

Nelson, Kay Hoyle and Nancy Huse, eds. *The Critical Response to Tillie Olsen*. New York: Greenwood Press, 1994.

Orr, Elaine Neil. *Tillie Olsen and a Feminist Spiritual Vision*. Jackson: University Press of Mississippi, 1987.

Pearlman, Mickey and Abby H. P. Werlock. *Tillie Olsen*. Boston: G. K. Hall, 1991.

Pfaelzer, Jeanne. "Tillie Olsen's *Tell Me a Riddle:* The Dialectics of Silence." *Frontiers,* forthcoming.

Rosenfelt, Deborah. "Rereading *Tell Me a Riddle* in the Age of Deconstruction." In Hedges and Fishkin.

Rubin, Naomi. "A Riddle of History for the Future." Interview with Olsen in *Sojourner* (June 1983): 3–4.

Yalom, Marilyn. "Tillie Olsen." In *Women Writers of the West Coast: Speaking of Their Lives and Careers*, edited by Marilyn Yalom. Santa Barbara: Capra, 1983.

❑ Permissions ∎